QuickBooks
Premier 2016
Level 1

QuickBooks 2016 Product Registration for Students

In order for students to access their one year free QuickBooks 2016 software students must register online here:
http://www.intuit.ca/education/students.jsp

Students must add notify@quickbase.com and iepcanada@intuit.com to their safe sender list otherwise the email will be blocked by spam filters.

Students must install QuickBooks Desktop 2016 and register the product online immediately after installation. Failure to register the product will result in the software access expiring after 30 days.

For any support issues, students must visit the Support page on the Intuit Education website:
http://education.intuit.ca/education-program/support.jsp.

September 2016

QuickBooks Premier 2016 – Level 1

Developer(s): Valerie Tribes

Editor(s): George Tribes

Publisher(s): Kelly Hegedus

This courseware is one in a series prepared by CCI Learning Solutions Inc. for use by students and instructors in courses on computer software applications. CCI designed these materials to assist students and instructors in making the learning process both effective and enjoyable.

This training manual is copyrighted and all rights are reserved by CCI Learning Solutions, Inc. No part of this publication may be reproduced, transmitted, stored in a retrieval system, modified, or translated into any language or computer language, in any form or by any means, electronic, mechanical, magnetic, optical, chemical, manual or otherwise without written permission of CCI Learning Solutions, Canada: 1-800-668-1669.

The information in this courseware is distributed on an "as is" basis, without warranty. While every precaution has been taken in the preparation of this courseware, neither the author nor CCI Learning Solutions Inc. shall have any liability to any person or entity with respect to any liability, loss, or damage caused or alleged to be caused directly or indirectly by the instructions contained in this courseware or by the computer software and hardware products described therein.

Funded by the Government of Canada | Canada

Working With the Data Files

The exercises in this courseware require you to use the data files provided for the book. Follow the instructions shown to download the data files for this courseware.

1   Launch your Browser and navigate to the CCI Web site location http://www.ccilearning.com/data.

2   Enter: 1761 in the Courseware # box and click the **Find Data** button.

3   Click **Save** in the File Download – Security Warning window.

4   Navigate to the desktop (or the preferred save location as indicated by your Instructor) and click **Save**.

The *1761-1-student-files.exe* file is downloaded to your computer.

5   Close the Browser window and double-click the *1761-1-student-files.exe* file. The Open File – Security Warning window appears.

6   Click **Run**. The WinZip Self Extractor will open. The file needs to be unzipped to the required folder.

7   Click the **Browse** button to navigate to the folder identified by your instructor and click **Unzip**. The message that the files successfully unzipped will appear.

8   Click **OK**, then click **Close** to close the WinZip Self Extractor.

It is recommended that the folder be renamed using your own name before starting the exercises in this courseware. You can reinstall and use the work files as many times as you like.

QuickBooks Desktop Files

QuickBooks desktop data can be stored as three different file types: company files, backup files and portable company files. A company file (extension .qbw) is the type in which you will work with your business. A backup file (extension .qbb) is used to store a copy of your file and can be used to restore the file if the main company file is corrupted. A portable company file (extension .qbm) is much smaller than either of the other two, and can be used to send your information by email. The company file can be stored anywhere on your computer, but it is recommended that you also store a backup or portable company file on either an external hard drive, or flash drive kept in a safe place.

Table of Contents

About This Courseware

Lesson 1: Introduction

Lesson 2: Inventory and Services

Lesson 3: Vendors and Accounts Payable

Lesson 4: Customers and Accounts Receivable

Lesson 5: Employees and Payroll

Lesson 6: Reporting, Miscellaneous and Year End Procedures

Appendices

Course Description

QuickBooks Premier 2016 Level 1 teaches you how to perform daily accounting tasks in the General Ledger, Accounts Receivable, Accounts Payable, and Payroll. This course is geared towards someone who will be primarily doing data entry in QuickBooks.

Course Series

QuickBooks Premier 2016 Level 1 is the first course in the MasterTrak Accounting series. MasterTrak Accounting consists of the following two courses:

- QuickBooks Premier 2016 Level 1
- QuickBooks Premier 2016 Level 2

Course Length

QuickBooks Premier 2016 Level 1 is an 18-24 hour course that can be implemented in three to four days.

Course Prerequisites

Students must have completed *Microsoft Windows Level 1* or be able to demonstrate equivalent basic PC and Windows knowledge. In addition, it is important to understand how a business functions to fully understand the concepts discussed.

Classroom Setup

Your instructor will have set up the classroom computers based on the system requirements to run the software for this course. Most software configurations on your computer are identical to those on your instructor's computer. However, your instructor may use additional software to demonstrate network interaction or related technologies.

This courseware was developed with QuickBooks Premier 2016 and Windows 10. Some figures may vary depending on the tax deduction tables used for the release of QuickBooks in your lab or on your computer.

The data files used in this courseware are set up for companies in British Columbia, Alberta, and Ontario using the GST/HST rates relevant to those Provinces at the time the data files were created. If you wish you can change the GST/HST or PST tax rates but take note that your figures will then differ from those provided in the courseware.

Course Objectives

After completing this course, you will be able to:

- start and exit QuickBooks Premier
- manage QuickBooks files
- understand the Chart of Accounts
- create, modify, find, edit, and delete General Ledger accounts
- save changes to company data files
- enter, adjust, and delete General Journal transactions
- create and recall memorized transactions
- produce a General Journal report
- backup company data
- change company information
- create and change inventory and service items
- run Inventory reports
- create and modify vendor records
- enter and modify bills
- write cheques
- issue and fill purchase orders
- receive items and bills
- pay vendor bills and print cheques
- run Vendor reports
- create new and modify existing customers
- enter new cash and credit sales invoices for customers
- issue and fill sales orders
- work with sales taxes
- record and modify payments received from customers

- record deposits of customer payments in order to update your bank balance
- process refunds and credits
- print invoices, and related forms for customers
- make deposits
- run customer reports
- set up the payroll module and preferences
- set up and modify the employee defaults
- create payroll items
- edit individual employee data
- add a new employee
- create and use payroll schedules
- produce and print payroll cheques and paystubs
- create payroll reports
- remit government and other payroll liabilities
- understand and work with the Report Centre
- run reports on accounts, inventory, customers, vendors, and employees
- run financial reports
- remit sales tax
- use the Calendar
- work with the Company Snapshot
- use the Reminders list
- verify data integrity
- understand year end procedures

Course Design

This courseware was developed for instructor-led training and will assist you during class. Together with comprehensive instructional text and objectives checklists, this courseware provides easy-to-follow hands-on lab exercises and a glossary of course-specific terms.

This courseware is organized in the following manner:

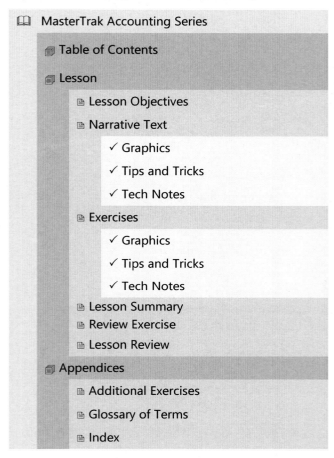

When you return to your home or office, you will find this courseware to be a valuable resource for reviewing exercises and applying the skills you have learned. Each lesson concludes with questions that review the material. Lesson review questions are provided as a study resource only and in no way guarantee a passing score on a certification exam. Appendices in the back of this courseware provide additional information, resources, and answers to review questions.

Hands on, comprehensive assignments are provided in the Appendix. Students are required to apply all their knowledge of features learned in the courseware to accomplish tasks as in a real working environment. These exercises can be used as additional hands on practice, challenging exercises for the advanced student, or as a final exam to test skills.

The instructor has access to additional exercises, and a project based on the concepts covered in this course.

Conventions and Graphics

The following conventions are used in CCI learning materials.

File Names or Database Field Names	File names or database field names are indicated in *italic* type.
Exercise Text	Content to be entered by the student during an exercise appears in Consolas font.
Procedures	Text that appears in **bold** indicates menu choices or field names.
Menu Options and Features	Menu options and features are listed in left hand columns and corresponding descriptions are in the right hand column.

The following graphics are used in CCI learning materials.

 Specific Keyboard Graphics to easily identify the key to press on the keyboard.

Technical Notes point out exceptions or special circumstances that you may find when working a particular procedure, or may indicate there is another method to complete the task.

Learn the Skill
Learn the Skill graphics signal the start of step-by-step hands-on exercises or other activities.

Practice the Skill
Practice the Skill graphics signal the start of hands-on exercises at the end of each lesson that can be used to review the concepts learned.

Overview
What is QuickBooks?

QuickBooks is a product of Intuit Canada. QuickBooks Premier is an integrated accounting package suitable for most small to medium-sized businesses needing such accounting modules as the General Ledger, Accounts Payable, Accounts Receivable, Canadian Payroll, and Inventory accounting.

QuickBooks Editions

QuickBooks provides several editions, all of which perform the basic tasks required for small-business bookkeeping. It is wise to evaluate just what you need QuickBooks to do for your business before you decide which edition to purchase. The following is a sample list of the editions available in QuickBooks 2016:

- Premier Edition (General Business)
- Accountant Edition
- Contractor Edition
- Manufacturing & Wholesale Edition
- Non-profit Edition

- Professional Services Edition
- Retail Edition
- QuickBooks Pro
- QuickBooks Easy Start

QuickBooks

Lesson 1: Introduction

Lesson Objectives

The objective of this lesson is to introduce you to the basic operation of QuickBooks Premier. Upon successful completion of this lesson, you should know how to:

- ☐ manage QuickBooks files
- ☐ open and restore QuickBooks files
- ☐ explain the QuickBooks screen components
- ☐ understand the Chart of Accounts
- ☐ create, modify, find, edit and delete general ledger (GL) accounts
- ☐ work with QuickBooks Preferences

- ☐ find and amend the company information
- ☐ input dates into QuickBooks
- ☐ input, adjust, and delete General Journal transactions
- ☐ create, recall and delete memorized transactions
- ☐ produce a General Journal report
- ☐ back up company data files

Using the Exercise File in Each Lesson

For each lesson in this courseware you'll restore a copy of the exercise file *We Are Music Ltd - Your Name.qbb* and use that file to complete the lesson. The qbb file that you copy into the directory on your hard disk is a QuickBooks backup copy. This means that at the start of each lesson, you'll be restoring a new lesson file. This also means that entries done in a previous lesson will not show in a later one. This will not affect the results of each lesson.

This manual has been developed using QuickBooks Premier 2016. Please note that if you are using a different edition your screen may look slightly different from those displayed in this courseware. The Tax Tables used are those as of June 30, 2016. If you are using different Tax Tables, your results will be slightly different from those displayed in this manual. The Sales Tax is based on the current taxes in British Columbia – GST 5% and PST 7%.

Managing QuickBooks Files

Understanding some basic file management tasks will allow you to work more effectively in the QuickBooks environment. This section will show you how to start the program, open and restore files, and understand the basic types of files.

Starting QuickBooks

There is always more than one way to do things on a computer, and starting QuickBooks is no exception. Ask your instructor the preferred method of starting QuickBooks in the computer lab where you are working. There may be a shortcut on the desktop, or you may have to go through the All Programs menu which can be accessed by the Start button.

QuickBooks has the ability to remember which data file was used most recently. If you do not close the data file before closing QuickBooks, the program will automatically open that data file when it is started. Closing the opened company file will then result in the **No Company Open** window as shown below. You may then choose from the options offered.

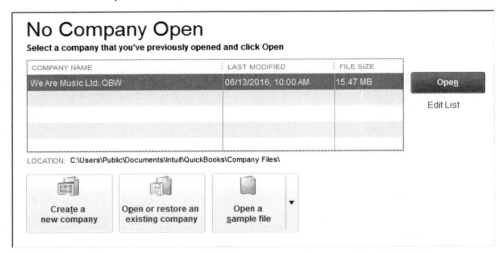

This screen offers three options:

Create a new company	This will begin the process of creating a new data file.
Open or restore an existing company	This will begin the process of opening or restoring a company file.
Open a sample file	This will open a sample company to provide an opportunity to explore QuickBooks.

Opening and Restoring QuickBooks Files

The command to open or restore a company file can be accessed from the **File** menu as well as the **No Company Open** window. This command will display the following window, which allows you to choose which type of file to open.

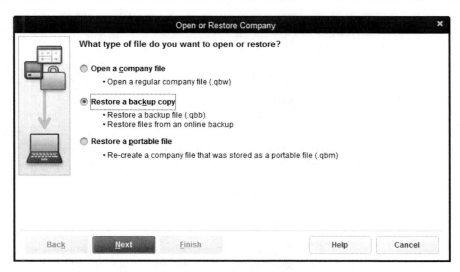

To Open a company file proceed as follows:

1. Choose **File**, **Open or Restore Company** from the menu bar.

2. Choose **Open a company file**, click **Next**.

3. Navigate to the file location, select the desired file, and click **Open**.

    OR

1. Choose **File**, **Open Previous Company**.

2. Select the desired file from the drop-down list by clicking it.

To Restore a company file proceed as follows:

1. Choose **File**, **Open or Restore Company** from the menu bar.

2. Choose **Restore a backup copy**, click **Next**.

3. Choose **Local backup**, click **Next**.

4. Navigate to the file location, click **Next**.

5. Locate the backup file you wish to restore, and then click **Open**.

6. Click **Next**, choose the location to save the restored file, and then click **Save**.

Note: A similar procedure would be followed to restore a portable file.

To Start This Lesson

Before proceeding to the following steps, make sure the student data file has been properly saved to your hard disk. See *Working with the Data Files* in the Preface to this manual.

It is recommended that you make a copy of the exercise file and store it in a safe place in case the original becomes damaged.

Restoring the Exercise File

1. From the **File** menu in QuickBooks, choose **Open or Restore Company**.

    QuickBooks displays the Open or Restore Company window.

2. Select **Restore a backup copy** and click **Next**.

3. Select **Local backup** and click **Next**.

4. In the Open Backup Copy window navigate to your *1761 Student Files* folder.

5. Select *We Are Music Ltd 2016 - Student.QBB* file and then click **Open**.

6. In the Open or Restore Company window, click **Next**.

7. Navigate to your *1761 Student Files* folder.

8. In the **File name** field of the Save Company File as window, type: We Are Music Ltd - Your Name Lesson 1 and then click **Save**.

9. In the QuickBooks Login window enter the password: **Sys2016** , and click **OK**

   QuickBooks requires that the password must be at least 7 characters with one upper case letter and a number.

   If the 'Have a Question' window opens, click the **Close** button, click **Do not show this again** to activate the check box and then click **OK**.

   If a warning regarding the Payroll tax table being out of date appears click **OK** to continue.

10. Click **OK** when you see the message that the file has been successfully restored.

11. The QuickBooks Learning Centre window opens.

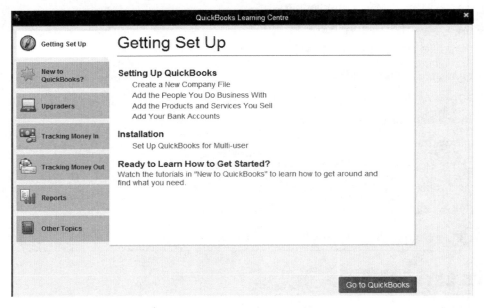

Getting Set Up	Links for setting up, installation, and tutorials.
New to QuickBooks	Getting around and finding what you need.
Upgraders	New features in 2016.
Tracking Money In	A list of everyday tasks, and Income Tracker.
Tracking Money Out	Everyday tasks on entering expenses.
Reports	A list of common reports on business activities.
Other Topics	Payroll and Handling Bounced Cheques.
Go To QuickBooks	Click on this button to close this window and return to the main screen.

Looking at the QuickBooks Screen

When you open a company data file in QuickBooks, you will see a screen similar to the following:

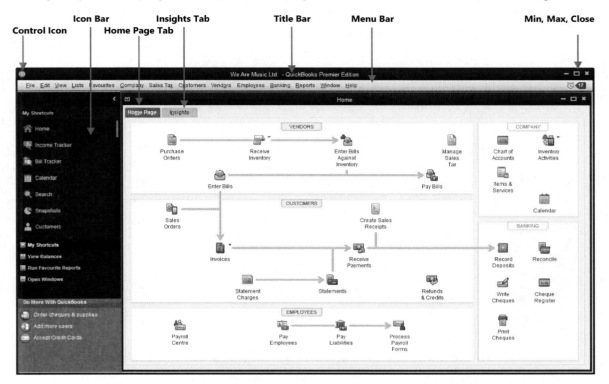

Control Icon	Located in the top left corner, this displays the Control Menu to select such options as **Move**, **Size**, **Maximize**, **Minimize**, and **Close**. These are standard Windows options available on most Control Menus.
Icon Bar	The location of this bar can be adjusted by clicking View on the menu bar and choosing either Top or Hide. Using the left Icon bar is recommended as it offers more power and versatility. The Icon bar contains shortcuts to the tasks and reports you use most.
Title Bar	Located at the top of a window, the title bar displays the name of the currently active company data file, e.g., We Are Music Ltd., followed by the name of the selected application, in this case QuickBooks Premier Edition.
Minimize, Maximize/ Restore or Close Buttons	Located in the top right corner of a window, these buttons control a window's display size. Use the ▬ (**Minimize**) button to minimize the QuickBooks window to the taskbar, ▭ (**Maximize**) to the screen, ▭ (**Restore Down**) to the original window size, or ✕ (**Close**) the program completely.
Menu Bar	Located below the title bar, this bar provides access to the main menu commands such as **File**, **Edit**, **View** and so on which, when displayed, contain different sets of commands to activate features or options.
Home Page Tab	This window displays sections for the various company areas such as Vendors, or Customers, for example, each of which contain icons for features used in each area.

Vendors	Contains icons for transactions such as: Purchase Orders, Enter Bills, Receive Inventory, Enter Bills Against Inventory, Pay Bills, Manage Sales Tax.
Customers	Contains icons for transactions such as: Sales Orders, Invoices, Create Sales Receipts, Receive Payments, Statement Charges, Statements, Refunds & Credits.
Employees	Contains icons for Payroll Centre, Pay Employees, Pay Liabilities, Process Payroll Forms.
Company	Contains icons for Chart of Accounts, Items & Services, Inventory Activities (which includes Inventory Centre, Build Assemblies, Adjust Quantity/Value on Hand), and Calendar.
Banking	Contains icons for Record Deposits, Write Cheques, Print Cheques, Reconcile, and Cheque Register.

Insights Tab

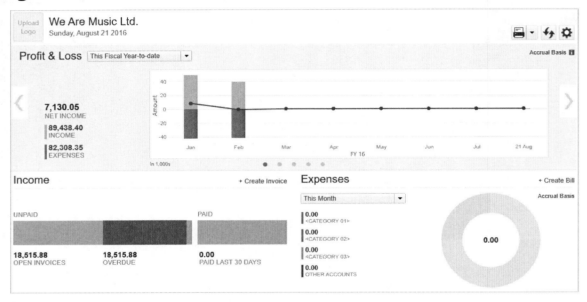

This window displays three panes, Profit & Loss with various reports, Income and Expenses. It can be used to view how the business is doing at a glance. To move between panes, click the left or right arrow. When a company file is set up, only the QuickBooks Administrator has access to Home page Insights. This tab provides similar information to that in the Company Snapshot; however, that window provides many more report options for management information. We will explore the Insights tab in greater detail in Level 2 of this course.

Moving Around Dialog Boxes

A *dialog box* is a window that appears when QuickBooks offers additional options or requires more information from you before carrying out a command. You can use either the mouse or keyboard to access the commands available in a dialog box.

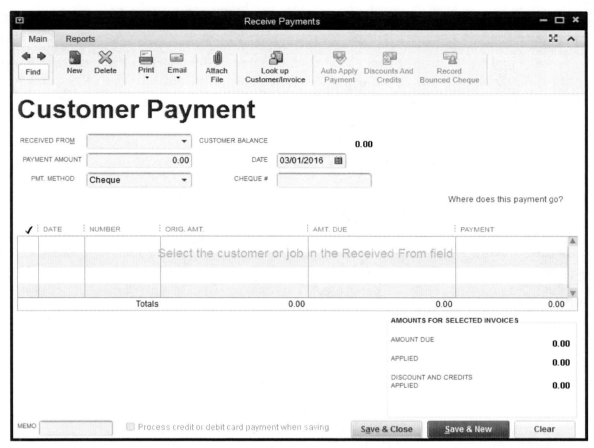

- When there is a check box beside an option, you can select or clear the option by clicking the check box or pressing the (Spacebar). A cleared check box will appear similar to ☐.

- To enter text in a text field, either click in the appropriate text field or use the appropriate keyboard method to move to that field and then type the text.

- To select items from a drop-down list, click the left mouse button on the drop-down arrow ▼ next to the option. This will display a list of available items to choose from.

- To increase or decrease amounts with an increment button, move to that command and either click the up or down arrow button or press the (↑) or (↓) keys. An increment button is sometimes referred to as a spin button. When you are on a command with increment buttons, the corresponding direction button will highlight (⬍).

- You can also select certain features by clicking the appropriate option button. Option buttons are always found in groups and only one option button from a group can be selected at any one time (◉). As you move to that option, it will appear similar to ◯. Either click the option button or the command name to select it. Depending on the placement of the option command, you may not be able to access that command using the keyboard methods.

- You can also select a date by clicking the calendar button 📅 next to a field. By default, the days of the current month will be displayed in a calendar format, and the entered date (today's date if a date has not been selected) will be marked. You can scroll forward to future months, or back to previous months.

- To choose a command button, click the button of your choice, or press ⌷Tab until at the command button and then press ⌷Enter. When a command button is selected, it will appear as [OK   ] and you can press ⌷Enter to activate all options selected in the dialog box. Alternatively, be sure to select Cancel or close the dialog box if you do not want to activate any options selected in the dialog box.
- To move to a command in the dialog box, you can either move the mouse cursor overtop of the command, or press ⌷Alt and the underlined character to move directly to the command. Alternatively, you can also press ⌷Tab to move from field to field.

When a dialog box contains tabs, move to the appropriate tab by clicking on the desired tab.

Using the QuickBooks Menus

The QuickBooks menus not only display the menu choice, but additionally provide an icon for reference and a keyboard shortcut beside some of the menu commands. An ellipsis (...) at the end of a menu option indicates a dialog box will appear when you select this command.

Use the following methods to access a menu:

- Click the menu command.
- Press ⌷Alt or ⌷F10 to move to the menu bar and highlight the first menu command (e.g., ⌷File).

To access a command on a menu, use one of the following methods:

- Click the command in the menu.
- Press the underlined character for the menu command.
- Press the ⌷↓ arrow to move to the menu command to use and then press ⌷Enter.

If a menu is displayed and you no longer need it, use one of the following methods to close the menu:

- Click in a blank area away from the menu.
- Press ⌷Esc to close the menu, and then press ⌷Esc once more to deselect the menu bar.

> **Note:** Any menu item in black on the menu bar means that particular item is active; a menu item in grey indicates the feature is unavailable at this time.

A feature provided in QuickBooks is the shortcut menu which can be accessed by pointing at an area of the active window, then pressing the right mouse button once. A different shortcut menu may be displayed, depending on what the mouse cursor is pointing at.

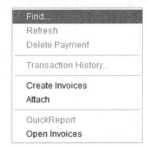

Using the QuickBooks Icon Bar

The Icon bar contains buttons you can access using the mouse. These buttons provide shortcuts for accessing many QuickBooks features. When you place the mouse cursor over a button in the Icon bar, a ScreenTip appears to identify the purpose of the button. Many of the menu items appear as buttons on the Icon bar to enable you to use QuickBooks more quickly and efficiently. To choose a button on the Icon bar, click it with the left mouse button.

There are four sections on the icon bar:

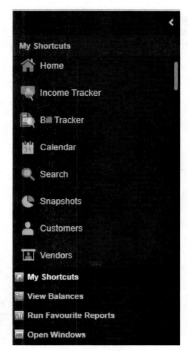

My Shortcuts: Click any icon in this section to open the feature, place the mouse pointer over the icon to display the icon's function. To add, edit, or remove icons from the My Shortcuts section, scroll to the bottom of the section and click "Customize Shortcuts"

View Balances: This section shows balances in your most important accounts.

Run Favourite Reports: This section displays the reports you marked as favourite.

Open Windows: This section displays the list of open windows.

Use the mouse to select the desired section.

Learn the Skill

In this lesson you will explore the QuickBooks program. (If necessary, see page ii in the Preface for detailed instructions on downloading the required data files).

1 If necessary, start QuickBooks and open *We Are Music Ltd. - Your Name* company file.

2 Select the My Shortcuts section of the Icon bar, and move the mouse to point to each of the icons and read the descriptions that appear.

3 Click **Customers** in the Icon bar.

The Customer Centre window is displayed.

4 Click **Vendors** in the Icon bar.

The Vendor Centre window is displayed.

5 Select **View** from the menu bar and then click **Open Window List** from the menu.

6 Click **Customer Centre** in the Open Windows list.

The Customer Centre window is redisplayed.

7 Select **Vendors**, **Enter Bills** from the menu bar.

The Enter Bills window is displayed in the main window, and is now added to the Open Windows List.

8 Select **Customers**, **Customer Centre** from the menu bar.

The menu bar is another way of selecting or opening a window.

9 Select **Customers**, **Create Sales Orders** from the menu bar.

The Create Sales Orders window is displayed in the main window, and is added to the Open Windows List.

10 Select **Enter Bills** in the Open Windows List.

The Enter Bills window is now shown, and it appears at the top of the Open Windows List.

11 Click ❌ **(Close)** at the top right corner of the Enter Bills window to close it. If necessary, click **No** in the Recording Transaction window.

12 Close the Create Sales Orders window. If necessary, click **No** in the Recording Transaction window.

13 Close the Customer Centre and Vendor Centre windows.

14 Select **My Shortcuts** to close the Open Windows List.

15 Select **View Balances** to view some account balances, and then select **My Shortcuts**.

The Chart of Accounts
How the Chart of Accounts Works

Before making entries within QuickBooks, you must first define a Chart of Accounts for your company. This Chart of Accounts works using five main account groups. These are:

Balance Sheet			Income Statement	
o Assets	o Liabilities	o Equity	o Revenue	o Expenses

The Chart of Accounts will contain accounts such as bank accounts, accounts receivable and payable, inventory accounts, equity accounts, revenue, and expense accounts. Your Chart of Accounts can be simple or complex but each account must be identified as one of the QuickBooks Account Types. This table will help describe what each QuickBooks Account Type is and how it relates to financial statements:

QuickBooks Account Type	Account Group	Shows in Financial Statement	Example
Bank	Asset	Balance Sheet	Bank Chequing Account
Accounts Receivable	Asset	Balance Sheet	Accounts Receivable
Other Current Asset	Asset	Balance Sheet	Inventory
Fixed Asset	Asset	Balance Sheet	Equipment
Other Asset	Asset	Balance Sheet	Goodwill
Accounts Payable	Liability	Balance Sheet	Accounts Payable
Credit Card	Liability	Balance Sheet	Credit Card Payable
Other Current Liability	Liability	Balance Sheet	Sales Tax Payable
Long Term Liability	Liability	Balance Sheet	Mortgage Payable
Equity	Equity	Balance Sheet	Owner's Equity
Income	Revenue	Income Statement	Sales Revenue
Cost of Goods Sold	Expense	Income Statement	Cost of Goods Sold
Expense	Expense	Income Statement	Utilities Expense
Other Income	Revenue	Income Statement	Interest Revenue
Other Expense	Expense	Income Statement	Interest Expense

Most Charts of Accounts use account numbers to uniquely identify each account and to identify the account type. In QuickBooks, you can turn this feature on or off; however, most accountants prefer to have the accounts numbered. If you do turn it on, you must follow the numbering convention shown below.

For **Balance Sheet** accounts:

- For **Asset** accounts, assign account numbers from 10,000-19,999.

- For **Liability** accounts, assign account numbers from 20,000-29,999.

- For **Equity** accounts, assign account numbers from 30,000-39,999.

For **Income Statement** accounts:

- For **Revenue** accounts, assign account numbers from 40,000-49,999.

- For **Cost of Goods Sold** and related accounts, assign account numbers from 50,000-59,999.

- For **Expense** accounts, assign account numbers from 60,000-69,999.

Within QuickBooks, it is possible to assign account numbers in the 70,000 and 80,000 ranges. However, it is standard practice to keep account numbers within the ranges listed above.

If you do use account numbers, you should also adhere to the following recommended general ledger account structure:

- Leave plenty of room between account numbers to allow for future growth. For example, if you number accounts without any spaces or gaps between the numbers you assign them, you may have a problem should you later want to add an account within a particular range. Remember that you have 10,000 account spaces for each type of account (Assets, Liabilities, Equity, Revenue, and Expenses).

- Place accounts in the order of liquidity. For example, when you are entering the current asset accounts, place your petty cash and bank account before your accounts receivable and inventory. This is a standard practice, so that external readers of your financial statements can easily determine the "liquidity" of your balance sheet accounts (that is, the relative ease with which you could convert them into cash). Do the same for the liabilities—you should place them in order of timing of payment. For example, you will pay your accounts payable before you make your current bank loan payment; therefore, you should list the accounts payable first. The Chart of Accounts has already been set up for you for the exercises in this courseware. We are going to make a few minor changes and additions to the Chart of Accounts.

> Most business enterprises consult and are guided by the advice of an accountant when creating a Chart of Accounts. The accountant will normally provide a suggested Chart of Accounts, as well as a recommended format and layout for the Balance Sheet and Income Statement. This is important, as it will determine the Account Type (see below) to be allocated in QuickBooks.

 Learn the Skill

In this exercise, you will learn to access the Chart of Accounts window.

1 On the Home Page, in the Company section, click **Chart of Accounts** to open the Chart of Accounts window.

> To display the Chart of Accounts you can also select **Lists**, **Chart of Accounts** in the menu bar, or press Ctrl + A on the keyboard.

The Chart of Accounts window will be displayed as follows:

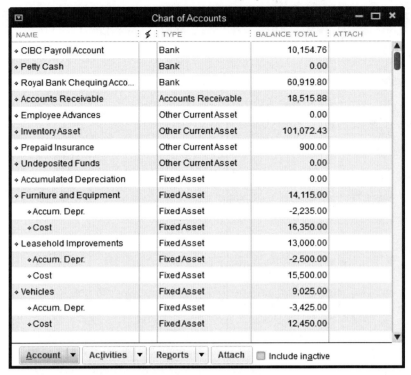

The Accounts window displays the General Ledger accounts that have already been created. It contains the following headings and tabs:

Name	Name of the account.
Type	The type or group of accounts: Bank, Accounts Receivable, Other Current Assets, Fixed Assets, etc.
Balance Total	Current balance in the account.
Account	Where you would create, edit, delete, and make accounts inactive.
Activities	Where you can process transactions such as writing cheques, making deposits, transferring funds and processing journal entries, and so on.
Reports	Where you can access reports such as QuickReport, income tax preparation list, account listing and financial reports.
Attach	This allows you to attach documents from Outlook, desktop, or folders to a particular account.

> Additional columns can be added to the display view, by clicking **View** in the menu bar, and selecting **Customize Columns**. A window is displayed which allows additional columns to be displayed in the Chart of Accounts window.

2   Double-click any account with a **Balance** value that is not **0.00** (zero) or blank.

A new window, the account register, opens showing the detailed transactions in that account.

3   Close the account register.

4   Select **Edit**, **Preferences** in the menu bar.

5   If necessary, select **Accounting** in the list at the left side.

6   If necessary, select the **Company Preferences** tab.

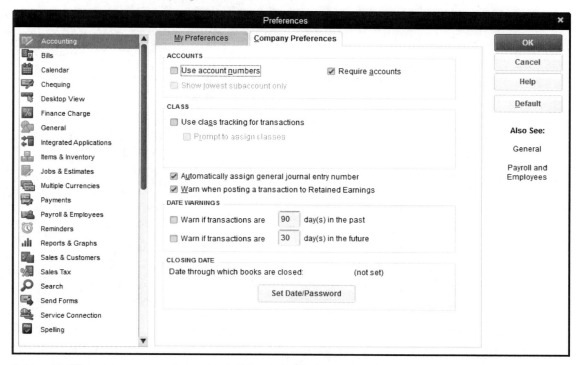

7   Select the **Use account numbers** check box, and click **OK**.

The account numbers will now be displayed for accounts with account numbers. The remaining accounts will not show an account number because these numbers have not been previously entered. Now turn off the account number display again.

8   Select **Edit**, **Preferences** in the menu bar.

9   Clear the **Use account numbers** check box and click **OK**.

Change the sort sequence of the Chart of Accounts.

10   Click the **Name** title bar to sort all of the accounts in alphabetical sequence by name.

11   Click the **Name** title bar again to re-sort all of the accounts into descending sequence.

12   Click the **Balance Total** title bar to sort the accounts in ascending order based on the account balance.

13   Click the **Type** title bar to re-sort the accounts by their type. This is the default setting and is recommended.

14   Close the Chart of Accounts window.

Account Type

The design of the Chart of Accounts is a very important aspect of QuickBooks because you not only want to track financial information at a level of detail to help you determine your financial state of affairs quickly, but also be able to format the financial statements (Balance Sheet and Income Statement) presentation, as desired. Consider the following partial sample Balance Sheet:

Beauty Aesthetics Inc.

Balance Sheet

Jan. 1, 2016

Assets

Bank Account	$7,000.00
Float	200.00
Petty Cash	50.00
Accounts Receivable	2,630.00
Advances Receivable	0.00
Prepaid Expense	1,200.00
Furniture & Fixtures	5,600.00
Accum. Depreciation - Furniture/Fixtures	(1,425.00)
Total Assets	**$15,255.00**

While this Balance Sheet is correct, it does not display the accounts in an easy-to-read format. All the company's assets are grouped together (current and fixed assets), and it is not that easy to determine the total cash in this business. It is also difficult to determine the net value of the fixed assets (Furniture/Fixtures and Accum. Depreciation – Furniture/Fixtures).

However, you cannot simply decide to keep the number of accounts to a minimum because doing so will eliminate the details, such as the following:

Beauty Aesthetics Inc.

Balance Sheet

Jan. 1, 2016

Assets

Current Assets	$11,080.00
Fixed Assets	4,175.00
Total Assets	**$15,255.00**

To overcome this problem, you can make use of the Subaccount option in QuickBooks so that you can have both sufficient detail and also the ability to see a bird's eye view of the financial state. For example, you may want to track all of your cash in three accounts: bank account, float (cash on hand to conduct daily business), and petty cash (to pay minor expenses). These three accounts can be designated as subaccounts of another account named as Cash, which simply includes all transactions from these three accounts as its own, including the final balance. The Cash account is a summary account of the three subaccounts.

The account type is also used to designate how the accounts are grouped together on the balance sheet or income statement. For example, accounts of types such as Bank, Accounts Receivable, and Other Current Asset are grouped together under Current Assets.

By using subaccounts and account types, the partial balance sheet will now look like this:

Beauty Aesthetics Inc.
Balance Sheet

Jan. 1, 2016

Assets

Current Assets

Cash

Bank Account	$7,000.00	
Float	200.00	
Petty Cash	50.00	
Total Cash		$7,250.00

Receivable

Accounts Receivable	2,630.00	
Advances Receivable	0.00	
Total Receivable		2,630.00
Prepaid Expense		1,200.00
Total Current Assets		**$11,080.00**

Fixed Assets

Furniture/Fixtures

Furniture & Fixtures	5,600.00	
Accum. Depreciation	(1,425.00)	
Total Furniture/Fixtures		$4,175.00
Total Fixed Assets		**$4,175.00**
Total Assets		**$15,255.00**

 Learn the Skill

In this exercise, you will learn to change the way the information in the Accounts window is displayed.

1   Click **Lists** in the menu bar, then **Chart of Accounts** to display the Chart of Accounts.

2   Click **Account** at the bottom of the window. Select **Flat View** from the pop-up menu.

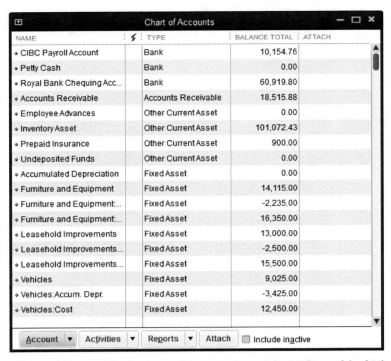

3 Click **Account** at the bottom of the window. Select **Hierarchical View** from the pop-up menu.

4 Click **Reports** at the bottom of the window. Select **Reports on All Accounts**, **Balance Sheet**, **Standard** from the pop-up menu to display the Balance Sheet report.

5 In the **Dates** drop-down list select **Custom**, and in the **As of** box, select **Feb 29, 2016**. If necessary, click **Refresh**.

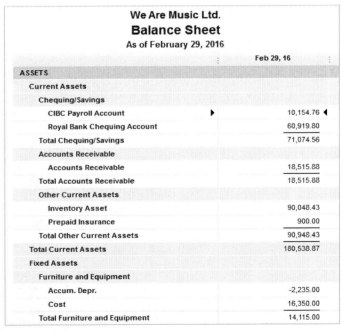

6 Use the scroll bar to view the entire report. Close the Balance Sheet and, if a window appears asking if you wish to memorize the report settings, click **No**.

7 Close the Chart of Accounts window.

General Ledger Accounts
Creating GL Accounts

From the Chart of Accounts window, you can create more General Ledger accounts as you need them.

 Learn the Skill

In this exercise, you will create General Ledger accounts.

1   From the **Lists** menu, select **Chart of Accounts**.

2   Click **Account** at the bottom of the window, and select **New** from the pop-up menu.

> You can also right-click in the Chart of Accounts window and select **New** in the shortcut menu, or press `Ctrl`+`N` to display the Add New Account window.

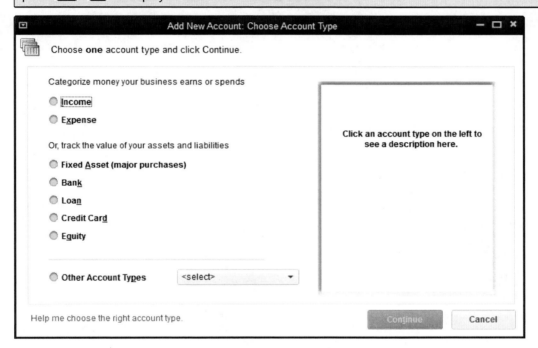

Income	Categorizes money earned from normal business operations.
Expense	Categorizes money spent in the normal course of business operations.
Fixed Asset	Tracks the value of significant items that have a useful life of more than one year.
Bank	Create one account for each cash account needed.
Loan	Tracks the principal owed on loans or lines of credit.
Credit Card	Create one for each credit card your business uses or accepts.
Equity	Tracks money invested in or taken from the company by owners or investors.
Other Account Types	Select an account type from the list that includes: accounts receivable, current assets, other assets, accounts payable, current and/or long term liabilities, cost of goods sold, other income, other expenses.

3   Click to select **Bank**, and then click **Continue** to open the Add New Account window.

Account Type	This field is automatically completed from the previous window choice. There is an option to change this by clicking the down arrow beside the field and choosing from the options provided. The Account Type field serves two functions in your account setup. First, it identifies the various types of accounts. Second, it will categorize them in the correct sections of your Financial Statements.
	The accounts are also sorted in alphabetic order within each type.
Account Name	Name of the account (maximum 31 characters).
Subaccount of	Identifies whether the account being created is part of a group of accounts. If the account is part of a group, you are required to provide the Parent Account (the main account).
Description	This is an optional field to expand on the name of the account.
Bank Acct. No.	The Company Bank Account number. This is also an optional field.
Tax-Line Mapping	If you plan to export your tax information to income tax preparation software such as Intuit's QuickTax or ProFile you can choose the correct tax line from the options offered in the drop-down menu. Otherwise, in general, you should not use tax-line mapping.
Enter Opening Balance	The historical account balance from your previous accounting system, if applicable.

4   In the Account Name field, type: BMO Chequing.

> As with other standard Windows applications, you can use the (Tab) key or the mouse to move between fields.

5   Enter the following data for the remaining fields in the dialog box:

     Description   Bank of Montreal Chequing
     Bank Acct. No.   40987

Do not enter an opening balance. Do not use the Tax-Line Mapping option.

Your screen will be similar to the following:

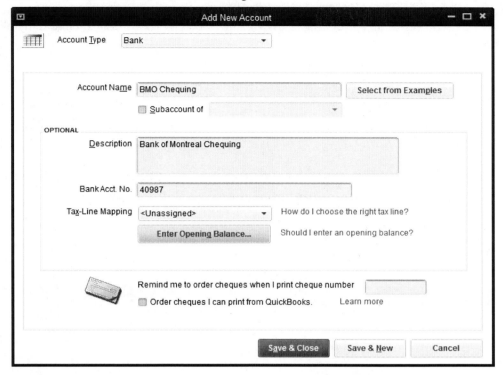

At this point, you have two choices in saving your information:
- Save & Close will save the new account and close the Chart of Accounts window.
- Save & New will save the account and provides the opportunity to input a new ledger account.

6   Click **Save & New**.

> At any time in the process, you can cancel the creation of an account by clicking **Cancel** or by pressing (Esc).

7   Use the method outlined previously to create the following new account:

Account Type	Bank
Account Name	Cash
Description	Cash Summary

8   Click **Save & Close**.

9   When the Set Up Bank Feed window appears, click **No**. Remain in the Chart of Accounts window and proceed with the next exercise.

Modifying GL Accounts

Within the Chart of Accounts window, you can access, modify, and delete previously entered General Ledger accounts.

 Learn the Skill

In this exercise, you will modify General Ledger accounts.

1   Right-click the Royal Bank Chequing Account and select **Edit Account** to display the Edit Account window.

> You can also select the account in the Chart of Accounts window, then click **Account** and select **Edit Account** in the pop-up menu or press Ctrl + E to display the Edit Account window.

2   Enter the following data into the Edit Account window:

Subaccount of   Yes   Cash

The completed window should appear similar to the following:

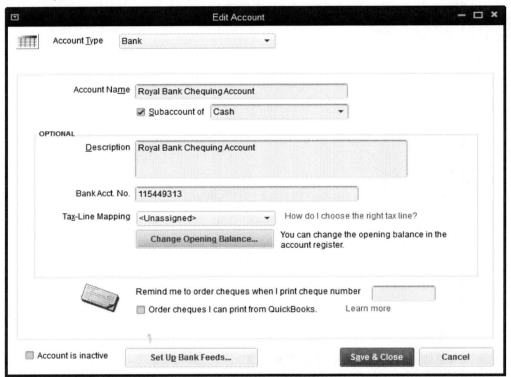

3   Click **Save & Close** to save the changes.

Now change the other two bank accounts and the Petty Cash account to be subaccounts of Cash.

4   Right-click the BMO Chequing account and select **Edit Account** from the shortcut menu.

5   Make the following changes in the Edit Account window:

Subaccount of   Yes   Cash

6   Click **Save & Close** and repeat steps 4 through 6 for the CIBC Payroll Account, and the Petty Cash account.

Learn the Skill

Use the methods outlined previously to set up and modify the following accounts:

1 From the Chart of Accounts window, click **Account**, select **New** and complete as follows:

Account Type	Expense
Account Name	Trade Publications
Subaccount	Dues & Subscriptions
Description	Subscriptions to trade magazines
Sales Tax Code	S

2 Click **Save & Close**.

3 In the Chart of Accounts window, select **Membership Dues**, right-click and select **Edit Account**. Complete as follows:

Subaccount   Dues & Subscriptions

4 Click **Save & Close**.

The Chart of Accounts window should now appear similar to the following:

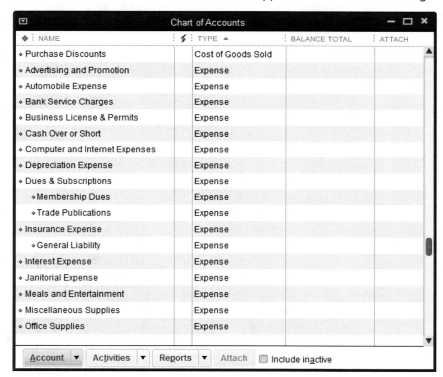

5 Leave the Chart of Accounts window open for the next exercise.

Deleting or Removing GL Accounts

You can delete or remove an existing General Ledger account if it does not have a current balance or a transaction history and it does not have subaccounts under it. This feature is useful if you had created a General Ledger account in error, or circumstances had turned out that the account was never needed.

If transactions have been recorded against it in the past, you should simply make it inactive if it is no longer needed.

Learn the Skill

In this exercise you will learn how to delete an account.

1   In the Chart of Accounts window, right-click the **Uniforms** account and select **Delete Account** from the pop-up menu.

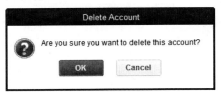

2   Select **OK** to confirm this action.

3   Close the Chart of Accounts window.

QuickBooks Preferences

Through preferences, you can customize QuickBooks to suit the needs of your business and your personal style of working. For most Preference categories, there are two options, My Preferences, and Company Preferences. To access QuickBooks Preferences, select **Edit**, **Preferences** from the menu bar.

The screen below displays the options for General under My Preferences

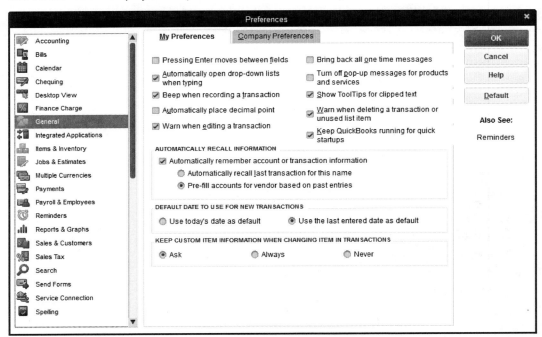

On the left side of the Preferences dialog box is a listing of the various categories. Clicking on each category opens windows where you can choose a variety of functions relevant to each feature. The following overview provides a brief introduction to the options available, many of which will not be discussed further until the Level 2 course.

> The settings entered on the My Preferences tab only affect your QuickBooks sessions, not those of other users. Settings on the Company Preferences tab affect all users, and only the QuickBooks Administrator can enter changes on this tab.

Accounting	This category deals with such items as accounts, account numbers, class tracking, general journal entry numbers, and date warnings.
Bills	The Company Preferences tab allows settings for entering and paying bills, such as due dates, warnings regarding duplicate bill numbers, and using credits and or discounts.
Calendar	The QuickBooks Calendar is a quick way to view transactions and tasks you've entered into QuickBooks.
Chequing	The My Preferences tab allows settings for default bank chequing accounts, and settings for deposit entries. The Company Preferences tab allows settings for defaults on cheques, and chequing accounts for pay cheques, and pay liabilities.
Desktop View	This category allows you to customize your view of the QuickBooks desktop to reflect how you move around QuickBooks, find features, and switch between windows.
Finance Charge	Settings for charges relative to overdue customer accounts.
General	Tabs in this category allow settings for a wide variety of features for entering data, moving around dialog boxes, information recall, default dates, and time formats.
Integrated Applications	Settings for managing applications that interact with the company file. You can integrate key QuickBooks data with a variety of QuickBooks compatible software solutions. Sales, customer, and other financial data can be shared between QuickBooks and certain QuickBooks-compatible software.
Items & Inventory	Settings for purchase orders and inventory, as well as units of measure.
Jobs & Estimates	Settings for job status, estimates, and progress invoicing.
Multiple Currencies	Settings for the use of more than one currency.
Payments	Settings for how payments are applied, and how the funds are deposited.
Payroll & Employees	Settings for payroll and employees.
Reminders	Use the Reminders list to track all the QuickBooks tasks you need to do. It shows you all of the things that are due (such as bills) or that you need to act on (such as To Do notes). You can choose which tasks to be reminded of, and how and when you'll see the reminder.
Reports & Graphs	Settings for a variety of defaults for reports and graphs.
Sales & Customers	Settings for sales forms, price levels, sales orders, and templates.
Sales Tax	Settings for customer and vendor tax codes, display taxes, and assigning tax code defaults.
Search	Settings for search preferences.
Send Forms	Settings for sending by email, including content defaults.
Service Connection	Settings for internet connections.
Spelling	Settings for spelling defaults.
Time & Expenses	The Company Preferences tab allows settings for time tracking, and invoicing options.

Learn the Skill

In this exercise you will learn how to modify preferences.

1   If necessary, select **Edit**, **Preferences** from the menu bar to open the Preferences window.

2   Select **Chequing** from the list, and click the **Company Preferences** tab.

3   Click the checkbox to activate Open the Create Pay Cheques... ensure the **CIBC Payroll Account** is entered. Click the checkbox to activate Open the Pay Payroll Liabilities... ensure the **Royal Bank Chequing Account** is entered.

4   Click the **Desktop View** category, if necessary, click **Yes** in the Save Changes warning.

5   In Desktop View, under **My Preferences**, change the colour scheme to one of your choice, click **OK**.

6   View the screen, observe the difference, and then change the scheme back to the default.

7   In Desktop View, under **Company Preferences**, in the Customers section, click the checkbox for **Statements and Statement Charges** to deselect it.

8   Click **OK**, and **OK** again in the warning screen.

9   Click **Home** on the Icon bar to open the Home Page again, and view the changes. (The icons for Statements and Statement Charges are not displayed.)

10 Open the Preferences window and then click the checkbox to select and turn the icons on again. Click **OK** and **OK** again, and click **Home**.

Both icons should now be displayed.

Company Information

The Company Information function allows you to view all the important information for the company you are working with.

 Learn the Skill

In this exercise you will modify the company information so each student's work can be identified when printed.

1   Select **Company**, **Company Information** from the menu bar.

2   Change the company name to include your name by adding your own name to the end of *We Are Music Ltd.* (for example: We Are Music Ltd. – Jane Black).

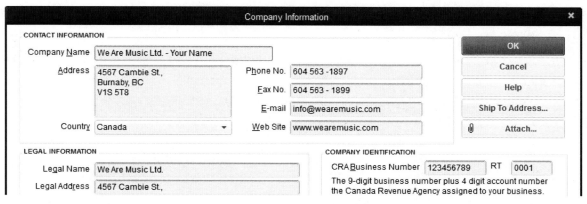

3 When done, click **OK**. If necessary, click **Continue anyway** in the Invalid Business Number warning.

Printing the Chart of Accounts Listing

In order to ensure that you have entered the Chart of Accounts correctly, you should view a listing of the accounts.

 Learn the Skill

In this exercise you will learn how to print a list report.

1 Select **Reports**, **List**, **Account Listing** from the menu bar.

The Account Listing window is displayed. This is one of the pre-built reports that QuickBooks supplies as part of the program. You can modify the format and content of the report to suit your individual needs as well. The default date setting will always be the current date.

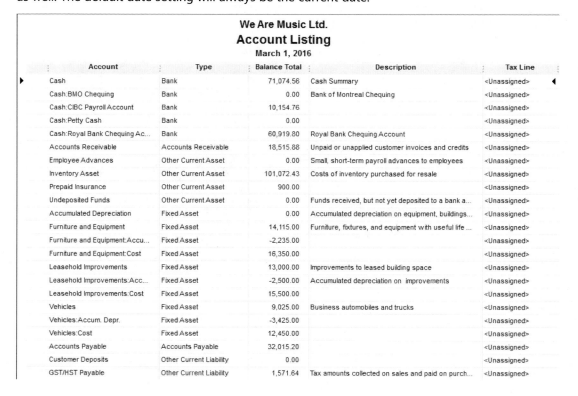

We Are Music Ltd.
Account Listing
March 1, 2016

Account	Type	Balance Total	Description	Tax Line
Cash	Bank	71,074.56	Cash Summary	<Unassigned>
Cash:BMO Chequing	Bank	0.00	Bank of Montreal Chequing	<Unassigned>
Cash:CIBC Payroll Account	Bank	10,154.76		<Unassigned>
Cash:Petty Cash	Bank	0.00		<Unassigned>
Cash:Royal Bank Chequing Ac...	Bank	60,919.80	Royal Bank Chequing Account	<Unassigned>
Accounts Receivable	Accounts Receivable	18,515.88	Unpaid or unapplied customer invoices and credits	<Unassigned>
Employee Advances	Other Current Asset	0.00	Small, short-term payroll advances to employees	<Unassigned>
Inventory Asset	Other Current Asset	101,072.43	Costs of inventory purchased for resale	<Unassigned>
Prepaid Insurance	Other Current Asset	900.00		<Unassigned>
Undeposited Funds	Other Current Asset	0.00	Funds received, but not yet deposited to a bank a...	<Unassigned>
Accumulated Depreciation	Fixed Asset	0.00	Accumulated depreciation on equipment, buildings...	<Unassigned>
Furniture and Equipment	Fixed Asset	14,115.00	Furniture, fixtures, and equipment with useful life ...	<Unassigned>
Furniture and Equipment:Accu...	Fixed Asset	-2,235.00		<Unassigned>
Furniture and Equipment:Cost	Fixed Asset	16,350.00		<Unassigned>
Leasehold Improvements	Fixed Asset	13,000.00	Improvements to leased building space	<Unassigned>
Leasehold Improvements:Acc...	Fixed Asset	-2,500.00	Accumulated depreciation on improvements	<Unassigned>
Leasehold Improvements:Cost	Fixed Asset	15,500.00		<Unassigned>
Vehicles	Fixed Asset	9,025.00	Business automobiles and trucks	<Unassigned>
Vehicles:Accum. Depr.	Fixed Asset	-3,425.00		<Unassigned>
Vehicles:Cost	Fixed Asset	12,450.00		<Unassigned>
Accounts Payable	Accounts Payable	32,015.20		<Unassigned>
Customer Deposits	Other Current Liability	0.00		<Unassigned>
GST/HST Payable	Other Current Liability	1,571.64	Tax amounts collected on sales and paid on purch...	<Unassigned>

2   Once QuickBooks displays the report, you can maximize the window and move around the report using the vertical scroll bar on the right.

3   Select **Print** at the top of the Account Listing window to display the **Print Reports** dialog box, which allows you to change your printer and page settings for the report.

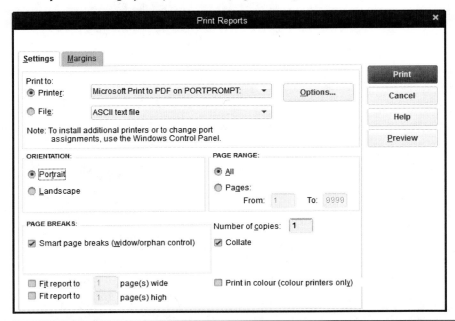

> You can also get to the Print Reports dialog box by selecting **File**, **Print Report** from the menu bar. Review the Print Reports window to choose which orientation you wish. Usually, portrait is the preferred option, but a preview before printing will show which will work best for your purposes.

4   Click **Preview** to view the report before it is printed.

We Are Music Ltd.
Account Listing
March 1, 2016

Account	Type	Balance Total	Description	Tax Line
Cash	Bank	71,074.56	Cash Summary	<Unassigned>
Cash:BMO Chequing	Bank	0.00	Bank of Montreal Chequing	<Unassigned>
Cash:CIBC Payroll Account	Bank	10,154.76		<Unassigned>
Cash:Petty Cash	Bank	0.00		<Unassigned>
Cash:Royal Bank Chequing Acc...	Bank	60,919.80	Royal Bank Chequing Account	<Unassigned>
Accounts Receivable	Accounts Receivable	18,515.88	Unpaid or unapplied customer invoices and credits	<Unassigned>
Employee Advances	Other Current Asset	0.00	Small, short-term payroll advances to employees	<Unassigned>
Inventory Asset	Other Current Asset	101,072.43	Costs of inventory purchased for resale	<Unassigned>
Prepaid Insurance	Other Current Asset	900.00		<Unassigned>
Undeposited Funds	Other Current Asset	0.00	Funds received, but not yet deposited to a bank acco...	<Unassigned>
Accumulated Depreciation	Fixed Asset	0.00	Accumulated depreciation on equipment, buildings a...	<Unassigned>
Furniture and Equipment	Fixed Asset	14,115.00	Furniture, fixtures, and equipment with useful life bey...	<Unassigned>
Furniture and Equipment:Accum...	Fixed Asset	-2,235.00		<Unassigned>
Furniture and Equipment:Cost	Fixed Asset	16,350.00		<Unassigned>
Leasehold Improvements	Fixed Asset	13,000.00	Improvements to leased building space	<Unassigned>
Leasehold Improvements:Accu...	Fixed Asset	-2,500.00	Accumulated depreciation on improvements	<Unassigned>
Leasehold Improvements:Cost	Fixed Asset	15,500.00		<Unassigned>
Vehicles	Fixed Asset	9,025.00	Business automobiles and trucks	<Unassigned>
Vehicles:Accum. Depr.	Fixed Asset	-3,425.00		<Unassigned>
Vehicles:Cost	Fixed Asset	12,450.00		<Unassigned>

5   Click **Next page** to go to the last page of the report.

6   Click **Zoom In** to magnify the page, then click **Zoom Out**.

7   Click **Close** to close the Preview window.

8   Click **Print** in the Print Reports dialog box to print the report.

9   Close the Account Listing window. If necessary, click **No** if asked to memorize the report settings.

Now display and print the Chart of Accounts.

10 Display the Chart of Accounts window by clicking **Chart of Accounts** in the Company section of the Home Page.

11 Select **File**, **Print List** from the menu bar. If a List Reports warning screen is displayed, click **Do not display this message in the future**, and then **OK**.

12 In the Print Lists dialog box, click **Preview**.

Chart of Accounts

Account	Type
Cash	Bank
BMO Chequing	Bank
CIBC Payroll Account	Bank
Petty Cash	Bank
Royal Bank Chequing Account	Bank
Accounts Receivable	Accounts Receivable
Employee Advances	Other Current Asset
Inventory Asset	Other Current Asset
Prepaid Insurance	Other Current Asset
Undeposited Funds	Other Current Asset
Accumulated Depreciation	Fixed Asset
Furniture and Equipment	Fixed Asset
Accum. Depr.	Fixed Asset
Cost	Fixed Asset
Leasehold Improvements	Fixed Asset
Accum. Depr.	Fixed Asset
Cost	Fixed Asset

13 Click **Close**.

14 In the Print Lists dialog box, click **Print**.

15 Close the Chart of Accounts window.

Using Dates in QuickBooks

QuickBooks uses an 8-digit date format for its operations. The format used is dictated by the settings in the Region and Language settings in the Windows operating system. For the purpose of this courseware, the mm/dd/yyyy format is used.

The following are acceptable ways of keying in the date January 31, 2016 (with Windows set in mm/dd/yyyy format):

Format	Examples
MM/DD/YY	01/31/16
MM/DD/YYYY	01/31/2016
MMDDYY	013116
M/D/Y	1/31/16

◄	March 2016	►

SU	MO	TU	WE	TH	FR	SA
		01	02	03	04	05
06	07	08	09	10	11	12
13	14	15	16	17	18	19
20	21	22	23	24	25	26
27	28	29	30	31		

You can also use the pop-up calendar by clicking the ▦ icon at the right of any date field.

Using the icon ensures an accurate date entry format. When you use the ▦ icon to select a date, use the arrows at the left and right of the current month to move to another month. Then click on the day you want to use in the date field.

As dates are used to calculate discounts, due dates and interest charges, absolute accuracy is required when inputting date data into any computerized bookkeeping program.

General Journal Transactions
Creating Journal Transactions

Within QuickBooks, you should always select the appropriate document for a particular type of transaction. For example, you would choose the Create Invoice icon when you are entering a sale and the Pay Bills icon when you want to enter a payment to one of your vendors.

The General Journal is slightly different—you will use it for miscellaneous transactions that are not handled by any of the other transactions. Note that you must enter all purchases and sales either into the Create Invoices or the Enter Bills transaction windows, rather than the General Journal. This is because QuickBooks does not automatically track the GST/HST entered within the General Journal. If you enter purchases and sales into the appropriate transaction windows, then QuickBooks can keep accurate records of the GST/HST you have charged and paid, and create accurate Customer and Vendor records.

The types of transactions that might be entered in the General Journal include:

- loan interest
- depreciation transactions
- accruals
- General Ledger adjustments
- transfers from one bank to another
- owner's loans and changes to the capital structure of the business.

 Learn the Skill

In this exercise you will learn how to create General Journal Entries.

1   Select **Company**, **Make General Journal Entries** from the menu bar.

2   In the **Date** field, type: 3/1/16 (March 1, 2016) as the date for this General Journal entry and press Tab two times. This will bypass the automatic Entry No.

3   In the **Account** field, click the drop-down button and select **BMO Chequing** and press Tab.

4   Type: 5000 as the **Debit** and press Tab twice.

> QuickBooks assumes that you are working with dollar amounts, so that if 5000 is keyed in, the program recognizes it as $5,000.00. You only need to key in a decimal point if there is a cent amount, for example, $10.50 should be entered as 10.5 or 10.50.
>
> If you wanted to enter a credit for this account, you would press Tab without an entry in order to move to the Credit column.

5   In the **Memo** field, type: Transfer from Royal chequing as a descriptive comment for this transaction and press Tab twice to jump to the Account field on the next line.

QuickBooks now defaults to a $5,000.00 credit in order to try to balance this entry.

6   For this second Account, select **Royal Bank Chequing Account** and press Tab three times.

7   Type: Transfer to BMO chequing in the memo column.

Your entry should be similar to the following:

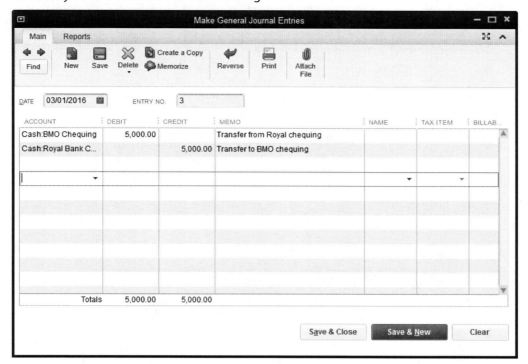

8   Click **Save & New**.

9   Input the following General Journal entry:

        Date   3/01/16 (March 1, 2016)

Account	Debit	Credit	Memo
Petty Cash	300.00		Establish Petty Cash
BMO Chequing		300.00	

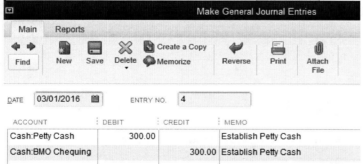

10   Click **Save & New** to keep the General Journal window open for the next exercise.

Creating Memorized Journal Transactions

When an entry is a standard entry that recurs on a regular basis, you can save time by creating a memorized transaction. This function lets you instruct QuickBooks to make a copy of the transaction for future use so that you will not have to rethink the bookkeeping entries or re-enter most of the information.

Learn the Skill

In this exercise you will learn how to memorize a General Journal transaction.

1   Enter the following General Journal transaction, but do not save.

Date   3/15/16 (Mar 15, 2016)

Term Loan	500.00		Loan payment
Royal Bank Chequing		500.00	

2   Select the memorize icon **Memorize** from the Main ribbon at the top of the dialog box.

3   Enter the following values or options in the Memorize Transaction dialog box:

Name   Term loan payment
How Often   Monthly
Next Date   4/15/16 (Apr 15, 2016)

The completed dialog box should appear similar to the following:

4   Click **OK** to return to the General Journal window.

5   Click the **Save & Close** button in the General Journal window.

Recalling Memorized Journal Transactions

You have created a recurring transaction for the monthly loan payment. Now you can reuse this transaction without having to re-enter any of the information, with QuickBooks inserting the next due date for you.

 ## Learn the Skill

In this exercise you will recall and post a memorized transaction.

1   Click **Lists** on the menu bar and then select **Memorized Transaction List**.

The Memorized Transaction List window displays the memorized transactions, including the new one just entered, along with such information as the frequency and the next due date.

2   If necessary, click **LRS Property Management** to highlight it, and click **Enter Transaction**.

QuickBooks now creates a new transaction, using the memorized transaction data. QuickBooks has also automatically adjusted the transaction date to Mar 1, 2016 for this new transaction.

3   Accept the date of **03/01/2016** and click the **Print Later** check box to enable the To Print option. Adjust the memo to read: March rent and the Expenses memo to read: Store rent for March 2016.

4   Click **Save & Close** to save this entry then close the Memorized Transaction List.

Now create another General Journal transaction, but this one will be automatically processed by QuickBooks.

5   Select **Company**, **Make General Journal Entries** from the menu bar.

6   Enter the following General Journal transaction, but do not save.

Date   03/01/16 (Mar 1, 2016)

Account	Debit	Credit	Memo
Insurance Expense:			
General Liability . . .	150.00		Monthly portion of annual premium
Prepaid Insurance		150.00	

7   Right-click in the Make General Journal Entries window, select **Memorize General Journal** from the menu.

8   Enter the following values/options in the Memorize Transaction dialog box:

Name   Monthly Insurance cost
Automate Transaction Entry   On
How Often   Monthly
Next Date   04/01/2016 (Apr 1, 2016)

9   Click **OK** to save this memorized transaction.

10   Save the General Journal transaction by clicking **Save & Close**.

11   Select **Lists**, **Memorized Transaction List** from the menu bar.

The list now includes the additional memorized transaction. Notice the settings in the Frequency and Auto columns for each of the transactions that you selected.

12   Close the Memorized Transaction List window.

When you close down QuickBooks and start it up again later, you will see a message box similar to the following. This is displayed because QuickBooks compares the current system date to the dates set for the automated transaction(s) entered. You can then choose to process them or defer them. The number of entries to be made will depend on the current computer date when you open QuickBooks.

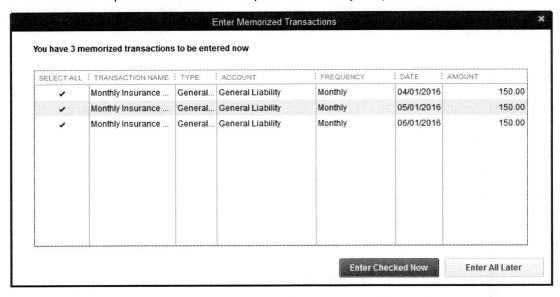

If you choose not to enter the Memorized Transactions, the following screen will be displayed.

Adjusting Previously Posted General Journal Entries

Journal entries that have already been posted may be easily adjusted if errors are found later.

 ## Learn the Skill

In this exercise you will learn how to adjust a previously posted journal entry.

The journal entry for the petty cash entry posted on Mar 1, 2016 was subsequently found to be incorrect. The amount should have been taken from the Royal Bank Chequing Account, not the BMO Chequing Account.

1   Click **Edit** on the menu bar, then **Find**. If necessary, select the **Simple** tab.

Assume that you do not remember any details about the transaction except that you know it was recorded in the General Journal, and the amount was entered as $300.00.

> You should avoid this situation of not having details of recorded transactions. For example, you should have recorded (as a minimum) the transaction entry number, date of entry, amount, and your initials (or whoever entered the data) on the source document—the accountant's memo as an example. These documents are required to be stored in any case for audit reasons.

2   Click **Transaction Type**, and select **Journal**.

3   In the **Amount** field type: 300.00.

4   Click **Find** to search for all transactions that meet these criteria.

The Find window should appear similar to the following:

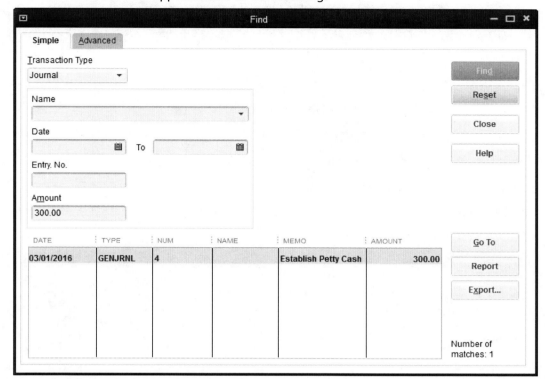

5   Select anywhere on the journal entry number 4 (dated Mar 1) row, and click **Go To**.

The General Journal transaction is now displayed.

6   Change the bank account from BMO Chequing to **Royal Bank Chequing Account** then click **Save & Close**.

A message box appears to inform you that: You have changed the transaction. Do you want to record your changes? Click **Yes** to close the message box.

> Use this same procedure if an entry was originally posted with an incorrect date. Recall the original transaction, amend the date instead of the amount, and save the transaction again.

7   Close the Find window.

Reversing General Journal Entries

To remove a General Journal entry that has already been saved, you can either void or delete it. You should always choose to void a transaction because this action will simply change the amount values to zero but otherwise leave the transaction in the records.

If you need to completely remove the transaction from the records, you can choose to delete it. However, the transaction number will not be re-used, and an audit of your records will reveal that a transaction has been deleted.

Learn the Skill

In this exercise you will reverse a previously posted General Journal entry.

You have renegotiated a loan with the bank. You would like to void the loan payment that was generated on Mar 15, 2016.

1   Click **Edit** on the menu bar, then **Find**.

2   Click the **Transaction Type** drop-down button, and select **Journal**.

3   Select the first **Date** field, and select **Mar 15, 2016**.

4   Click **Find** to search for all transactions that meet these criteria.

5   Select the **Loan Payment** that is displayed (Journal entry number 5) and click **Go To**.

6   Right-click anywhere in the Make General Journal Entries window, and select **Void General Journal**. Your window should resemble the following:

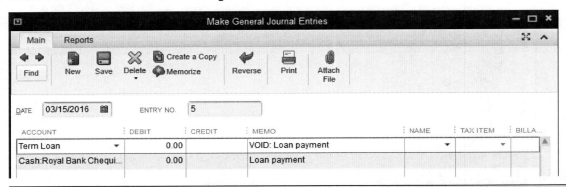

You can also void the transaction by selecting **Edit**, **Void General Journal** from the menu bar.

7   Click **Save & Close**.

8   Click **Yes** to close the changed transaction message box.

9   Close the Find window.

10   We still have a memorized transaction for the voided loan payment, which will have to be deleted. Click **Lists**, **Memorized Transaction List** on the menu bar.

11   Right-click the **Term loan payment**.

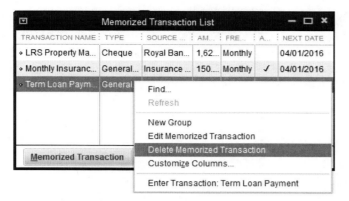

12 Select **Delete Memorized Transaction**.

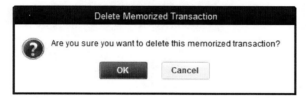

13 Click **OK** in the Delete Memorized Transaction window, and then close the Memorized Transaction List window.

General Journal Report

 Learn the Skill

In this exercise, you will learn how to generate a general journal report, review the entries that have been posted, and check that QuickBooks has made the necessary adjustments for the correction shown above.

1 Select **Reports**, **Accountant & Taxes**, **Journal** from the menu bar.

The Journal report is immediately generated and displayed on screen. If a message regarding Collapsing and Expanding Transactions is displayed, click "Do Not display...". By default, it chooses the current month for the report. For this exercise, the report dates must be changed to March 2016 because the transactions were entered for those dates.

2 At the top of the Journal report window, in the **Dates** field, select **Custom**, change the **From** date to **Mar 1, 2016** and the **To** date to **Mar 31, 2016**.

3 Click **Refresh** to display the data.

4   Compare with the following report by scrolling down to view these transactions:

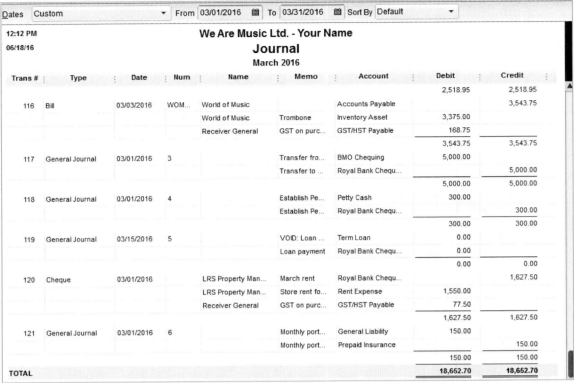

Look at Journal entry 4 which shows the adjusted Petty Cash entry (change of bank account) and Journal entry 5 which was the voided loan payment.

8   Close the Journal report window.

The following message box may display because you had made a change to one of the report selection criteria.

9   If necessary, click to select the check box and click **No** to close this message box.

Backing Up QuickBooks Data Files

Backups should be done every time you complete a work session where you have made changes of any sort to the QuickBooks data. The importance of backups cannot be over-emphasized. Hard disk drives do crash and data files do become corrupted. Imagine having to re-enter a whole year's work because a backup wasn't done—it has happened!

Using QuickBooks Backup allows you to stay with the original file as opposed to using Create Copy, which saves the data as a new file. QuickBooks contains a feature to schedule regular backups. For more information, search *back up* in the Help index, and select the topic Schedule Backups.

 ## Learn the Skill

In this exercise you will learn to create a backup copy of the data file.

1   Click **File** from the menu bar, and then select **Create Backup**.

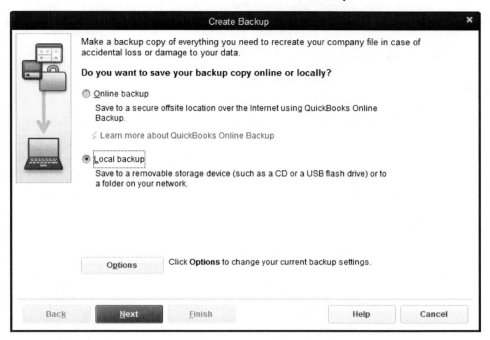

2   Since this is the first time you will be backing up the data file, select the **Options** button to specify the location for the backup.

3   Click the **Browse** button to navigate to the student data files location.

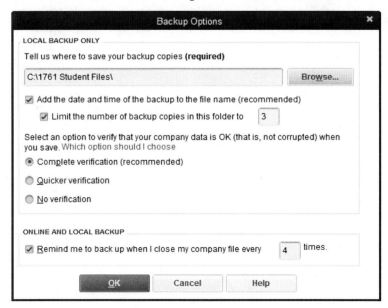

4 Review this screen to ensure you have selected the appropriate options. Ensure the check boxes for date and time and number limits are selected, and the **Complete verification** option button is selected. You may set the number of backup files you prefer. You may also select to have the program remind you about backing up the file every so often.

> It is recommended that you add the date of the backup to the filename. This allows you to keep multiple versions of the backup file on the same disk—if you encounter problems with your most recent backup, then you can select an older backup version.

4 Click **OK** to proceed. If you are backing up to the C: drive, the next warning message will appear.

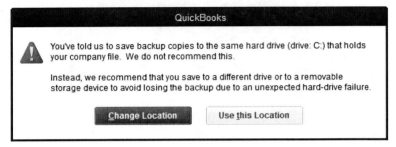

5 To continue to use the C: drive click **Use this Location**.

6 If available insert a USB flash drive into the computer, click **Change Location** and select that drive as the backup destination for your file, if not use the C: drive.

> With today's new technology, a backup is best done using a portable hard drive or USB flash drive, and stored away from the company's location. Although no storage media are guaranteed to preserve their contents for a very long period of time, these types are fairly reliable. This exercise uses the C: drive here for demonstration purposes only.

7 In the Create Backup window, click **Next**.

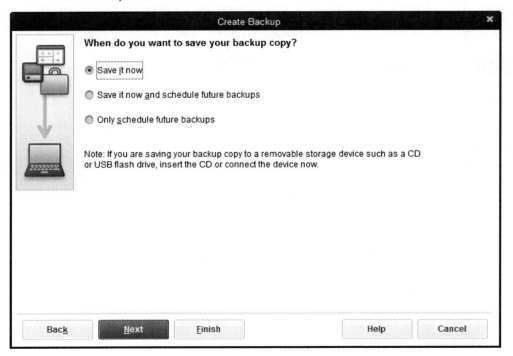

8 Select **Save it now**, and then **Next**

9 In the Save Backup Copy window, if necessary select the desired location, and in the File name field type: `We Are Music Ltd. - Your Name Lesson 1`.

10 Click **Save** to save and close the window.

The following message confirming the backup and the relevant information regarding the location and the name of the file will appear.

10 Click **OK** to acknowledge that the backup is complete.

> Backup files are compressed before they are copied, thus taking less space on your disk. If you wish to use your backup file for any reason, select **File**, **Open or Restore Company** or **Restore Previous Local Backup** from the menu bar.

Lesson Summary

In this lesson, you learned about the basic functions and features of QuickBooks Premier. In particular, you learned how to:

- ☑ manage QuickBooks files
- ☑ open and restore QuickBooks files
- ☑ explain the QuickBooks screen components
- ☑ understand the Chart of Accounts
- ☑ create, modify, find, edit and delete general ledger (GL) accounts
- ☑ work with QuickBooks Preferences

- ☑ find and amend the company information
- ☑ input dates into QuickBooks
- ☑ input, adjust, and delete General Journal transactions
- ☑ create, recall and delete memorized transactions
- ☑ produce a General Journal report
- ☑ back up company data files

 ## Practice the Skill

The following additional exercise covers many of the items discussed in this Lesson. The Practice the Skill exercises are included as extra practice and may be completed by the students in class or on their own. Your instructor has access to the Answer Key for these exercises.

1. Create the following new account:

Type	Expense
Name	License
Subaccount	Yes - Vehicle Expense
Description	Annual vehicle license

2. Create and process the following memorized transaction:

Date	Mar 4, 2016			
Account	Owners Draw	Debit:	500.00	Memo: Weekly draw
Account	Royal Bank Chequing	Credit:	500.00	
Name	Owner's Draw			
Automatically	Weekly			
Next Date	Mar 11, 2016			

3. Delete the following Accounts:
   Automobile Expense
   Cash Over or Short

4. Create the following General Journal entry:

Date	March 7, 2016		
Account	CIBC Payroll Account	Debit:	5,000.00
Account	Royal Bank Chequing	Credit:	5,000.00
Memo	Transfer of funds		

5. Backup the data file as: `We Are Music Ltd. - Your Name Lesson 1 Practice.`

Review Questions

1. Name five items that can be found on the Lists menu.

2. Where is a good location to save a backup copy of your QuickBooks company data?

3. Which menu option would you access to change your company's address or name?

4. List the different ways you can access a command within QuickBooks.

5. Why would you want to create a backup copy of your company data?

6. How do you open an existing set of data files?

7. What are the two different ways of creating accounts in QuickBooks?

8. What conditions need to exist before you can delete an account in QuickBooks?

9. Name the two tabs displayed on the Home screen.

10. The General Journal is used to input bookkeeping transactions that do not obviously fit into one of the other modules.

    a. True   b. False

11. Once you have posted a General Journal entry, the only way to adjust it is to void the original entry, and then create a new transaction.

    a. True   b. False

12. What report is used to print the General Journal transactions posted between specific dates?

Lesson 2: Inventory and Services

Lesson Objectives

In this lesson, you will learn how to set up the Inventory and Services module of QuickBooks Premier. Upon successful completion of this lesson, you will be able to:

☐ work with the Inventory Centre

☐ create inventory accounts

☐ work with the Item list

☐ create inventory parts and service items

☐ set Units of Measure

☐ manage inventory and service item data

☐ run inventory reports

To Start This Lesson

Restoring the Exercise File

1. From the **File** menu in QuickBooks, choose **Open or Restore Company**.

   QuickBooks displays the Open or Restore Company window.

2. Select **Restore a backup copy** and click **Next**.

3. Select **Local backup** and click **Next**.

4. In the Open Backup Copy window navigate to your *1761 Student Files* folder.

5. Select *We Are Music Ltd 2016 - Student.QBB* file and then click **Open**.

6. In the Open or Restore Company window, click **Next**.

7. Navigate to your *1761 Student Files* folder.

8. In the File name field of the Save Company File as window, type: We Are Music Ltd - Your Name Lesson 2 and then click **Save**.

9. In the QuickBooks Login window enter the password: **Sys2016**.

10. Click **OK** when you see the message that the file has been successfully restored.

11. If necessary close the QuickBooks Learning Centre and Have a Question windows.

Inventory
Working with the Inventory Centre

QuickBooks makes it easy to manage your inventory with the Inventory Centre.

To open the Inventory Centre:

- Choose **Vendors**, **Inventory Activities**, then **Inventory Centre** from the menu bar; or

- Click the **Inventory Activities** icon in the Company section of the Home page, and select **Inventory Centre** from the drop-down list.

> If you don't see this option, you need to turn on inventory tracking – click **Edit**, **Preferences**, **Items & Inventory**.

When you open the Inventory Centre the following screen appears:

The Tool bar buttons allow access to a variety of tasks, including creating new items and transactions.

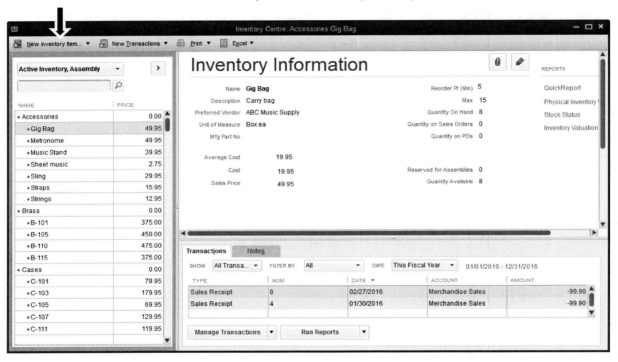

The Inventory Centre is divided into three panes:

- The left pane lists your inventory and inventory assembly items. To filter or sort this list, click the top drop-down arrow and select an option.

- The top-right pane shows the details for the selected inventory item, and provides quick access to several reports.

- The bottom-right pane has tabs that show transactions and notes related to the selected item.

The Inventory Centre can be used for a variety of activities such as:

- Working with inventory items:
    - Searching an item
    - Adding new items
    - Editing items
    - Adding a picture to an item
- Adding transactions
- Running inventory reports

Managing the Inventory List

There are a variety of lists in QuickBooks. All list management tasks are performed in a similar manner in these lists. Some lists are incorporated into a QuickBooks Centre, and some are accessed via a list option on the menu bar. Lists that are in the centres are not accessible separately from the menu bar. Entries in these lists can be added, edited, or deleted as needed. There are four centres in QuickBooks, Customers, Vendors, Inventory and Employees.

 Learn the Skill

In this exercise you will work with the Inventory list to adjust the list views.

1 Click the **Inventory Activities** icon in the Company section of the Home page, and select **Inventory Centre** from the drop-down list.

2 Click the top drop-down arrow in the left pane and view the options in the list.

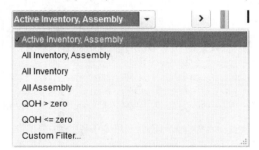

Active Inventory, Assembly	Displays only active inventory, assembly items.
All Inventory, Assembly	Displays all inventory assembly items.

All Inventory	Displays all items (active and inactive).
All Assembly	Displays only assembly items.
QOH>zero	Displays the items whose quantity on hand is greater than zero.
QOH<=zero	Displays the items whose quantity on hand is equal to or less than zero.
Custom Filter	Allow a search of items with specific parameters, such as: item name, company name, account number, custom fields, and so on.

3 Select **QOH<=zero** and view the list.

4 Select **QOH>zero** and view the list.

5   Select **Active Inventory, Assembly**.

6   Select item **Music Stand** in the list and view the right pane to see the information for this item.

7   Double-click invoice 10 to view the invoice.

8   Close the invoice, and the Inventory Centre.

Creating Inventory Accounts

In QuickBooks every inventory and service item type is uniquely recorded and tracked in your inventory. This capability allows you to:

- Manage your inventory to an optimum level so that stock outs are prevented, while preventing you from having too much of your capital tied up in inventory.

- Manage the price you charge for each item by monitoring the gross profit earned on these items. You will then have more information when deciding on prices to be charged.

- Run financial reports at any time to monitor your overall business profitability.

- Calculate any inventory shrinkage whenever a physical inventory count is done.

- Be warned when the current level of stock of an inventory item falls below a specified minimum and re-ordering is required.

You should understand that QuickBooks uses only the Moving Average Cost Method in valuing inventory. Other inventory valuation methods (such as First In First Out (FIFO), Last In First Out (LIFO), standard cost) are not supported. The Moving Average Cost Method means that:

- The book value cost of each item type is calculated as the average cost of each item type. For example, the inventory cost of a printer is calculated as the total cost of buying the printers currently in stock (e.g., $1,000) divided by the number of printers in stock (e.g., 10), which would then be $100.

- The average cost moves because new stock purchased may affect the average cost. If the new stock costs more than the current average (e.g., $110), then the new average cost will move higher. Conversely, if the new stock costs less, then the new average cost will move lower.

- The average cost is recalculated every time new stock is purchased, or inventory adjustments are made.

- The current average cost is automatically used for the accounting transaction whenever goods are sold.

Creating Inventory and Service Items saves time, in that, when buying or selling merchandise, and selling services, QuickBooks enters the items from a list, rather than the user having to type each item in.

Before you add an inventory item you need to create the different types of accounts associated with inventory items. The necessary accounts are *Asset*, *Revenue,* and *Expense*.

You may also need a Transfer Costs account, a Variance account, an Inventory Adjustment account and a Purchases Discount account. If Inventory items are used to assemble finished components, then an Item Assembly Costs account may be required. Note that accounting treatment of purchase-related costs varies from company to company in how these are recorded and allocated in the financial statements.

Learn the Skill

In this exercise you will create the accounts required for inventory management.

1   If necessary, start QuickBooks and ensure the *We Are Music Ltd - Your Name Lesson 2* company file is open.

2   From the **Lists** menu select **Chart of Accounts** to display the Chart of Accounts.

A series of new accounts must be added to the Chart of Accounts for inventory accounting. Some of them have already been done for you. Examples of the necessary accounts include:

Account Name	Account Type
Inventory-Asset	Other Current Asset
Merchandise Sales	Income
Service Sales	Income
Cost of Goods Sold*	Cost of Goods Sold
Freight Charges	Cost of Goods Sold
Purchase Discounts	Cost of Goods Sold
Inventory Variance	Cost of Goods Sold
Item Assembly Costs	Cost of Goods Sold
Adjustment Write-off	Cost of Goods Sold

*the abbreviation COGS (Cost of Goods Sold) may be used in this account name.

Now add the new inventory accounts.

3   In the Chart of Accounts window, click **Account**, and then **New** from the pop-up menu. Enter the following data for this new account:

Other Account Types	Name	Sales Tax Code
Cost of Goods Sold	Inventory Variance	G

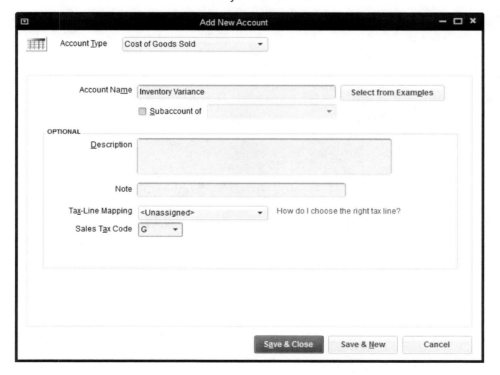

4   Click **Save & New** to save this new account.

5   Repeat steps 3 and 4 to add these new accounts: click **Save & Close** after the second account.

Other Account Types	Name	Sales Tax Code
Cost of Goods Sold	Item Assembly Costs	G
Cost of Goods Sold	Inventory Adjustment Write-off	G

6   Close the Chart of Accounts window.

> Where a business has separate departments or divisions, Asset, Revenue and Expense accounts may be set up for each department, for example, Inventory – Computers, Inventory – Printers, Inventory – Software and Inventory – Copiers, with similar Sales and Expense accounts.

Creating Inventory Items

In order to create invoices, there must be items to include on the invoice. An item can be defined as a product or service that is sold or resold by your company in the course of doing business.

The total value of all the inventory items that are entered in the Inventory Ledger has to match the same value that is shown in the balance of the inventory asset account(s) in the General Ledger. This is part of the procedure to set up data files, and will be discussed in the Level 2 courseware.

To accurately track inventory, each type/piece of merchandise that is stocked as inventory must be listed as a separate item in the Inventory Ledger. Each item must have its own unique reference name or number consisting of letters, digits, or a combination of these. You should be aware that each company uses its own inventory numbering scheme based upon specific volumes and needs, with the exception of Universal Product Codes (UPCs) on grocery items.

Item List

This list contains the items you have set up for the services and goods you buy and sell, as well as special items that perform calculations (subtotals, discounts, and sales tax). These items appear as line items on your sales and purchase forms.

Entries in the list can be added, edited, deleted, moved and merged. There are several lists in QuickBooks, Item, Vendors, Customers, Employees; and entries in all lists can be managed in a similar manner. This will be dealt with in succeeding lessons.

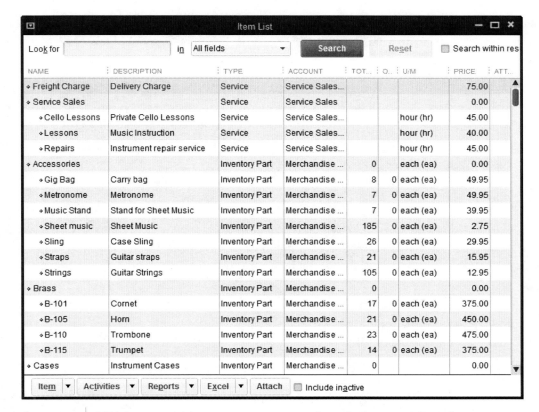

Item	This button provides access to commands such as: New, Edit, Delete, etc.
Activities	This button provides access to commands such as: Create Invoices, Enter Sales Receipts, Change Item Prices, etc.
Reports	This button provides access to commands such as: QuickReport, Price List, Item Listing, etc.
Excel	This button allows you to import, export and/or paste from Excel.
Attach	This button allows you to attach documents or other relevant files to the selected item.

Service Items

Service items in QuickBooks can be used to track services that you sell and purchase. For example, this company sells repair services to clients, but purchases services such as cleaning services. You must create a service item for each type of service your company sells. However, in order to provide more detail, you can also create sub-items of particular services. The primary difference is that services generally cannot be kept on the shelf or in storage until they are sold, nor be verified by physical count.

Non-Inventory Items

In QuickBooks, a non-inventory part is one of the types of line items you can use when you are filling out a sales form or purchase form. Use non-inventory part items to track merchandise that:

- You purchase but do not resell.
- You sell but do not purchase.
- You purchase and resell but do not stock in inventory or track as inventory.

You can use purchase orders to obtain non-inventory items if you wish to track items that you use in the business, but do not sell to customers. Purchase orders will be dealt with in Lesson 3 of this courseware.

Inventory Part Items

In QuickBooks, an inventory part is one of the types of line items you can use when you are filling out a sales or purchase form. You use inventory items to track merchandise your business purchases, keeps in stock as inventory, and then resells. For each inventory item, QuickBooks tracks the current number in stock and the average value of your inventory after each purchase and sale.

Units of Measure

QuickBooks is also able to track items by different units of measure. Most retailers sell their goods in smaller units than those they purchase. For example, they may purchase goods by the pallet. Each pallet will have 30 cases containing 12 or 24 items each. The retailer will then price and sell each item as an individual unit. In this example, the buying unit of measure (UOM) is the *pallet*, the stocking UOM is the *case*, and the selling UOM is *each*. Generally, units of measure include weight (e.g., kilograms, grams, pounds), volume (e.g., litres, cubic feet), length (e.g., km, metres, feet), time (e.g., days, hours, minutes), and count (e.g., each, packages, bundles). QuickBooks has three types of UOMs:

Inventory Unit	How the items are stocked and counted (each, box, pack, etc.) while stored in inventory.
Sales Unit	How the items are sold to customers.
Purchasing Unit	How the items are bought from suppliers.

For the purposes of the following exercise, the Units of Measure have been enabled in the data file. If it was necessary to enable the UOM, you would follow these steps:

1. From the menu bar select **Edit**, **Preferences**.

2. From the left side, select **Items & Inventory**.

3. Select the **Company Preferences** tab and under Unit of Measure, click the **Enable** button.

4. In the next window select **Multiple U/M Per Item**.

5. Click **Finish**. Click **OK** and **OK** again to accept the warning.

 ## Learn the Skill

In this exercise, you will learn how to work with the units of measure and to create new inventory items.

1   From the **Lists** menu select **Item List** to display the Item List window.

> You can also display this window by selecting **Vendors**, **Item List** from the menu bar, or by clicking the **Items & Services** icon in the Company section of the Home Page.

2   Click **Item** at the bottom of the Item List window, and then select **New** in the pop-up menu.

The New Item window opens. The contents of this window will change, depending on the type of item that you select.

> You can also display this window by right-clicking anywhere in the Item List window and selecting **New**, by pressing Ctrl + N on the keyboard, or by selecting **New Inventory Item** from the menu bar of the **Inventory Centre**.

This courseware will deal with two of the item types: Inventory and Service. A simple way of differentiating between these is to remember that a service is not stocked on the shelf, and cannot be verified by a physical count.

3   Click in the **Type** field and select **Inventory Part**.

4   In the **Item Name/Number** text box, type: C-115 (Each inventory item should have either a specific name or number) and press the Tab key.

5   Activate the **Subitem of** checkbox and then click the drop-down arrow and select **Cases**.

6   In U/M Set, select **Count in each:ea** and press the Tab key twice.

7   In the Description on Purchase Transactions text box, type: Cornet Case and press Tab.

8   Enter the remaining data for this window, ensuring the As of date shows **03/01/2016** (March 1, 2016).

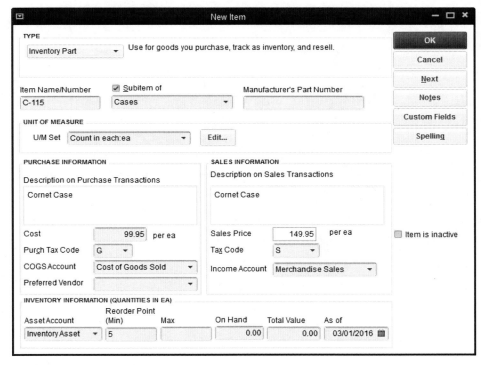

9   Click **OK** to save the new item.

The Item List window now includes this new item.

Cases	Instrument Cases	Inventory Part	Merchandise ...	0			0.00
◇C-101	Oboe Case	Inventory Part	Merchandise ...	6	0	each (ea)	79.95
◇C-103	Guitar cases	Inventory Part	Merchandise ...	11	0	each (ea)	179.95
◇C-105	Flute Case	Inventory Part	Merchandise ...	32	0	each (ea)	69.95
◇C-107	Trombone Case	Inventory Part	Merchandise ...	28	0	each (ea)	129.95
◇C-111	Trumpet Case	Inventory Part	Merchandise ...	18	0	each (ea)	119.95
◇C-115	Cornet Case	Inventory Part	Merchandise ...	0	0	each (ea)	149.95

Learn the Skill

In this exercise you will create an inventory item which uses a selling unit that is smaller than the buying and stocking units.

1 Create a new inventory part item: Violin Bows, Subitem of **Accessories**.

2 In the U/M Set, select **<Add New>**.

3 In the Unit of Measure window, select **Count** and then click **Next**.

4 For the Base Unit select **Each (ea)**, click **Next**.

5 In Add Related Units, click in the **Add** column beside **dozen** to select it.

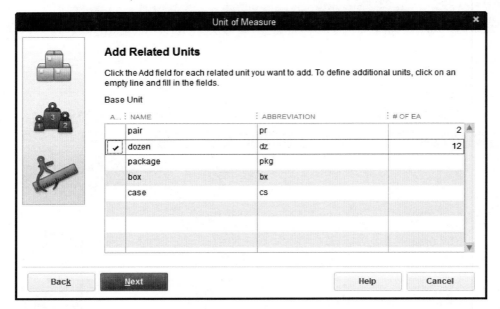

6 In the **# of Ea** column, accept the default of 12, and click **Next**.

7 In the Select Default Units of Measure window, for Purchase select **dozen** and for Sales select **each** and leave the shipping line blank. Click **Next**.

8 To give this set a name, type: Carton, and then click **Finish**.

9 Enter the following information for this new inventory item: watch the As of date and the Purch Tax Code.

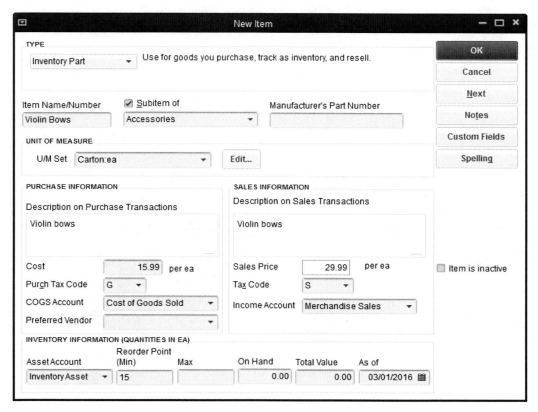

10 Click **OK** to save this new item. Leave the Item List window open for the next exercise.

Creating Service Items

Service items are like inventory part items in that they are sold to customers. The difference is that they cannot be stored on a shelf like physical inventory. Examples of services are the labour required for mechanical repairs, consulting services, or moving furniture. Other types of services include towing cars, hotel room rentals, and dry cleaning. The common factor is that there are a fixed number of resources available (e.g., staff, mechanics, tow trucks, hotel rooms) that will earn nothing if not purchased by a customer but will incur costs (e.g., staff salaries, gas for tow trucks) in any case. In addition, you cannot sell more than you have available unless overtime is utilized.

In comparison to an inventory part item, the New Item window contains different information which you must enter. These differences reflect how services are handled and sold.

> You must ensure that you select the correct accounts for each service item because QuickBooks will use these accounts for every sales transaction made. If you are uncertain in any way, you should consult your accountant.

 ## Learn the Skill

In this exercise, you will learn how to create a service item.

1 In the Item List window, click **Item**, then select **New**.

2 In the **Type** field select **Service**.

The New Item window will display the fields that are appropriate for a service item.

3   Enter the following information for this new service item:

Item Name	Violin Lessons
Subitem of	Service Sales
U/M Set	Time by the hour:hr
Description	Private Violin Lessons
Rate	45.00
Sales Tax Code	G
Account	Service Sales: Lessons

The completed window should appear similar to the following:

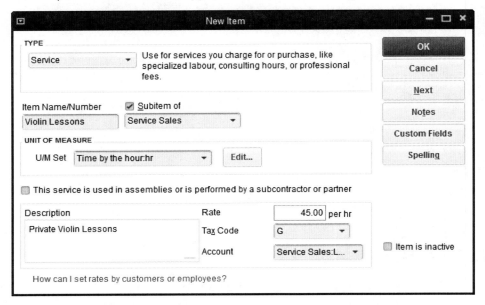

4   Click **OK** to save this new item.

5   Leave the Item List open for the next exercise.

Managing Inventory and Service Item Data

You can change almost any information about an inventory or service item at any time, except for any quantity on hand data—these are automatically maintained by QuickBooks. You can, therefore, change the description or the price of an item whenever necessary. You can add or delete items; however there are some parameters around deleting an item: for instance, you cannot delete an item if it has been used in a transaction or if there is inventory on hand. In most circumstances it is better to *Hide* the item.

 ## Learn the Skill

In this exercise, you will learn how to update inventory and service items.

1   In the Item List window, double-click **B110 - Trombone** to open the Edit Item window.

> You can also right-click the item name and select **Edit Item** or select **Edit**, **Edit Item** from the menu bar to open the Edit Item window for this inventory item.

Notice that there are four display-only fields at the bottom of the Edit Item window; On Hand, Average Cost, On P.O., and On Sales Order. This data is useful for helping you to manage your inventory of this item.

2   Select the **Reorder Point** text box, replace the current value with: 10 and click **OK**.

3   Repeat steps 1 to 2 for the following inventory item, selecting the **Max** text box:

   Inventory Item   Max
   P103 – Drum set   15

4   In the Item List window, right-click **Lessons: Music Instruction** and select **Edit Item**.

5   In the **Rate** field, change the amount to 45.00 and then press (Tab).

Your screen should resemble the following:

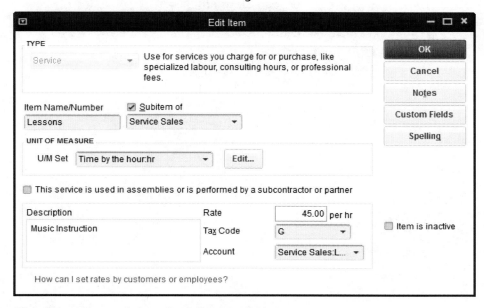

6   Click **OK** to save and close the Edit Item window.

7   In the Item List window, right-click **Freight Charge** and select **Edit Item**.

8   Make the item a **Subitem** of Service Sales and select **Count in each** as the U/M set.

9   Click **OK** to save the changes.

10   Keep the Item List window open for the next exercise.

Inventory Reports

A key component of successfully running your business is in inventory management. Even if you have superb abilities in marketing, finance, or other areas of expertise, you must manage your inventory of goods and employees to meet customer demands for your products and services, and at prices that will produce reasonable profits for your business. QuickBooks has a series of pre-set reports that can be used for this purpose.

Learn the Skill

In this exercise, you will learn how to display various inventory and services reports.

1   Click **Reports** at the bottom of the Item List window, and select **Price List**.

2   To customize the report to show only the desired columns, click **Customize Report**, and in the Modify Report window, on the Display tab, ensure only the following columns are selected:

(left margin); Item; Description; Price.

3   On the Header/Footer tab change the Subtitle to: March 1, 2016, and deselect the **Date Prepared** and **Time Prepared** options.

4   Click **OK** to display the modified report

This report can then be used as a price list for your sales staff to use.

We Are Music Ltd.
Item Price List
March 1, 2016

Item	Description	Price
Service Sales		0.00
Service Sales:Cello Lessons	Private Cello Lessons	45.00
Service Sales:Freight Charge	Delivery Charge	75.00
Service Sales:Lessons	Music Instruction	45.00
Service Sales:Repairs	Instrument repair service	45.00
Service Sales:Violin Lessons	Private Violin Lessons	45.00
Accessories		0.00
Accessories:Gig Bag	Carry bag	49.95
Accessories:Metronome	Metronome	49.95
Accessories:Music Stand	Stand for Sheet Music	39.95
Accessories:Sheet music	Sheet Music	2.75
Accessories:Sling	Case Sling	29.95
Accessories:Straps	Guitar straps	15.95
Accessories:Strings	Guitar Strings	12.95
Accessories:Violin Bows	Violin bows	29.99
Brass		0.00
Brass:B-101	Cornet	375.00
Brass:B-105	Horn	450.00
Brass:B-110	Trombone	475.00
Brass:B-115	Trumpet	375.00
Cases	Instrument Cases	0.00
Cases:C-101	Oboe Case	79.95
Cases:C-103	Guitar cases	179.95
Cases:C-105	Flute Case	69.95

Note that the default date for the above report is the real time date. In QuickBooks some reports will show the current real time date as the default date.

5   Double-click anywhere on the **Cases: C-103** row in the report.

The Edit Item window is now displayed for this item.

6   Close the Edit Item and Item Price List windows. Click **No** if asked to memorize this report.

7 Click **Reports** at the bottom of the Item List window, and select **Item Listing**. The default for this report is also the current real time date. The illustration below has been customized for demonstration purposes.

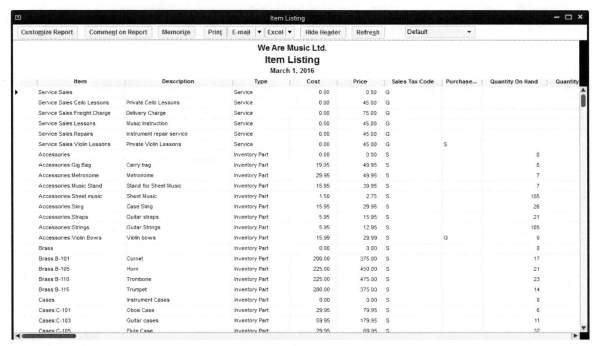

8 Scroll to the right of the report to see the data displayed there.

You can also double-click any of the item rows to display it in the Edit Item window.

9 Close the report and click **No** if asked to memorize the report.

10 Close the Item List window.

Now we will run a report from the Inventory Centre.

11 Click the down arrow beside **Inventory Activities** in the Company section of the Home Page, and select **Inventory Centre** from the list.

12 In the Reports section, click **Stock Status** to display the Inventory Stock Status by Item window.

13 Select **Custom** in the Dates field, and set the From date to **March 1, 2016** and the To date to **March 31, 2016** and click **Refresh**.

This report shows the following information about each item in your inventory: item description, preferred vendor, reorder point, quantity on hand, quantity on sales order, number available, u/m, which items are below their reorder point, and so on. This is a useful report to verify which items are short stocked and should be reordered.

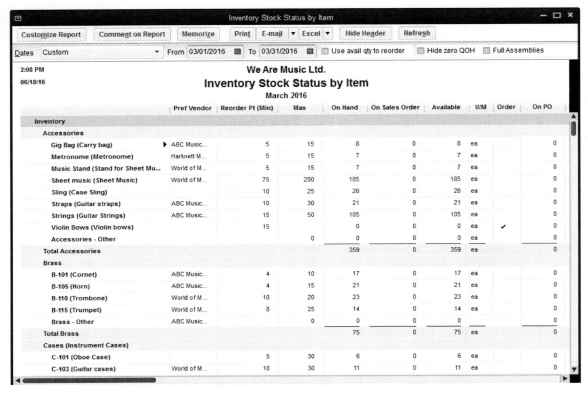

14 Scroll down to see just which items need to be reordered

15 Close the report, say **No** to the memorize report message, and then close the Inventory Centre window.

16 Backup the file as: We Are Music Ltd. – Your Name Lesson 2 following the same steps learned in Lesson 1.

Lesson Summary

In this lesson, you learned how to set up the Inventory and Service Items in QuickBooks Premier. In particular, you learned how to:

☑ work with the Inventory Centre

☑ create inventory accounts

☑ work with the Item list

☑ create inventory parts and service items

☑ set Units of Measure

☑ manage inventory and service item data

☑ run inventory reports

Practice the Skill

The following additional exercise covers many of the items discussed in this Lesson. The Practice the Skill exercises are included as extra practice and may be completed by the students in class or on their own. Your instructor has access to the Answer Key for these exercises.

Create and/or modify these items as of **March 7, 2016**.

1. Create the following inventory item:

Type	Inventory Part
Item Name	P-111
Subitem	Percussion
UOM	Count in each:ea
Description	Xylophone with stand
Cost	89.95
Purchase Tax	G
COGS Account	Cost of Goods Sold
Sales Price	149.95
Tax code	S
Income Account	Merchandise Sales
Reorder Point	10

2. Create the following service item:

Type	Service
Item Name	Piano Tuning
Subitem	Service Sales
UOM	Time by the Hour:hr
Description	Piano tuning
Rate	45.00
Tax code	G
Income Account	Service Sales: Repair Services

3. Modify the following inventory items:

C-101	Change the reorder Point to 8
I-107	Change the cost to 29.95
B-110	Change the Preferred Vendor to ABC Music Supply

4. Backup the data file as: `We Are Music Ltd. - Your Name Lesson 2 Practice`.

Review Questions

1.   How do you open the Item List?

   a.   Click the Items & Services icon on the Home Page.

   b.   Click Lists, Item List.

   c.   Click Vendors, Item List.

   d.   All of the above.

2.   What three options are available from the Inventory Activities list?

3.   What is the difference between an inventory and a service item?

4.   A Non-Inventory Part item is used for merchandise you buy but do not sell to customers.

   a.   True   b.   False

5.   Which report will show the item description and price of each item in inventory?

6.   In the Reports section of the Inventory Centre, which of the following is **not** a completed report?

   a.   Quick Report

   b.   Physical Inventory Worksheet

   c.   Stock Status

   d.   Inventory Valuation Summary

7.   Which of the following options does **not** open a New Item window?

   a.   Right-click in the Item List window, and select New.

   b.   Click the Inventory Activities icon in the Home screen.

   c.   Click the Item button in the Item List window, and select New.

   d.   All of the above.

QuickBooks
Premier 2016
Level 1

Lesson 3: Vendors and Accounts Payable

Lesson Objectives

In this lesson, you will learn how to work with the Vendor Centre, how to manage vendor information and how to move around and process transactions in the Vendor Centre. Upon successful completion of this lesson, you should know how to:

- ☐ work with the Vendor Centre
- ☐ understand the workflow
- ☐ create and modify vendor records
- ☐ make purchases by entering vendor bills
- ☐ work with Sales Tax codes
- ☐ make purchases by writing cheques
- ☐ create memorized payment transactions

- ☐ issue and fill purchase orders
- ☐ receive items
- ☐ receive vendor bills
- ☐ find and modify vendor bills
- ☐ pay vendor bills
- ☐ print cheques
- ☐ run vendor reports

To Start This Lesson

Restoring the Exercise File

1. From the **File** menu in QuickBooks, choose **Open or Restore Company**.

   QuickBooks displays the Open or Restore Company window.

2. Select **Restore a backup copy** and click **Next**.

3. Select **Local backup** and click **Next**.

4. In the Open Backup Copy window navigate to your *1761 Student Files* folder.

5. Select the *We Are Music Ltd 2016 - Student.QBB* file and then click **Open**.

6. In the Open or Restore Company window, click **Next**.

7. Navigate to your *1761 Student Files* folder.

8. In the File name field of the Save Company File as window, type: `We Are Music Ltd - Your Name Lesson 3` and then click **Save**.

9. In the QuickBooks Login window enter the password: **Sys2016**.

10. Click **OK** when you see the message that the file has been successfully restored.

11. If necessary close the QuickBooks Learning Centre and Have a Question windows.

Vendors
Working with the Vendor Centre

The Vendor Centre is a single place that gathers all of the relevant transactions as well as other information, such as the names and addresses of your vendors.

To access the Vendor Centre:

- Click the **Vendors** icon on the Icon bar; or
- select **Vendors, Vendor Centre** from the menu bar; or
- click the **Vendors** button in the Vendors section of the Home Page.

The tool bar buttons allow access to a variety of tasks, including creating new vendors and transactions.

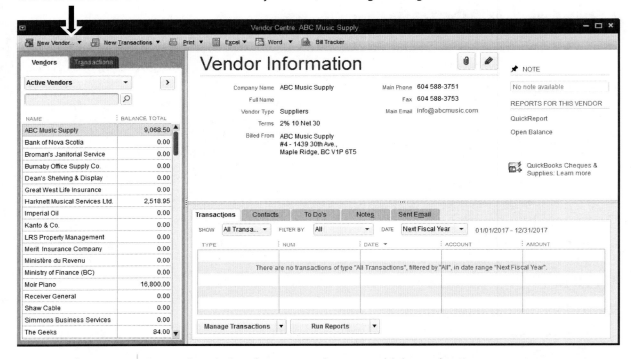

New Vendor	Opens the window for new vendors, or multiple vendors.
New Transactions	Enter bills, pay bills, purchase orders, receive items and enter bill, receive items, enter bill for received items.
Print	Vendor List, Vendor Information, Vendor Transaction List.
Excel	Export Vendor List, export transactions, import from Excel, paste from Excel.
Word	Prepare letter to selected vendor, prepare vendor letters, customize letter templates.
Bill Tracker	Tracks your outstanding payables by date, due date, and status

The Vendor Centre is divided into three panes:

- The left pane contains two tabs, Vendors and Transactions. The Vendors tab lists your vendors, and can be sorted by clicking the top drop-down arrow and selecting an option. The Transaction tab lists the types of transactions available in QuickBooks.

- The top-right pane shows the details for the selected vendor, and provides quick access to several reports.

- The bottom-right pane has tabs that show Transactions, Contacts, To Do's, Notes, and Sent Email related to the selected vendor.

Managing the Vendors List

There are a variety of lists in QuickBooks. All list management tasks are performed in a similar manner in these lists. Some lists are incorporated into a QuickBooks Centre, and some are accessed via a list option on the menu bar. Lists that are in the centres are not accessible separately from the menu bar. Entries in these lists can be added, edited, or deleted as needed.

 Learn the Skill

In this exercise you will work with the Vendors list to adjust the list views, and view various transactions in the Transactions list.

1   Click the **Vendors** icon from the Icon bar to open the Vendor Centre.

2   With the **Vendors** tab selected, click the **Name** title bar twice to sort the list of vendors by name in descending order.

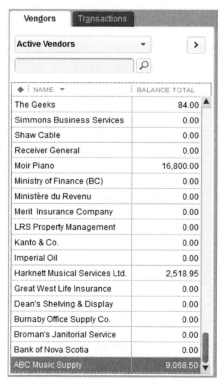

3   Click the **Balance Total** title bar to sort the list of vendors by the balance owing in ascending order.

4   Click **Balance** again to sort in descending order.

5   Click the **Name** title bar to sort in ascending order.

6   In the left pane of the Vendor Centre, click the **Transactions** tab.

7   Click the **Bills** icon to view the bills that have been processed.

8   Click the **Cheques** icon to view the cheques that have been processed.

9   Select the **Vendors** tab, and keep the Vendor Centre open for the next exercise.

Creating Vendor Records

A vendor is a supplier of goods and/or services to your business in exchange for payment. These items may be used for resale to your customers or consumed directly by your business (such as stationery, utilities, or contract services). QuickBooks also treats government bodies and agencies as vendors because payments are made to these organizations for services such as property taxes, workers compensation premiums, and other taxes and fees.

QuickBooks uses the vendor record for tracking purchase orders (also known as PO's), quotes, and debts owed to vendors. It will then remind you when it is time to pay the bills.

The vendor record has five sections (called tabs) to record basic information about each vendor.

Address Info	Vendors name, address, and contact information.
Payment Settings	Account number, credit limit, payment terms, billing rate level, print name on cheque as.
Sales Tax Settings	Vendor is a sales tax agency, tax code, country, business number.
Account Settings	Fields to enter prefill accounts when entering a bill for a vendor.
Additional Info	Vendor type, and custom fields.

This information stays constant no matter how many purchase orders, quotes, or purchases on account are made.

Learn the Skill

In this exercise you will learn how to create a new vendor record.

1   Click **New Vendor** from the toolbar at the top left of the window and select **New Vendor** from the drop-down list to display the New Vendor window.

You can also display this window by right-clicking anywhere in the list of Vendors and selecting **New Vendor** or by pressing `Ctrl`+`N` on the keyboard.

2　In the Company Name text field, type: Danby Marketing Co. and press `Tab`.

3　In the Opening Balance field, type: 0.00 and press `Tab`.

4　In the As Of date field, type: 03/01/2016.

The content of the Company Name field is automatically copied into the Bill From field as well as into the Vendor Name field at the top of the window.

5　Click in the first line of the Billed From field, press the `End` key to jump to the end of the line, and press `Enter` to create a new line.

6　Enter the rest of the mailing address:
```
100 - 18th Street
Burnaby, BC V1S 5T7
```

7　Click the 🖉 (**Edit**) button beside the Billed From address to display the Edit Address Information window.

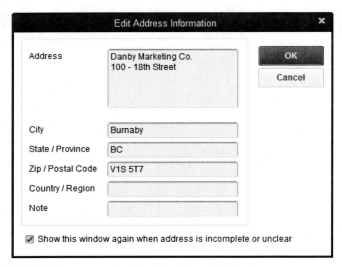

8   Click **OK** to return to the New Vendor window.

9   Enter the remaining vendor data using the (Tab) key to jump to the next field.

Main Phone	604 403-5634
Main Email	info@danbymarketing.ca
Mobile	604 626-3584
Website:	www.danbymarketing.ca
Fax	604 403-5659

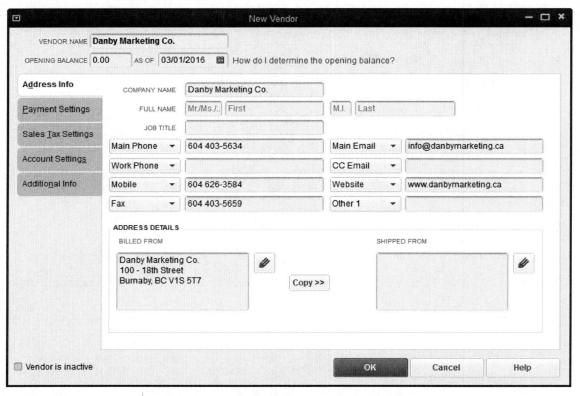

Vendor Name	Used to sort the Vendor List alphabetically.
Opening Balance, As Of	The total amount owing to the vendor for goods and services delivered up to and including the as of date.

Company Name	Use this field if the vendor is a company or partnership.
Mr./Ms., First Name, M.I., Last Name	Use these fields if the vendor is an individual person.
Address Details	The mailing address where purchase orders and cheques are to be sent.
Phone, Fax, Email	The phone, fax, and email address of the business.
Vendor is inactive	If this indicator is turned on, then this vendor will no longer appear on lists or reports to prevent you from creating new purchase orders and payments for this vendor. You should preferably not delete a vendor that you are no longer using because you will then lose all of the historical information for this vendor.

10 Click the **Payment Settings** tab.

11 Enter the following vendor data using ⌨Tab to jump to the next field:

      Account No.   654321
      Credit Limit   2,000
      Payment Terms 2% 10 Net 30

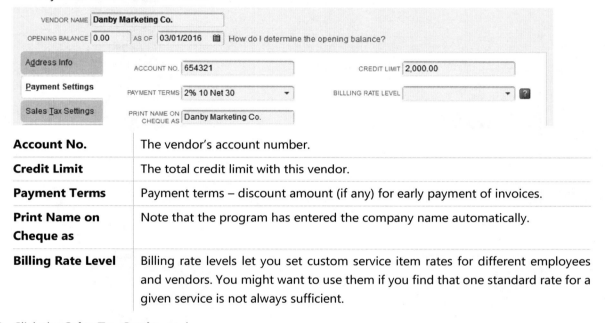

Account No.	The vendor's account number.
Credit Limit	The total credit limit with this vendor.
Payment Terms	Payment terms – discount amount (if any) for early payment of invoices.
Print Name on Cheque as	Note that the program has entered the company name automatically.
Billing Rate Level	Billing rate levels let you set custom service item rates for different employees and vendors. You might want to use them if you find that one standard rate for a given service is not always sufficient.

12 Click the **Sales Tax Settings** tab.

13 Enter the following vendor data using ⌨Tab to jump to the next field:

      Tax Code   S
      Country   Canada
      Business Number 123456

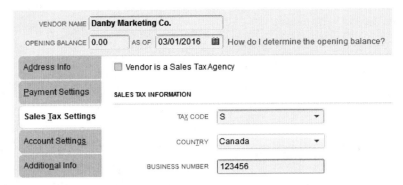

14 Click the **Account Settings** tab.

15 In the first field, click the arrow and select **Advertising and Promotion** from the list.

16 Click the **Additional Info** tab, and in the Vendor Type field select **Service Providers**.

17 Click **OK** to save and close the New Vendor window.

18 In the lower right pane of the Vendor Information section click the **Contacts** tab. Right-click in the first row of the **Contact Name** column, and select **Add New.**

> **Note:** You can also open the New Contact window by clicking the **Manage Contacts** button and selecting **Add New** from the drop-down list.

19 Complete the Contacts window as follows:

20 Click **Save and Close**.

Your screen should resemble the following:

Modifying Vendors

You can update the information about a vendor whenever something about them has changed or to correct mistyped information. However, you cannot change the Current Balance (owed to this vendor)—this is calculated automatically by QuickBooks after the vendor record is created.

To locate and modify a vendor's record, select the vendor from the Vendors list, and then either double-click the vendor or right-click and select the desired option from the menu that is displayed. You can also access this menu by selecting a vendor, and then selecting **Edit Vendor** from the menu bar.

You will not be able to remove a vendor if it contains any open items (unpaid invoices).

 ## Learn the Skill

In this exercise, you will learn how to modify the information recorded for an existing vendor.

1   On the **Vendors** tab in the Vendor Centre window, double-click **Walters & Associates** to display the Edit Vendor window.

Assume that this vendor has just accepted a new partner, and the name of the company must be changed.

2   If necessary, select the **Vendor Name** text field and change the name of the vendor to: Walters Browne & Associates.

3   Enter the new name for the Company Name, and Address.

Now, assume that you want to begin recording some personal information for each of your vendors but QuickBooks does not have a predefined field to store this value. You can solve this by creating your own customized field.

4   Select the **Additional Info** tab and in the Custom Fields area, click **Define Fields**.

The Set up Custom Fields for Names window is displayed, showing all customized fields.

5   In the first blank Label field, type: Owner's Birthday and click in the **Vendors** column to turn it on for all vendor records.

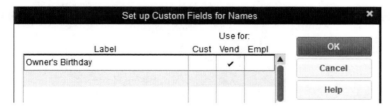

6   Click **OK** to save this field definition.

An information message may appear: You have activated custom fields for the list... Read the message, select the **Do not display** checkbox, and then click **OK** to close it.

7   In the Owner's Birthday field, type: October 21.

The completed Edit Vendor window should now appear similar to the following:

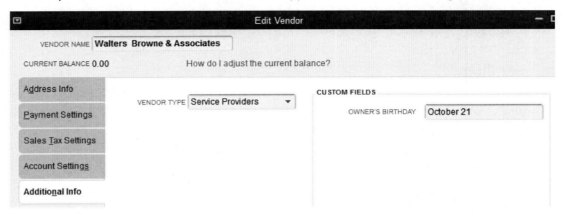

8   Click **OK** to save and close the Edit Vendor window.

We want to add the new partner as the primary contact.

9   In the Vendors list, select **Walters Browne & Associates** and then click the **Contacts** tab in the Vendor Information section.

10   Right-click in the **second** row, select **Add New**, and complete the Contacts window as follows:

11   Click **Save and Close.** The Vendor Information section should resemble the following:

12   Leave the Vendor Centre open for the next exercise.

Modifying a Credit Limit

Learn the Skill

In this exercise, you will edit a vendor credit limit.

You have negotiated a new credit limit with Valley Wind & Reed. Your new credit limit is $8,000.00.

1   In the Vendor Centre window, right-click **Valley Wind & Reed** and select **Edit Vendor**.

2   Select the **Payment Settings** tab and change the 5,000.00 Credit Limit to 8,000.00.

3   Enter the Account No. 58237, and change the Payment Terms to **2% 10 Net 30**.

4   Click **OK** and close the Vendor Centre.

Making Purchases

Understanding the Workflow

The Vendors section of the Home Page tab has a diagram that clearly describes how QuickBooks handles the Purchases and Accounts Payable functions.

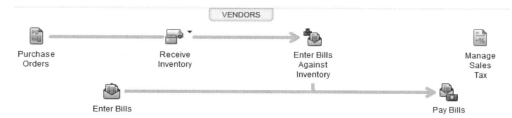

This diagram shows that there are two main streams: Enter Bills and Purchase Orders. Both streams lead to the Pay Bills process. There are definitive workflows for the different operations and transactions conducted by the company. It is critical to follow the steps as outlined in certain transactions. If you receive an invoice (bill) from a vendor that will be paid in the future, it must be entered as a bill. When the time comes to pay the bill, it must be paid via the Pay Bills process in order to properly clear the entry. If a Write Cheque process is used instead, the original bill will not be cleared, and the expense will be recorded twice.

Enter Bills	This process involves entering the vendor bill into QuickBooks. The bill (or invoice) may be for the purchase of inventory goods for resale. In any case, a purchase order was not used and the goods or services were delivered at the same time as the bill. Before entering the bill into QuickBooks, you should verify that the items and quantity match what was delivered, if possible.
Purchase Orders	It is important to note that by issuing a purchase order, you have not actually bought anything. As a result, there is no accounting entry required to record the purchase order.
	However, by issuing the purchase order you are making a firm commitment to the vendor that you will accept the goods and services when they are delivered and you will pay for them according to the payment terms offered to you on the invoice. From a legal perspective, a vendor can take legal action against a customer that has issued a purchase order for failure to accept the goods or services.

A purchase order is a request to buy inventory or other items from a vendor. QuickBooks lets you prepare, store, and print purchase orders.

When you complete a purchase order, the program automatically updates the quantity on order. When a shipment arrives, you can quickly fill all or part of the order. If you receive a partial shipment, the program keeps track of the back-ordered items and quantities.

Receive Inventory	This process involves receiving the goods from the vendor. The shipment will always include a packing list that describes what the shipment contains. Some vendors include the invoice with the shipment. QuickBooks allows you to accept/receive inventory with or without a bill.
Enter Bills Against Inventory	This process involves entering the vendor bill into QuickBooks. An important step here involves comparing the items, quantity, and cost listed on this bill against the packing list and the original purchase orders. Any discrepancies must be resolved before the bill is entered into QuickBooks. Shorted items are expected to be delivered at a later date and must not be billed at this time.
Pay Bills	This process involves paying the vendor bill, i.e., generating the cheque. It is always advantageous to maximize the time between when the bill is received to when it is paid. Most vendors, once a business relationship has been established, will offer payment terms as long as the vendor is willing to grant credit to you. The payment terms are recorded in the vendor record (e.g., 2% discount if paid within 10 days, otherwise the full amount is due in 30 days), and redisplayed at the bottom of the input window. If the terms for this specific invoice are different than other invoices from the same vendor, you can change it. In order to create an invoice for later payment, the vendor must be in the Vendors list.
Manage Sales Tax	This is a periodic process that involves submitting the sales taxes collected from customers to the appropriate government agencies. This icon opens a window that shows tax accounts and payments, sales tax codes and rates, as well as links to areas for sales tax adjustments, and set up.

Entering Vendor Bills

This topic discusses how to enter a bill for the immediate purchase of resale inventory (without using a purchase order). Payment will be made later, even though the bill is being recorded now (because the purchased goods are now assets). In accounting terminology, this type of invoice is known as a payable, and the amount owed is recorded in the Accounts Payable account. The accounting entry for this would be:

DR	Inventory	2,500.00	
DR	GST Paid on Purchases	130.00	
DR	Freight Expense	100.00	
CR	Accounts Payable		2,730.00

These amounts were calculated as follows:

Inventory	$2,500.00 for the inventory items.
GST Paid on Purchases	$125.00 for GST on the inventory items, plus $5.00 for GST on freight.
Freight Expense	$100.00. This total value is expensed in the current fiscal year.
Accounts Payable	The total value at the bottom of the purchase invoice (agrees with the paper invoice).

The Enter Bills window allows you to enter purchase orders, quotes, and invoices for inventory and non-inventory purchases (such as services) in an invoice-style window.

Learn the Skill

In this exercise, you will learn how to enter a bill to be paid later.

1 In the Vendors section of the Home Page tab, click **Enter Bills.**

> You can also display this window by clicking **Vendors** in the menu bar and selecting **Enter Bills**, or by displaying the Vendor Centre window, right-clicking on the vendor and selecting **Enter Bills** from the shortcut menu.

2 In the Vendor field, select **Harknett Musical Services Ltd.**

3 Click the 🗒 **(Calendar)** button for the Date field, and select **March 15, 2016** and press ⌷Tab⌷.

> Notice that QuickBooks automatically selects Apr 14 as the Bill Due date, as the data base preference is set for 30 days. This default can be changed by selecting **Edit**, **Preferences** on the menu bar, and then **Bills**, and **Company Preferences**.

4 In the Ref. No. field, type: HMS 598.

The Ref. No. field is used by the vendor—when they receive your cheque—to match the payment to their invoice. Therefore, you should enter their invoice number into this field.

5 Click the **Items** tab.

6 Click in the first blank cell in the Item column. Click the drop-down list button, and under Accessories select **Metronome**.

7 Ensure the Qty cell for this item displays: **1** (note the U/M shows "bx").

8 Ensure the Tax field shows **G**.

> In the province of B.C., for a retail outlet that purchases goods for resale, no PST is charged on these items. This tax is assessed on the user of the goods/services, and will be charged to the customer who purchases the inventory from the store. Therefore, inventory-part items purchased by the store will only be charged GST.

Your Enter Bills window should be similar to the following:

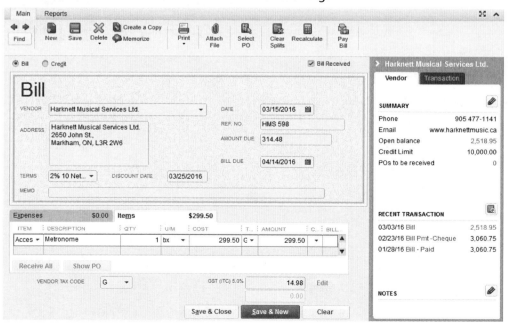

The top of the window contains a menu bar with two tabs, Main and Reports. Each tab displays a ribbon containing links to various activities.

Main	Access to Find, New, Save, etc.
Reports	Access to Quick Report, Transaction History, Transaction Journal.

To the far right of the menu bar, there are two icons:

Maximize your work area – This icon will enlarge the window to full-screen.

Hide the ribbon – This icon hides the ribbon.

Show the ribbon – This icon will display the ribbon.

QuickBooks provides useful detail on the right side of certain transactions (purchase orders, bills, sales orders, estimates, invoices, and sales receipts). Clicking on the arrow at the left of this tab hides/displays this section. It contains two tabs, Vendor and Transaction.

The Vendor tab displays up to date information on the vendor in this transaction.

Summary	Contact information, open balance, credit limit, purchase orders outstanding.
Recent Transactions	Bills and payments, further information is displayed by placing the cursor on the item.
Notes	The notes section allows any pertinent notes, To Do's to be entered.

The Transaction tab shows more details about the transaction.

Summary	The magnifying glass opens an Audit Trail report.
Related Transactions	Displays a Transactions History Report.
Notes	A field in which to enter any relevant notes.

Now, record the cost of shipping the goods to your location, assuming that shipping costs are recorded in a separate Cost of Goods account.

9   Click the **Expenses** tab.

10 Select the first blank Account cell, click the drop-down list button and select **Freight Charges** from the Cost of Goods Sold section.

11 In the Tax cell for this row ensure **G** - GST only is selected.

12 In the Amount cell for this row, type 25 and press (Tab).

Your Expenses tab in the Enter Bills window should now be similar to the following:

13 Verify the data has been entered correctly, the Amount Due should be 340.73, and then click **Save & Close**.

 ## Learn the Skill

In this exercise you will learn how to enter bills for non-inventory purchases (such as paying for goods and services that are not for resale to customers).

Assume for the purpose of this exercise that the vendor is not in the current Vendors list.

1 On the Home Page tab, click **Enter Bills** in the Vendors section. Select **March 16** as the date.

2 Click **Vendor** and select **<Add New>**.

The New Vendor window is displayed to allow you to enter the new vendor information. When you enter a bill, the vendor must be on the Vendors list because the amount(s) payable is tracked by vendor, even if you do not plan on making more purchases from this vendor in the future.

3 In the New Vendor window, enter the data as follows:

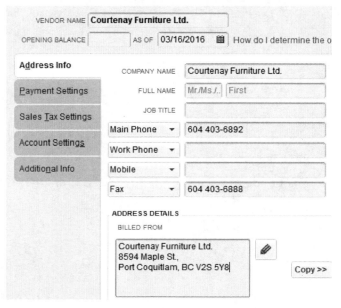

4   Select the **Payment Settings** tab and set the payment terms as: **Net 30**.

5   Select the **Sales Tax Settings** tab and complete as follows:

6   Click **OK** to save and close the New Vendor window. The updated information for this vendor now displays.

7   With the Expenses tab selected in the Enter Bills window, click the drop-down list button in the first Account cell, and select **Furniture and Equipment: Cost** in the Fixed Asset section.

> For most bills, you will be selecting an expense account in the **Expenses** tab. In some situations, you may be purchasing non-inventory assets. QuickBooks allows you to select any account to be debited, but you will normally select expense or asset accounts.

8   Complete your invoice as follows:

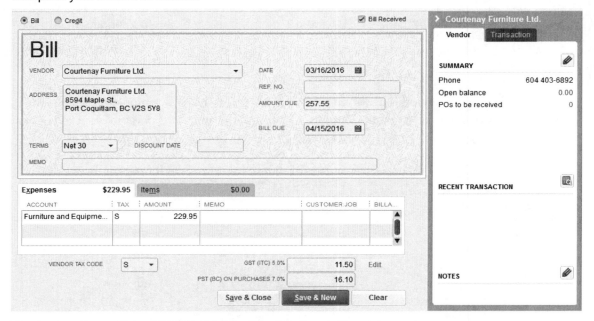

The Amount Due will be $257.55 (this is automatically calculated for you).

Note that since this non-inventory item will be used by the store, both taxes, GST and PST have been charged.

9   Click **Save & Close**, and close the Vendor Centre (if necessary).

Writing Cheques

Another type of purchase is COD (Cash On Delivery) when the item(s) being purchased are paid for at the time they are delivered. No purchase order is created in advance and nothing is owed to the vendor afterwards. When you create the bill, QuickBooks can immediately print the cheque for you. Alternatively, you can record the number of the manual cheque that you wrote to pay the invoice. The Bank, and not Accounts Payable, will be the credit entry for this transaction.

To save time, most QuickBooks users no longer make out cheques by hand, but prefer to print them directly from the system. To do this, special pre-printed cheque forms are required—these can be ordered from most large stationery outlets.

 Learn the Skill

In this exercise, you will learn how to create a purchase invoice for a COD purchase and issue a cheque for payment.

We are going to purchase stock display units from a supplier. It is very easy to miss the step of printing the cheque when processing the entry. QuickBooks can be set to produce a reminder to print at the appropriate time.

1 Click **Write Cheques** in the Banking section of the Home Page tab.

2 If necessary, click the Bank Account drop-down list button and select **Royal Bank Chequing Account**.

3 Click the Pay to the Order of drop-down list button and select **Dean's Shelving and Display**.

4 In the Write Cheques window, set the date to **March 18, 2016**, ensure **Print Later** is selected.

5 Select the **Expenses** tab, and click the drop-down list button for the first blank Account cell. Scroll up in the list, and select **Leasehold Improvements: Cost**.

6 Enter the remaining data into the Write Cheques window:

Tax	S
Amount	289.95
Memo (column)	Display shelving
Print Later	Yes
Memo (on cheque)	Dean - 257

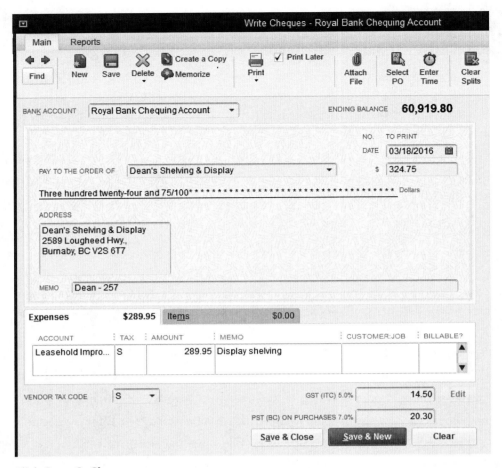

7   Click **Save & Close**.

Memorized Payment Transactions

Memorized payment transactions can be created for those payments that need to be made on a regular basis. This means that you do not have to re-key all of the data that is repeated on every transaction once the memorized transaction has been created.

 ## Learn the Skill

In this exercise, you will create a memorized transaction for the monthly janitorial expense as per the new arrangement with Broman's Janitorial Services.

1   Click **Write Cheques** in the Banking section of the Home Page tab.

2   If necessary, click **Bank Account** and select **Royal Bank Chequing Account**.

3   Click the Pay to the Order of drop-down list button and select **Broman's Janitorial Service**.

4 In the Write Cheques window, enter the following data:

Date   March 15, 2016

Account   Janitorial Expense

Tax   S

Amount   400.00

Memo   Monthly cleaning contract

Print Later Yes

The Total Amount will be $448.00.

5 Click the 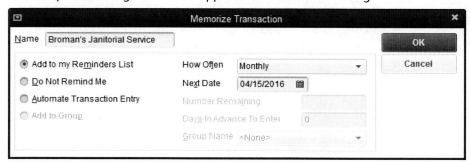 icon in the ribbon.

6 Enter the following values or options in the Memorize Transaction dialog box:

Add to my Reminders List   Yes

How Often   Monthly

Next Date   04/15/2016 (Apr 15, 2016)

The completed dialog box should appear similar to the following:

7 Click **OK**.

8 Click **Save & Close** in the Write Cheques window.

Creating Purchase Orders

A purchase order is a request to buy inventory or other items from a vendor. QuickBooks lets you prepare, store, and print purchase orders.

However, by issuing the purchase order, you are making a firm commitment to the vendor that you will accept the goods and services when they are delivered, and you will pay for them according to the payment terms offered to you on the invoice. From a legal perspective, a vendor may sue a customer who has issued a purchase order, for failure to accept the goods or services.

When you fill in a purchase order, the program automatically updates the quantity on order. When a shipment arrives, you can quickly fill all or part of the order. If you receive a partial shipment, the program keeps track of the back-ordered items and quantities.

Learn the Skill

In this exercise, you will learn how to create a purchase order for goods to be delivered in the future.

1   Select the **Purchase Orders** icon in the Vendors section on the Home Page tab.

> You can also display this window by selecting **Vendors**, **Create Purchase Orders** from the menu bar.

Automatically, QuickBooks assigns a P.O. No. (This number was entered when setting up the system).

2   Click the Vendor drop-down list button and select **Valley Wind & Reed**.

3   Complete the Purchase Order as follows:

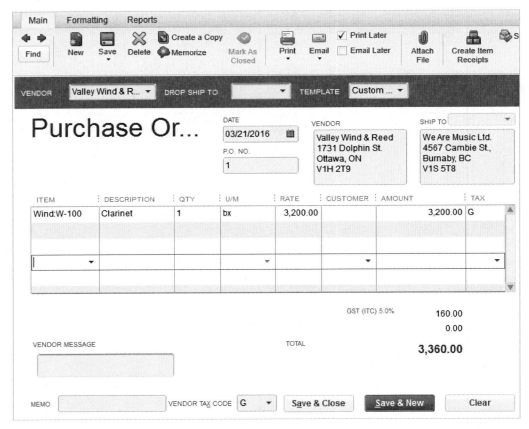

A purchase order does not result in an accounting transaction because no actual goods have been received yet.

4   Click **Save & Close**.

Filling a Purchase Order
Receiving Items

This function is used when a vendor has shipped goods to you to fulfill your purchase order. The shipment will include a packing slip that itemizes what was included in the shipment. You must check the packing slip carefully, and look for two possible problems:

- Does the packing slip agree with what was actually delivered? The shipment may be missing some items, but if you do not check carefully, then you will be paying for goods that were not received.

- Does the packing slip agree with the purchase order? If you were short-shipped (fewer items received than ordered), then the vendor will usually have back-ordered the remainder. The purchase order should then stay open until those items are delivered later. If you were over-shipped, then you are not obligated to accept any of the excess items. In all of these cases, be sure to record in QuickBooks the actual number of items that you received and accepted. In some rare cases, the vendor may ship goods that you did not order, and you may not want to accept.

From an accounting perspective, a shipment of goods with only a packing slip is a non-event. That is, the invoice is being sent separately and so you do not recognize the debt to them until it arrives.

If the invoice is included with the shipment, you would use the Enter Bills function instead.

 Learn the Skill

In this exercise, you will learn how to record the receipt of goods delivered to fill your purchase order.

1   In the Vendors section of the Home Page tab, click **Receive Inventory**, and then select **Receive Inventory without Bill**.

   The Create Item Receipts window is displayed.

   > You can also display this window by selecting **Vendors**, **Receive Items** from the menu bar.

2   In the Vendor field, select **Valley Wind & Reed**. Click **Yes**, in the Open POs Exist window.

   The Open Purchase Orders dialog box is displayed. This window will display all outstanding purchase orders from the selected vendor. This window allows you to select one or more purchase orders at the same time.

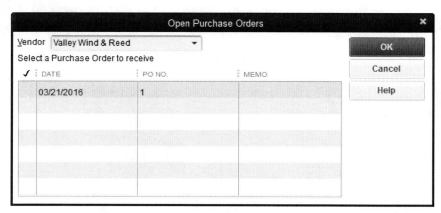

3   Click anywhere on the first purchase order row in the displayed list to display the check mark in the ✓ column, and click **OK**.

4   In the Create Item Receipts window, change the receipt Date to **March 24, 2016** as the date when the shipment of goods was received.

The completed window should appear similar to the following:

Note the words **Item Receipt** in large font to remind you that you are using the Item Receipt function. This is necessary because the window looks similar to the Enter Bills window.

For the purpose of this exercise, we will assume that all items listed on the purchase order were received in good condition. If you were short-shipped, then you would need to change the quantity of the items on this receipt window.

5   Click **Save & Close**.

Receiving Vendor Bills

This function occurs after the vendor has received your purchase order, filled the order, and delivered the items to you. The shipment may include an invoice from the vendor, or, if not, it will be delivered to you soon afterwards. QuickBooks is able to convert your previously issued purchase order into a bill for payment now or later (according to the payment terms offered by the vendor).

Once you process the bill, QuickBooks will produce the necessary accounting entry to recognize the receipt of the goods or services (if not done earlier), and the money owed or paid to the vendor. If you are paying later, the amount owed is recorded as a payable.

Learn the Skill

In this exercise, you will learn how to enter a bill for goods received earlier, i.e., an Item Receipt is on file.

1 In the Vendors section of the Home Page tab, click **Enter Bills Against Inventory**.

   The Select Item Receipt window is displayed.

   > You can also display this window by selecting **Vendors**, **Enter Bill for Received Items** from the menu bar.

2 Click the Vendor drop-down list button and select **Valley Wind & Reed**.

3 Leave the Use item receipt date for the bill date unselected, as we will use a different date.

4 Click the item receipt listed, to select it.

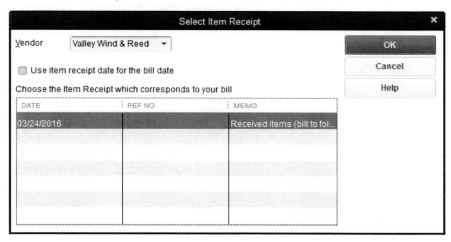

5 Click **OK**.

6 In the Enter Bills window, enter the following values:

Date	March 28, 2016
Ref. No.	P.O. #1
Account (Expenses tab)	Freight Charges
Tax	G
Amount	35.00

   > If you change or add any data in this window, be sure to click **Recalculate** (located on the ribbon) to recalculate the Amount Due amount. This amount is calculated when the window is first displayed, and may not change automatically when making changes on the screen.

7   Click **Recalculate.**

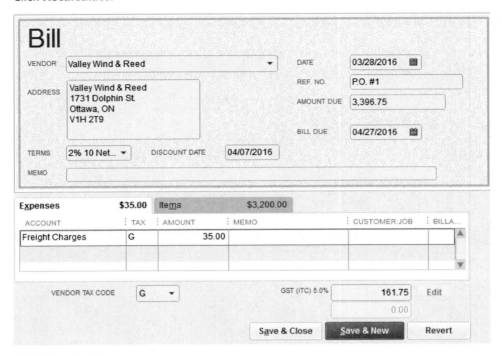

8   Click **Save & Close**.

The following message will be displayed because you are entering a bill that will close off the related purchase order and item receipt records.

9   Click **Yes** in the Recording Transaction message box.

 Learn the Skill

In this exercise, you will learn how to enter a bill from a Purchase Order in a different way.

In this instance, the Purchase Order will only be partially filled, and the invoice was included in the shipment.

1   Select **Vendors**, **Create Purchase Orders** from the menu bar.

2   Click the Vendor drop-down list button and select **World of Music**.

3 Enter the following values into the Create Purchase Orders window:

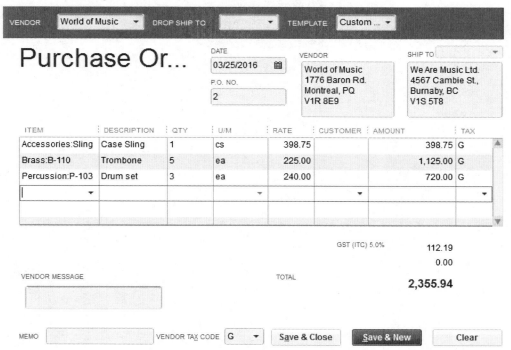

4 Click **Save & Close**.

5 In the Vendors section on the Home Page tab, click **Receive Inventory**, and then **Receive Inventory with Bill**.

6 In the Enter Bills window, click the Vendor drop-down list button, and select **World of Music**.

7 Click **Yes** in the Open POs Exist dialog box.

8 In the Open Purchase Orders dialog box, click anywhere in the purchase order row displayed to activate the check mark, and click **OK**.

Assume that the delivery is only a partial shipment of the goods ordered. You have received only two (2) B-110 Trombones, and one (1) Drum set. QuickBooks will automatically calculate the number of items on back-order.

9 Enter the following data into the Enter Bills window:

Bill

VENDOR	World of Music ▼		DATE	03/25/2016 🗓
			REF. NO.	
ADDRESS	World of Music 1776 Baron Rd. Montreal, PQ V1R 8E9		AMOUNT DUE	1,143.19
			BILL DUE	04/24/2016 🗓
TERMS	2% 10 Net.. ▼	DISCOUNT DATE 04/04/2016		
MEMO				

Expenses	$0.00	**Items**	$1,088.75						
ITEM	DESCRIPTION	QTY	U/M	COST	T...	AMOUNT	C...	B...	PO NO.
Accessories:Sling	Case Sling	1	cs	398.75	G	398.75			2
Brass:B-110	Trombone	2	ea	225.00	G	450.00			2
Percussion:P-103	Drum set	1	ea	240.00	G	240.00			2

Clear Qtys	Show PO

VENDOR TAX CODE	G ▼	GST (ITC) 5.0%	54.44	Edit
			0.00	

Save & Close	Save & New	Clear

10 Now enter the following data into the **Expenses** tab to add the shipping costs:

Account	Freight Charges
Tax	G
Amount	30.00

11 Click **Recalculate**. The new amount due is $1,174.69.

12 Click **Save & Close**.

13 On the Home Page tab, click **Purchase Orders**.

14 In the Create Purchase Orders window click ◀ **(Previous)** to display P.O. 2 (World of Music).

This window displays the number of items that have been received, as well as the order items that have been received in full, shown under CLSD column.

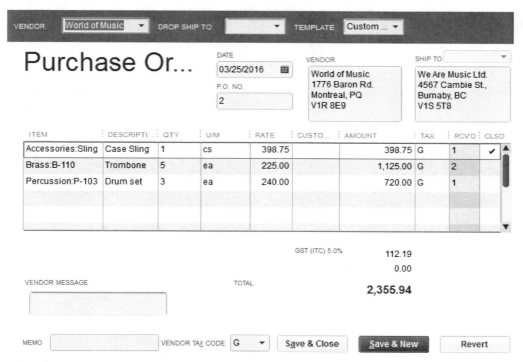

15 Close the Create Purchase Orders window.

Finding and Modifying Bills

You can modify bills after they have been entered and saved. The basic process involves redisplaying the bill, making the necessary changes, and then saving it again.

If you wish to cancel the entire vendor bill, you can simply select **Edit**, **Void Bill** from the menu bar.

The same procedure applies to adjust or void any purchase orders that have been recorded in the system.

 Learn the Skill

In this exercise, you will learn how to modify a bill created earlier.

1 Select **Vendors**, **Enter Bills** from the menu bar.

In order to adjust a bill, you must first find and display it. In this exercise, a purchase order was never created and therefore there is no purchase order to use as a reference. Instead, you must find the bill using the vendor's invoice number.

2 Click **Find** on the ribbon of the Enter Bills window.

In the Find Bills dialog box you must tell QuickBooks which bill to retrieve for you. For the purpose of this exercise, assume that you only know that the vendor is Harknett Musical Services Ltd. and the bill was received in either June or March.

3 Click the Vendor drop-down list button and select **Harknett Musical Services Ltd**.

4 Click the 🗓 **(Calendar)** buttons for the two **Date** fields, and select the date range March 1, 2016 to March 31, 2016.

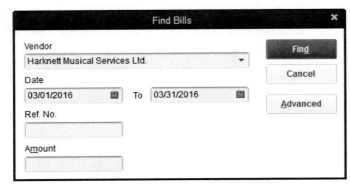

5 Click **Find**.

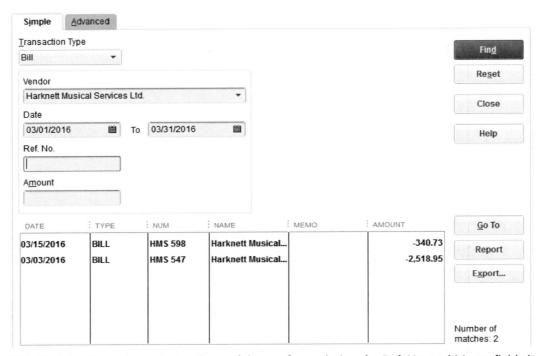

This Find function demonstrates the usefulness of completing the Ref. No. and Memo fields in the Enter Bills window—the data there helps you identify which is the correct bill you are looking for. For the purpose of this exercise, assume that you cannot remember which invoice is the one you are looking for.

6 Select the first invoice in the list (March 15, 2016) and click **Go To**.

> You can also double-click the invoice to select and open it.

The correct bill is now displayed: Invoice HMS 598. You have ordered 15 Metronomes, not one box. The vendor has made a mistake, and has issued an amended invoice.

7 Change the quantity value in the Qty column from 1 to 15, and the U/M to 15 **ea**.

8 Click **Recalculate**.

The updated bill should appear as follows:

9   Click **Save & Close**.

10 Click **Yes** in the message box that appears.

11 Close the Find window.

Paying Vendor Bills

The Pay Bills function is used to pay outstanding vendor invoices, pay credit card bill charges, and pay other types of bills. In this section, you will learn about paying outstanding vendor invoices.

A current payables report may be needed to ascertain how much is owed to a vendor.

Paying bills is a two-step process: the first step is to enter the bills into QuickBooks, which was demonstrated earlier in this lesson. The second step is to print the cheques. You can choose to have QuickBooks print the cheques for you, or to write the cheques manually and record the cheque numbers in QuickBooks.

IMPORTANT! You can print your cheques after you pay bills through the **File**, **Print Forms**, **Cheques** option. *Do not print cheques using the Write Cheques window after you have already recorded a bill payment to a vendor.* Otherwise, you will have two cheques recorded and your QuickBooks accounts will not be correct. Also, if bill payment cheques are to be manually written, be sure to verify the correct cheque numbers to use from the Chequing Account Register.

 Learn the Skill

In this exercise, you will learn how to generate an A/P Aged Summary report to examine how much is owed to each vendor based on their due dates. You will then learn how to process a payment on a bill.

1   In the Icon bar, click **Reports**, and then in the listing on the left of the window, select **Vendors & Payables**.

The screen has three viewing options.

2   Click on each option to see the differences ending with List View.

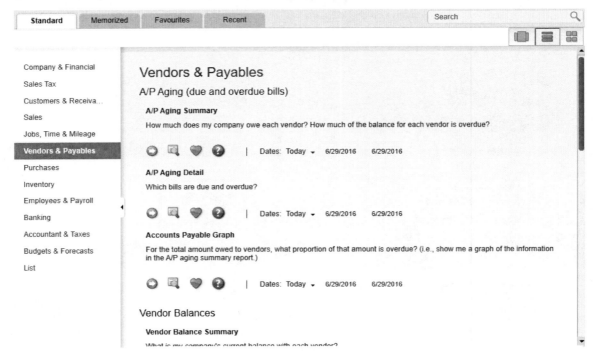

The report can be opened from this window by clicking the ⊙ **(Run)** button. Date ranges can also be set by clicking the arrow beside Dates. Desired date ranges can also be set once the report window is open.

3   Click the **Run** button for A/P Aging Summary to display the report.

> The report can be opened by double-clicking anywhere in the relevant section. Full modification/customization can be done once the report is opened. You can also display this report by selecting **Reports**, **Vendors & Payables**, **A/P Aging Summary** from the menu bar.

4 Select **Custom** in the Dates field, and then click the ▦ **(Calendar)** button to select **March 31, 2016** and click **Refresh**.

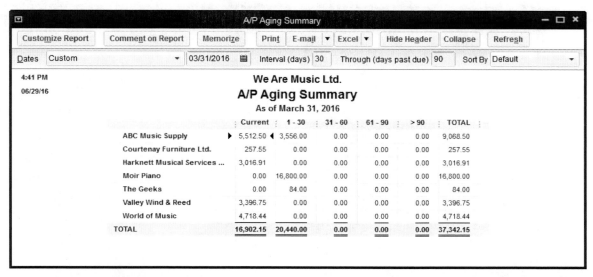

5 Review the numbers displayed, and then close the A/P Aging Summary window. Do not memorize the report.

6 Close the Report Centre.

Now pay one of the vendor bills.

7 In the Vendors section of the Home Page tab, click **Pay Bills**.

> You can also display this window by selecting **Vendors**, **Pay Bills** from the menu bar.

8 Click to select **Due on or before** and then click the ▦ **(Calendar)** button and select **March 31, 2016**.

9 Click the checkbox for the **Moir Piano** vendor bill with a Date Due of March 11, 2016.

10 If necessary, click **Account** and select **Royal Bank Chequing Account**.

11 Click the ▦ **(Calendar)** button for the Payment Date field, and select **March 22, 2016**.

12 Ensure **To be printed** is selected for the cheque.

Your screen should be similar to the following:

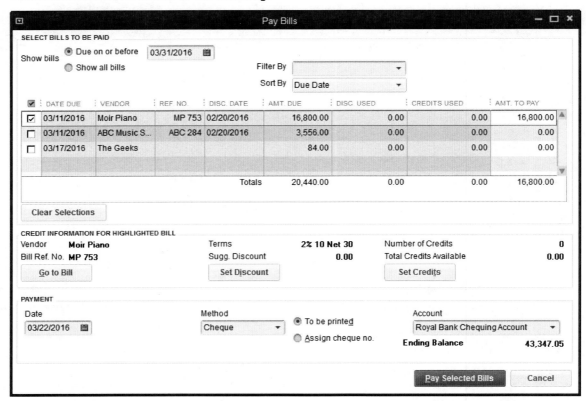

13 Click **Pay Selected Bills**.

14 The Payment Summary window gives you the option to Pay More Bills, to Print Cheques, or to finish by clicking Done. For this exercise, click **Done**.

At this point, you should stamp the vendor's invoice with the word "Paid" (or something similar) with today's date to indicate that this invoice has been recorded as paid in QuickBooks. Also, make a notation on the invoice of the cheque number used to make the payment.

Printing Cheques

Cheques can be printed in two ways using QuickBooks. If you selected the To be printed option in the Pay Bills window, then you can print cheques through the **File**, **Print Forms**, **Cheques** menu option.

IMPORTANT! The Print Cheques option is different than simply writing a cheque not associated with a bill, which is done through **Banking**, **Write Cheques**, or with the **Cheques** button in the Banking navigator.

Cheques can be printed in a batch or individually. When printing in the batch form, you will be required to select the cheque(s) you wish to print from the Select Cheques to Print dialog box. At this time you should confirm the bank account and the first cheque number.

 Learn the Skill

In this exercise you will learn how to print outstanding cheques.

1   Select **Print Cheques** in the Banking section of the Home Page tab.

> You can also display this report by selecting **File**, **Print Forms**, **Cheques** from the menu bar.

The Select Cheques to Print dialog box is displayed.

2   Confirm that the Bank Account selected is **Royal Bank Chequing Account**.

3   Ensure the **First Cheque Number** to be printed is: 119.

4   Ensure all bills in this window are selected.

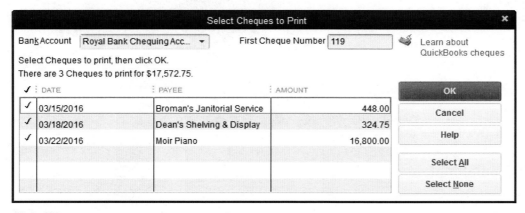

5   Click **OK**.

The Print Cheques window confirms your printer settings and how you are printing. It also informs you of how many cheques you are printing and the total value of these cheques.

QuickBooks has three types of cheques you can print. You are required to have pre-printed cheques for all three types.

Voucher	This form will print the cheque on the top portion of a letter size page. The middle section and the bottom section of the page provide the payment information.
Standard	This form will print three cheques to a letter size page. There is no payment information printed on the cheques.
Wallet	This form is similar to a personal cheque. It will print the Payee and the amount of the cheque on the stub portion.

6   If necessary, select the **Standard** cheque style.

7   Ensure **Print company name and address** is activated.

> If you should use pre-printed cheques, then you would not have to select **Print company name and address** or **Use logo**.

8   Number of copies should be 1. This cannot be changed for standard cheques.

> There should be no need to print more than one copy. It is normally cheaper and easier to make a photocopy. QuickBooks' register will provide you with the information about the payment.

9   Click **Print** to print the selected cheques.

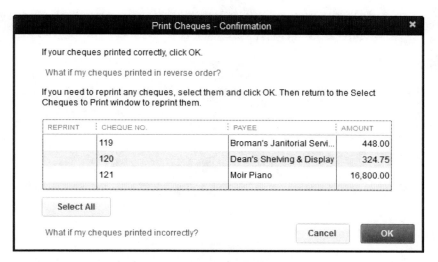

QuickBooks gives you an opportunity to reprint any of the cheques again if there was a problem with the print.

10 In this case we will assume all have printed correctly. Click **OK**.

Vendor Reports

QuickBooks has several built-in reports for vendors, purchases, and payments that are easy to run and read.

 ## Learn the Skill

In this exercise, you will learn how to run various vendor, purchases, and payments reports.

First print the list of all vendors entered in your system.

1 Select **Reports**, **Vendors & Payables**, **Vendor Contact List** from the menu bar.

The Vendor Contact List report displays the vendors and selected data about each of them, such as the balance owing to each of them and the address and phone numbers.

You will find that a printed copy of this list is very handy to refer to during the course of the day. You should print it on a regular basis (the frequency depends on how often it is updated) and place it where it is readily accessible to staff who need it. To improve its usefulness, you can modify this report by adding and removing fields and records.

2 Select **Customize Report**.

3 In the Display tab, click the **Fax, Bill from,** and **Account No**. columns to turn them off.

4 In the Header/Footer tab, change the Subtitle date to **March 31, 2016**. Deselect the Date and Time Prepared options, and click **OK**.

The customized report should appear similar to the following: The default date on the report will be the current computer date unless it is changed as directed above.

We Are Music Ltd.
Vendor Contact List
March 31 2016

Vendor	Primary Contact	Main Phone	Balance Total
ABC Music Supply	Jeremy Greene	604 588-3751	9,068.50 ◄
Bank of Nova Scotia			0.00
Broman's Janitorial Service	Gerry Broman	604 403-5634	0.00
Burnaby Office Supply Co.	Nancy Davies	604 403-3745	0.00
Courtenay Furniture Ltd.		604 403-6892	257.55
Danby Marketing Co.	Edward Danby	604 403-5634	0.00
Dean's Shelving & Display			0.00
Great West Life Insurance			0.00
Harknett Musical Services Ltd.	James Harknett	905 477-1141	3,016.91
Imperial Oil			0.00
Kanto & Co.		604 549-3698	0.00
LRS Property Management	Kathyrn Bogart	604 557-6534	0.00
Merit Insurance Company			0.00
Ministère du Revenu			0.00
Ministry of Finance (BC)			0.00
Moir Piano	Robert Borden	250 868-9537	0.00
Receiver General			0.00
Shaw Cable			0.00
Simmons Business Services	Jason Simmons	604 403-6892	0.00
The Geeks	Jim Contor	604 378-6534	84.00
The Phone Company			0.00
The Utility Co.			0.00

5   Close the report. Click **No** to the request to memorize the report.

Now run a report to graphically show the amount owing by vendor and by due date.

6   Select **Reports**, **Vendors & Payables**, **Accounts Payable Graph** from the menu bar.

7   Click **Dates**.

8   In the Change Graph Dates dialog box, click the 🗒 **(Calendar)** button and select **March 31, 2016**. Click
OK.

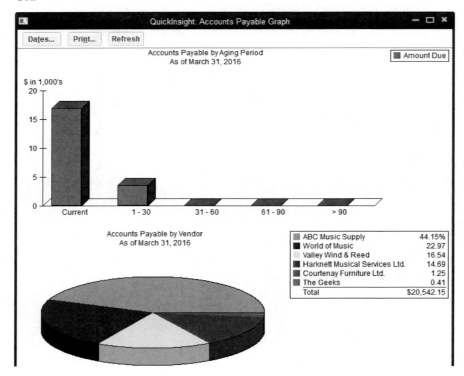

9 Close the Accounts Payable Graph window.

10 Select **Reports**, **Vendors & Payables**, **A/P Aging Detail** from the menu bar.

The A/P Aging Detail report shows all of the invoices outstanding that are included in the Accounts Payable Graph report. The information is also broken down into 30-day increments to help you recognize which invoices are overdue and by how much. Like the vendor list report, this should be printed on a regular basis to help you manage your payables and your cash balance.

11 Select **Custom** in the Dates field, then click the 📅 **(Calendar)** button for the Dates field, select **March 31, 2016** and click **Refresh**.

We Are Music Ltd.
A/P Aging Detail
As of March 31, 2016

Type	Date	Num	Name	Due Date	Aging	Open Balance
Current						
Bill	03/02/2016	ABC...	ABC Music Supply	04/01/2016		5,512.50 ◄
Bill	03/03/2016	HMS...	Harknett Musical S...	04/02/2016		2,518.95
Bill	03/03/2016	WOM...	World of Music	04/02/2016		3,543.75
Bill	03/15/2016	HMS...	Harknett Musical S...	04/14/2016		497.96
Bill	03/16/2016		Courtenay Furnitur...	04/15/2016		257.55
Bill	03/25/2016		World of Music	04/24/2016		1,174.69
Bill	03/28/2016	P.O. #1	Valley Wind & Reed	04/27/2016		3,396.75
Total Current						16,902.15
1 - 30						
Bill	02/10/2016	ABC...	ABC Music Supply	03/11/2016	20	3,556.00
Bill	02/16/2016		The Geeks	03/17/2016	14	84.00
Total 1 - 30						3,640.00
31 - 60						
Total 31 - 60						
61 - 90						
Total 61 - 90						
> 90						
Total > 90						
TOTAL						20,542.15

> The figures you see may vary, depending on the number of transactions you may have entered, including any adjustments or reversals.

12 If necessary, use the vertical scroll bar to see more. Close the A/P Aging Detail window. Click **No** to the request to memorize the report.

Another way of looking at the amounts owing is to re-sort the data by vendor.

13 Select **Reports**, **Vendors & Payables**, **Vendor Balance Detail** from the menu bar.

14 Select **Custom** in the Dates field, and set the dates to From **January 1, 2016** To **March 31, 2016**, click **Refresh**.

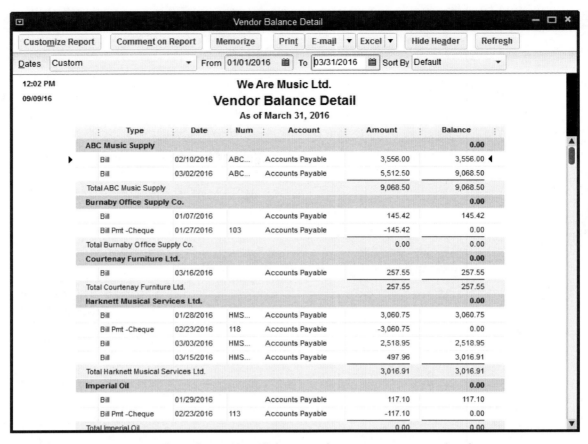

15 Scroll down to view more. Close the report. Click **No** to the request to memorize the report.

16 Backup the file as: We Are Music Ltd. – Your Name Lesson 3 following the same steps learned in Lesson 1.

Lesson Summary

In this lesson, you learned how to work with transactions in the Vendor Centre, including how to:

☑ work with the Vendor Centre   ☑ issue and fill purchase orders

☑ understand the workflow   ☑ receive items

☑ create and modify vendor records   ☑ receive vendor bills

☑ make purchases by entering vendor bills   ☑ find and modify vendor bills

☑ work with Sales Tax codes   ☑ pay vendor bills

☑ make purchases by writing cheques   ☑ print cheques

☑ create memorized payment transactions   ☑ run vendor reports

Practice the Skill

The following additional exercise covers many of the items discussed in this Lesson. The Practice the Skill exercises are included as extra practice and may be completed by the students in class or on their own. Your instructor has access to the Answer Key for these exercises.

1. Complete the following inventory purchases as of March 31, 2016 (Pay Later).
    a. Moir Piano, Invoice MP 539
        1 of item P-109 Piano @ 1,200 each
        Plus Freight charges of $75. Total invoice $1,338.75.

    b. Harknett Musical Services Ltd., Invoice HMS 6982
        1 bx of C-107, @ $599.50
        1 bx of I-107 @ $199.50
        1 **ea** of S-110 @ 850.00
        Freight charges of $55.00 apply. Total Invoice $1,789.20.

2. Using Cheque 122, complete the following non-inventory purchase dated March 31, 2016. Bought from Burnaby Office Supply, Invoice BOS 632, office supplies for a total of $154.80 plus GST @ 5% and PST @ 7%. Total cheque $173.38.

3. On March 31 receive the balance of items on back order from World of Music (P.O. #2). Create invoice #WOM 3587. No further freight charges, total invoice $1,212.75.

4. On March 31, 2016, pay the following bills. From Royal Bank Chequing Account: To be printed
    ABC Music Supply $3,556.00
    The Geeks $84.00

5. Backup the data file as: We Are Music Ltd. - Your Name Lesson 3 Practice.

Review Questions

1. To display the Vendor Centre you would:

    a. Click the Vendors icon on the Icon bar.

    b. Select Vendors, Vendor Centre from the menu bar.

    c. Click the Vendors icon in the Vendor's section of the Home Page tab.

    d. All of the above.

2. To pay an entered bill from a vendor you would:

    a. Write a cheque

    b. Use the General Journal

    c. Use the Pay Bills window

3. All purchases have to go through Enter Bills.

    a. True   b. False

4. What is the purpose behind memorized transactions?

5. Why is it important that you enter purchase entries through the Enter Bills and Write Cheques windows, rather than the General Journal?

6. To edit a Vendor record on the Vendor list you would:

    a. Right-click the Vendor name and select Edit Vendor.

    b. Double-click on the Vendor name.

    c. Select the Vendor name and click on Edit Vendor in the information section.

    d. All of the above.

7. The two steps required for adjusting an invoice are looking up the invoice, and then adjusting it.

    a. True   b. False

QuickBooks

Lesson 4: Customers and Accounts Receivable

Lesson Objectives

In this lesson, you will learn how to add customer information and how to move around and process transactions in the Customer Centre. Upon successful completion of this lesson, you should know how to:

- ☐ work with the Customer Centre
- ☐ add and modify customer records
- ☐ understand the workflow
- ☐ issue sales receipts
- ☐ record sales orders
- ☐ create, adjust and delete sales invoices

- ☐ work with price levels
- ☐ receive, adjust and delete payments
- ☐ process refunds and credits
- ☐ work with undeposited funds
- ☐ record deposits
- ☐ run customer reports

To Start This Lesson

Restoring the Exercise File

1. From the **File** menu in QuickBooks, choose **Open or Restore Company**.

   QuickBooks displays the Open or Restore Company window.

2. Select **Restore a backup copy** and click **Next**.

3. Select **Local backup** and click **Next**.

4. In the Open Backup Copy window navigate to your *1761 Student Files* folder.

5. Select the *We Are Music Ltd - 2016 - Student.QBB* file and then click **Open**.

6. In the Open or Restore Company window, click **Next**.

7. Navigate to your *1761 Student Files* folder.

8. In the File name field of the Save Company File as window, type: We Are Music Ltd - Your Name Lesson 4 and then click **Save**.

9. In the QuickBooks Login window enter the password: **Sys2016**.

10. Click **OK** when you see the message that the file has been successfully restored.

11. If necessary, close the QuickBooks Learning Centre and Have a Question windows.

Customers

A customer is anyone (people/companies) who purchases and pays for the services or products that your company sells. This definition is a general one, and applies to all types of organizations, even "not for profits" as they do not have "customers" in the traditional sense.

In this lesson, you will be using the Customer Centre of QuickBooks. In accounting terminology, you are using the *Accounts Receivable* module because you are selling goods and services to your customers, and some of them may be allowed to purchase on account and, therefore, owe money to your company.

Like the purchasing process, QuickBooks requires you to identify the customer on each sales transaction on invoice (on accounts receivable, as payment will arrive in the future). Even for cash sales (including other near-cash forms of payment such as cheques and credit card), you should still consider setting up a special customer record with a name like *Daily or Weekly Cash Sales* so you can track this group of sales as a single customer.

Customer records are required for sales transactions on invoice because you must be able to track how much they owe to you and when those payments are due. Failure to collect those payments will result in excessive delays in receiving cash and debt *write-offs* when these customers are unable to pay.

By tracking customer sales, you will be able to better understand your customers' buying patterns and increase your sales by anticipating their needs and offering incentives to encourage repeat business.

Before you can enter sales on invoice for your customers, you must first enter the customer information. This information includes such items as the customer's name, address, phone and fax numbers, email, and the credit limit your company has allowed the customer.

QuickBooks also allows you to use the customer function to track single jobs for a specific customer.

The Customer Centre

The Customer Centre provides similar information and performs similar tasks as the Vendor Centre. The Centre window provides information such as:

- the name of each customer and any jobs that have been created
- information relevant to the selected customer or job
- transactions that have occurred for the selected customer or job
- any balances owed by each customer

To open the Customer Centre click **Customers**, **Customer Centre** from the menu bar.

> You can also display this window by clicking the **Customers** button in the Customers section of the Home Page tab, or by clicking the **Customers** icon on the Icon bar.

The view within the window is consistent with that of the Vendor Centre.

The tool bar buttons provide access to a variety of tasks, such as creating new customers and jobs, transactions, and so on.

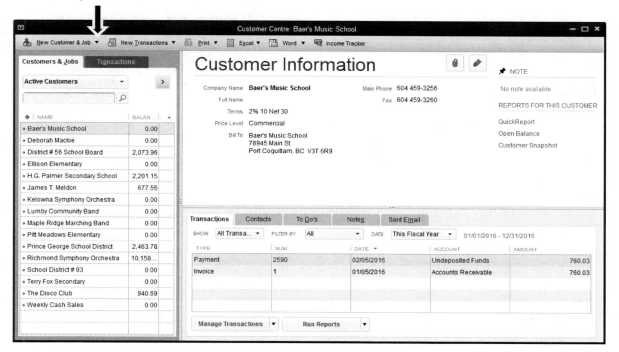

New Customer & Job	Opens the window for New Customer, Add Job, or Add Multiple Customers: Jobs.
New Transactions	Estimates, sales orders, invoices, sales receipts, statement charges, receive payments, credit memos/refunds.
Print	Customer & Job List, Customer & Job Information, Customer & Job Transaction List.
Excel	Export customer list, export transactions, import from Excel, paste from Excel.
Word	Prepare letter to selected customer, prepare customer letters, prepare collection letters, customize letter templates.
Income Tracker	The Income Tracker shows all unbilled sales (estimates, sales orders, and time & expenses), unpaid sales (open and overdue invoices, as well as payments and credits), and paid sales (payments and sales receipts).

Note: QuickBooks uses the current date to display the figures in the Income Tracker; therefore the figures and status below will be different, based on the current computer date.

Unbilled/Unpaid	Each coloured block shows the amount for transactions in that category. Click a block to see the transactions that make up that amount. Use the drop-down arrows below the coloured blocks to filter this list further. To reset the filters or see the complete list of transactions, click Clear/Show All.					
Action Column	Perform actions on a particular transaction. Click in the Action column and select an action from the drop-down menu.					
Batch Actions	This allows you to perform an action on a group of transactions of the same type.					
Manage Transactions	Allows you to create a new transaction by selecting the transaction type (estimates, sales orders, invoices, etc.) from the menu displayed by clicking the ▶ (chevron).					

The Income Tracker will be explored in greater detail in the Level 2 courseware.

The Customer Centre is divided into three panes:

- The left pane contains two tabs, Customers & Jobs and Transactions. The Customers & Jobs tab lists your Customers, and can be sorted by clicking the top drop-down arrow and selecting an option. The Transaction tab lists the types of transactions available in QuickBooks.

- If you track sites (warehouses) and/or bin locations (rows, shelves, or bins), a second drop-down arrow is available in the left pane to filter the list by location.

- The top-right pane shows the details for the selected Customer, and provides quick access to several reports.

- The bottom-right pane has tabs that show Transactions, Contacts, To Do's, Notes and Sent Email related to the selected customer. If you track bin locations (rows, shelves, or bins) in QuickBooks, the pane also contains a Bins tab, where you can set the default bin locations for purchasing and sales.

It is important to understand that QuickBooks uses lists to organize company information. Lists allow for an easy fill of necessary information into forms by the use of drop-down arrows. In some cases just starting to type in the entry causes QuickBooks to autofill the rest.

The Customers & Jobs List

The list management skills you learned in Lesson 3 can also be applied in this lesson, and will also be applied when working in the Employee Centre in a future lesson. The concepts for creating, editing and deleting a record work for Inventory, Vendors, Customers and Employee list entries.

Moving List Entries

You may occasionally need to move sub-entries to be under a different top-level entry. For example, if you entered a job under the wrong customer. You can move it under the correct customer.

- Move the mouse pointer so that it touches the small diamond in front of the entry that you want to move.

- While holding down the mouse button, drag the entry up, down, left, or right to its new location:

    - To move an entry with all of its sub-entries, drag the main (parent) entry.

    - To make a sub-entry a main entry, drag it to the left.

    - To make a main entry a sub-entry, drag it to the right.

◇ District # 56 School Board	2,073.96
◇ Ellison Elementary	0.00
◇ H.G. Palmer Secondary School	2,201.15

You can recognize the lists that can be reorganized by the small diamond that appears in front of each list entry. These lists are: Chart of Accounts, Class, Customers & Jobs, Customer Type, Item, Job Type, Memorized Transaction, and Vendor Type.

- On the Chart of Accounts, accounts of the same type must remain together. On the Item List, items of the same type must remain together.

- You cannot move entries in a list that has been sorted. Click the diamond column to return to the original sort order.

Removing List Entries

QuickBooks has three ways to remove list entries. The method listed below is used to demonstrate working with items, but this method also works with list entries for Vendors and Customers.

- Combine (merge) two entries:

    - For example, if you mistakenly entered the same item twice but with different names, you can merge the two items so that all of your transactions are associated with only one item name. The steps to merge two items are:

        o Open the Item List, open the Edit Item window for the item you do not wish to use.

        o Change the item name to the same name as the item you are combining it with.

        o Click **OK**, and then **Yes** to confirm.

> You cannot combine more than two items at a time, and you cannot combine items if both have sub-items. You must first remove the sub-items from the item you want to remove.

- Hide a list entry (by making it inactive):

    - For example, if you have customers that you no longer deal with, you can hide them so they do not appear in the list.

> o To hide a customer, right-click the customer in the Customers & Jobs list, and select **Make Customer:Job Inactive**.

- Delete a list entry:
    - Note: It's better for your records to hide a customer instead of deleting them. Also, there are limitations when you delete a list entry.
        - o To delete an entry, right-click the entry in the list, and select **Delete Customer:Job**.

> You must delete entries one at a time, and you cannot delete an entry that has been used in a transaction, or in the case of customers, one that also has an outstanding job, or jobs.

Learn the Skill

In this exercise, you will learn how to create a new customer record.

1 Start QuickBooks, if necessary, and ensure the Lesson 4 company data file is open.

2 If necessary, select **Customers** in the Icon bar to display the **Customer Centre**.

The customers displayed were previously created during the company data file setup process. As discussed previously, this screen provides an instant overview of the selected customer, with the balance owing, customer information, and a listing of this customer's transactions.

3 Click the **New Customer & Job** button and then select **New Customer** from the drop-down list to open the New Customer window.

> You can also display this window by right-clicking anywhere in the Customer: Job List area and selecting **New** or by pressing Ctrl + N on the keyboard.

Notice that the New Customer window resembles the New Vendor window. In the opening window, enter the basic information about the customer.

4 Enter the following data in the **Address Info** tab of the New Customer window:

Company Name	Seaton Street Band
Opening Balance	0.00
As of	March 01, 2016
Main Phone	604 942-3399
Main Email	edmaberly@shaw.ca

5 Add the rest of the address data in the **Invoice/Bill To** field:

c/o E. Maberly
123 Willow Avenue
Port Coquitlam, BC V3B 2J9

6 Click **Copy>>** to copy the Invoice/Bill To address to the Ship To address field.

7 In the window click **OK**.

The screen should appear similar to the following:

Customer Name	This field is used to sort the customer list alphabetically.
Opening Balance, as of	The total amount that this customer owes to you for goods and services delivered up to and including the as of date.
Company Name	Use this field if the customer is a company or a partnership.
Mr./Ms./..., First Name, M.I., Last Name	Use these fields if the customer is an individual person.
Phone, Fax, Email	The phone, fax, and email address of the contact person.
Website	The website address, if any.
Other	A variety of alternate contact options, such as Facebook, Twitter, etc.
Invoice/Bill To Address	The mailing address where invoices and statements are to be sent.
Ship To Address	Address information where goods and services are to be delivered.
Ship To Icons	The icons to the right of the Ship To address are: Add: additional addresses Edit: the address and Delete: an address.
Customer is inactive	If this indicator is turned on, then this customer will no longer appear on lists or reports to prevent you from creating new invoices and statements for this customer. You should preferably not delete a customer that is no longer buying from you because you will then lose all of the historical information for this customer.

8 Click the **Payment Settings** tab and enter the following data:

Account No.   56824
Credit Limit   1,000.00
Terms   1% 10 Net 30

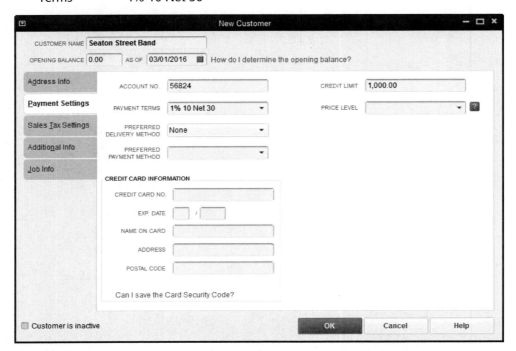

Account No.	The account number that you have assigned to this customer.
Payment Terms	Discounts (if any) for paying invoices within a specified period of time after the invoice date. These terms are usually printed on the invoices that you send.
Credit Limit	This is the credit limit you have authorized for this customer. QuickBooks advises you when the total amount owing from the customer exceeds this limit.
Price Level	Use this field to categorize your customers into different pricing groups, such as preferential and full price.
Preferred Delivery Method	This refers to the preferred delivery for invoices, Email, Mail, or None.
Preferred Payment Method	The payment method preferred by the customers, cash, cheque, credit card, etc.
Credit Card Information	This area would be completed if the customer preferred to pay by credit card. Clicking on the payment method field displays a drop-down menu of available credit cards.

9   Click the **Sales Tax Settings** tab and enter the following data:

Tax Code	S
Country	Canada
Business Number	12356897

Tax Code	A special tax code that this customer has. This code is used on invoices to override the tax code assigned to each item. For example, you can use this field to identify this customer as GST/HST-exempt.
Country	Specifies the country in which the customer is located for tax purposes.
Business Number	The customer's business number.

10   Click the **Additional Info** tab and complete as follows:

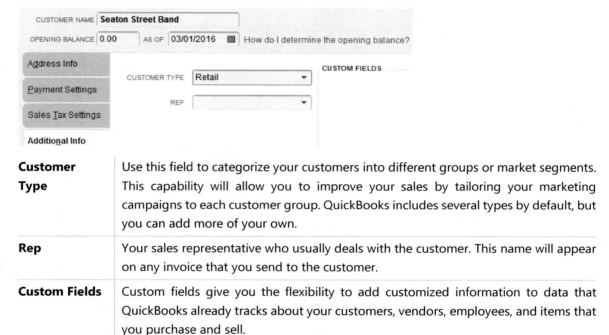

Customer Type	Use this field to categorize your customers into different groups or market segments. This capability will allow you to improve your sales by tailoring your marketing campaigns to each customer group. QuickBooks includes several types by default, but you can add more of your own.
Rep	Your sales representative who usually deals with the customer. This name will appear on any invoice that you send to the customer.
Custom Fields	Custom fields give you the flexibility to add customized information to data that QuickBooks already tracks about your customers, vendors, employees, and items that you purchase and sell.

11   Click the **Job Info** tab.

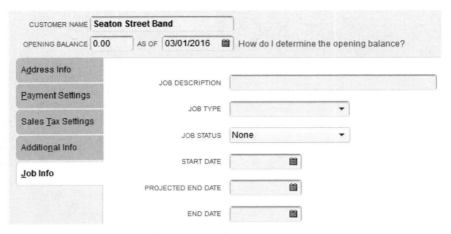

This information can be used to track a specific job or project for this customer.

Job Description	A short description of the job.
Job Type	Use this field to categorize this job.
Job Status	The current status of the job, such as Pending, or Awarded.
Start Date	The estimated or actual start date of the job.
Projected End Date	The estimated end date of the job.
End Date	The actual end date of the job.

12   Review the available fields, and then click **OK**.

Modifying Customer Records

You can update information about a customer any time something about them has changed or to correct mistyped information. However, you cannot change historical accounting information such as the outstanding balance as this is calculated automatically by QuickBooks.

 Learn the Skill

In this exercise, you will modify the information recorded about existing customers.

1   In the Customers & Jobs list, select **District # 56 School Board**, then click the ✎ **(Edit)** button in the customer information section of the Customer Centre.

> You can also double-click the customer row in the Customers & Jobs list or press Ctrl + E to open it.

In the Edit Customer window for District # 56 School Board enter additional data for this customer.

2   In the **Address Info** tab, add the following information:
        Main Email   admin@district56board.org

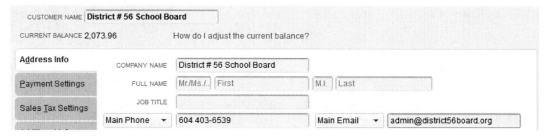

3 In the **Payment Settings** tab, add the following information:

Preferred Payment Method   Cheque

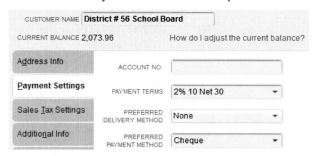

4 Click **OK**.

5 In the Customers & Jobs List select **H.G. Palmer Secondary School** and then click the  **(Edit)** button in the customer information section of the Customer Centre.

6 In the **Payment Settings** tab, type: 5,000.00 in the Credit Limit field.

7 Click **OK**.

8 Close the Customer Centre window.

Working with Price Level Lists

Price levels let you set custom pricing for different customers or jobs. Once you create a price level and associate it with one or more customers or jobs, each time you create an invoice, estimate, sales receipt, sales order, or credit memo for those customers or jobs, QuickBooks automatically pulls up the correct custom price. You create price levels, and then use them on sales forms to adjust the price of an item. You can also manually adjust the prices while creating a sales form.

 Learn the Skill

In this exercise, you will set the rate for a price level, and then modify customer records for future sales.

1 Click **Lists**, **Price Level List** on the menu bar.

2   If necessary, select **Commercial** and then click **Price Level**, select **Edit Price Level** from the drop-down list.

> You can also right-click **Commercial** and select **Edit Price Level** or press Ctrl+E to open the Edit Price Level window.

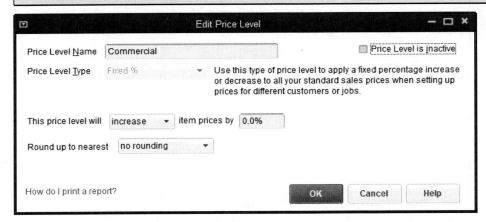

3   Select **decrease** in the This price level will field, and change the rate to 5% in the next field. Accept **no rounding**. Your screen should resemble the following:

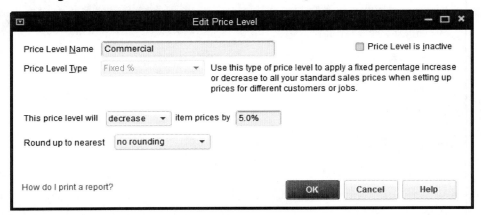

4   Click **OK**.

5   Follow steps 2 and 3 for the **Educational** price level, decreasing the level by 10%.

6   Click **OK**.

Your Price Level List should now resemble the following:

7   Close the Price Level List window.

8 Open the Customer Centre window, and click the **Edit** button for each of the following customers. Select the **Payment Settings** tab to set their Price Level as follows:

Customer	Price Level
Ellison Elementary	Educational
Kelowna Symphony Orchestra	Commercial
Prince George School District	Educational
Richmond Symphony Orchestra	Commercial
School District # 93	Educational

> You can also double-click the customer row in the Customers & Jobs list or press Ctrl+E to open the Edit Customer window.

9 Close the Customer Centre window.

Recording Sales

The Workflow

The Customers section on the Home Page tab has a diagram that clearly describes how QuickBooks handles the Sales and Accounts Receivable function.

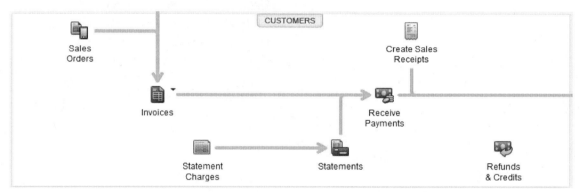

This diagram shows that there are two main streams: Invoices and Sales Receipts. Both streams lead to the Deposits process which can be accessed in the Banking section of the Home Page tab.

Sales Orders	Allows you to enter customer sales orders.
Estimates	Provides a bid, proposal, or estimate for a customer which can be converted to an invoice once the work is completed.
Create Invoices	Lists what you sold to a customer and shows the quantity and cost of each item. Use invoices if: • You sell goods or services and need to keep a detailed record of each item. • You sell to customers on account.
Receive Payments	Involves receiving payments from customers (cash, cheque, or credit card) for sales invoices issued previously. It is important to match payments received with the correct invoice to accurately record the payments.
Create Sales Receipts	Involves entering sales transactions in which payment was received immediately.
Statement Charges	Allows you to accumulate charges that will be included on a billing statement.

Statements	Allows you to create a new statement to show your customers a history of their account activity (charges, payments, balances).
Refunds & Credits	Issue a credit memo to a customer for merchandise returns, service credit, or credit toward an account.
Record Deposits	This icon in the Banking section allows you to deposit payments received from customers into your bank account. This process will be dealt with in detail later in this Lesson.

It is critical to follow the steps as outlined in certain transactions. If you create an invoice for a customer that will be paid in the future, it must be entered as an invoice. When the time comes to receive payment, it must be recorded via the Receive Payments process in order to properly clear the entry. If a Sales Receipts process is used instead, the original invoice will not be cleared, and the sale will be recorded twice.

Create Sales Receipts

This function is used to record transactions where a customer makes a purchase with immediate payment (by cash, cheque, debit, or credit card). A sales receipt is produced for each individual transaction. You can choose to select a customer (in which case that customer must be in the customer list) or manually enter the Sold To name to handle customers that may not return in the future, or handle multiple sales transactions.

Where a cash register or point-of-sale system is in use, one-off sales transactions may be recorded and receipted in that system, and then a summary sales invoice input into QuickBooks at the end of the day or the week. The total of this invoice should create a balancing total for the cash/cheque takings for the day. If this method is used, it may be helpful to create an *artificial* customer record called *Daily* or *Weekly Cash Sales* to assist in recording these transactions.

Because payment has been received immediately on these transactions, the bookkeeping embodies a debit to the bank account where the cash receipts will be deposited. Later in this Lesson we will cover sales with a debit to Accounts Receivable, when the customer pays later.

 ## Learn the Skill

In this exercise, you will learn how to create a sales receipt for a one-time customer where payment is received immediately.

1   In the Customers section on the Home Page tab, click **Create Sales Receipts**.

> You can also display this window by selecting **Customers**, **Enter Sales Receipts** from the menu bar.

This window now displays Summary and Transaction information, similar to that displayed in the Enter Bills window discussed in Lesson 3.

2   Enter the following data into the Enter Sales Receipts window:

Sold To	Joe Novak (Type name into the Sold To field and then click **Quick Add**)
Date	March 15, 2016
Cheque No.	104
Payment Method	Cheque

3 Enter the following data for the items sold:

Item	Description	Qty
B-110	Trombone	1
C-107	Trombone Case	1
I-103	Trombone Stand	1

4 Click the **Customer Message** drop-down list button and select **Thank you for your business**.

5 As this customer has no history with us, click the ▶ (chevron) on the right of the screen by the Summary section to Hide history.

The completed screen should appear similar to the following:

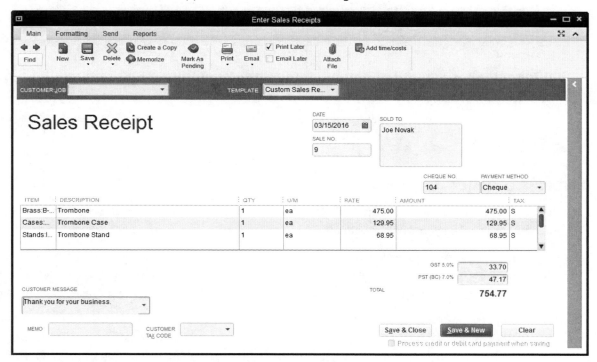

Each of the four tabs will display a ribbon when selected.

Main ribbon	Contains icons that link to a variety of tasks, such as New, Save, Print Later.
Formatting ribbon	Contains icons for Preview (Print), Template management, Customize Data Layout, Spelling etc.
Send ribbon	Contains the icon to allow the Sales Receipt to be emailed.
Reports ribbon	Contains icons for a variety of reports.
Customer:Job	The customer, from the Customers list.
Template	This field is used to select from the various customer sales receipt forms available. QuickBooks provides one standard form by default.
Sold To	The name and address of the customer retrieved from the customer record. Whether or not a customer is selected, the data in this field can be manually entered or changed.

Date	The date of the sales receipt.
Sale No.	The next sequential number available that will uniquely identify this sales receipt.
Cheque No.	If the customer paid by cheque, use this field to record the cheque number.
Payment Method	How the customer paid for the goods or services; e.g., cash, cheque, credit card.
Item	The item number of the goods or services sold. This item must be present in the Item List.
Description	The description of the selected item from the inventory record.
Qty	The quantity sold of this item.
U/M	The unit by which this item is sold.
Rate	The unit price of the item from the inventory record. It can be changed.
Amount	The calculated total of Qty multiplied by Rate.
Tax	The tax code of the item from the inventory record.
Customer Message	A freeform text message that is displayed on the printed sales receipt.
Memo	A freeform text message that is displayed in Find screens and company reports.

6   Click **Save & Close**.

Entering Sales Orders

If you are filling a customer's order immediately when receiving it (either by phone, email, or customer's purchase order), then you would create a sales invoice.

By issuing a sales order, however, you have not actually sold anything to anyone (and therefore you cannot record any sales revenue)—you created one in order to make the sale later on. Also, until the goods are shipped or the services are rendered, the customer may change his/her mind and cancel the sales order.

However, by issuing the sales order you are making a firm commitment to deliver the goods or services on the promised shipment date. If the goods have to be ordered from your vendor(s), you should place your purchase order immediately and obtain a firm delivery date from them. If you have some or all of the goods already in stock, you should physically move the inventory to a separate part of your storage area or warehouse and attach the sales order to the boxes to prevent them from being sold to another customer by accident. If you are promising services on a future date, you should ensure the required staff or subcontractors are scheduled for that date and time.

Examples to demonstrate the usefulness of a sales order:

* You can only fill part of the order and you must back order the remainder.
* You are supplying the same group of goods or services to a customer on a regular, repeating basis in the future.

Learn the Skill

In this exercise, you will learn how to create a sales order.

1   In the Customers section on the Home Page tab, click **Sales Orders**.

> You can also display this window by selecting **Customers**, **Create Sales Orders** from the menu bar.

2 Enter the following data:

Customer: Job	H.G. Palmer Secondary School
Date	March 15, 2016
Item	W-115
Description	Saxophone
Ordered	2
Customer Message	Thank you for your business.

The completed screen should appear similar to the following:

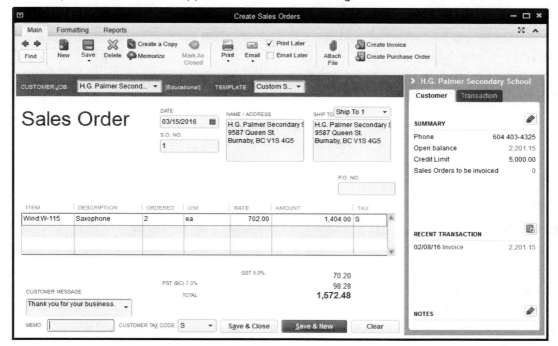

Customer: Job	The customer, from the Customers list.
Template	This field is used to select from the various customer sales receipt forms available. QuickBooks provides one standard form by default.
Date	The date of the sales order. This may be future-dated.
S.O. No.	The next sequential number available that will uniquely identify this sales order.
Name/Address	The name and address of the customer retrieved from the customer record. Whether or not a customer is selected, the data in this field can be manually entered or changed.
Ship To	The address where the goods and services are to be delivered. By default, QuickBooks uses the same address as the Name/Address field. It can be changed.
P.O. No.	The customer's purchase order number, if any.
Item	The name and number of the item to be ordered.
Description	The description of the ordered item.
Ordered	The number of items ordered.
U/M	The unit of measure is ea. for this particular item.

Rate	This customer receives a reduced rate (educational). To view that this is educational, click the drop-down arrow in this field.
Tax	The tax code of the item from the inventory record.
Customer Message	A freeform text message that is displayed on the printed sales receipt.
Customer Tax Code	The customer's tax code from the customer record.
Customer/Transaction History Section	As this customer has an account history, we will leave the history showing.

3   In the Create Sales Orders window click **Save & Close**.

Entering Sales on Invoice

When you record a sale as a sales invoice, you are allowing the customer to pay for the goods and services later. QuickBooks will automatically debit the Accounts Receivable account when you record this transaction.

You may have many customers who will pay later because you have established credit terms for them. The payment terms are recorded in the customer record (e.g., net due in 30 days), and redisplayed at the bottom of the screen as well as on the sales invoice. If you decide that the terms for this specific invoice should be different than the terms currently set up for the customer, you can change it just for this one sales invoice. In order to create a sales invoice for later payment, the customer must be in the customer list.

Sales transactions are normally handled in one of two ways. These are:

- Sales staff makes out manual invoices as sales are processed, and a copy of the manual invoice is handed to the bookkeeper to be input into QuickBooks.

- Sales staff has a user terminal on the sales floor and creates invoices by inputting the transaction details directly into QuickBooks. To do this, the QuickBooks Pro and higher versions software, which allows multiple users to access the same data file, may be used.

 ## Learn the Skill

In this exercise, you will learn how to create sales invoices that you expect to be paid later.

As there are several different templates for invoices, we will demonstrate the two most common. The first will be a service invoice.

1   Select **Customers**, **Create Invoices** from the menu bar.

2   In the Create Invoices window, click **Customer:Job** and select **Pitt Meadows Elementary**.

3   Enter the following data:

Template	Intuit Service Invoice
Date	March 16, 2016
Item	Lessons
Quantity	3
Description	Music Instruction
Tax	G
Customer Message	Thank you for your business.

The screen should appear similar to the following:

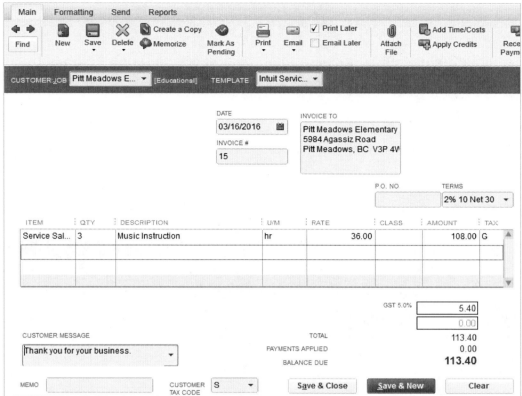

Template	This field is used to select from the various customer sales receipt forms available. QuickBooks provides seven standard forms by default. This invoice uses the Service template.
P.O. No.	The customer's purchase order number, if any.
Terms	The payment terms for this customer from the customer record.
Customer Tax Code	The tax code assigned to the customer, in this case it is different from the code assigned to each item.

Now record this invoice as a memorized transaction.

4   Right-click in the invoice, and select **Memorize Invoice** from the drop-down list.

5   Enter the following data into the Memorize Transaction window:

Name	Accept default
Add to my Reminders List	Yes
How Often	Weekly
Next Date	March 23, 2016

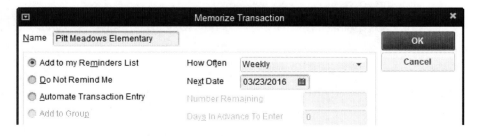

6 Click **OK**.

7 Click **Save & New** in the Create Invoices window.

This next invoice covers product sales.

8 In the Create Invoices window, click **Customer:Job** and select **Lumby Community Band**.

9 Enter the following data:

Template	Intuit Product Invoice	
Date	March 21, 2016	
	Item 1	**Item 2**
Quantity	2	1
Item	Gig Bag	B-101
Description	Carry bag	Cornet
Customer Message	Thank you for your business.	

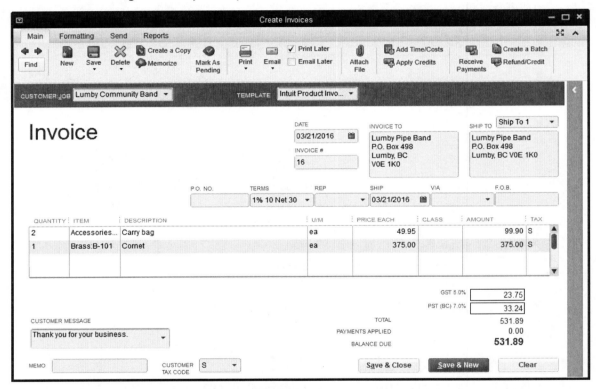

Template	This invoice uses the Product template, and several additional areas are shown.
Rep	Name or initials of the sales representative for this customer from the customer record.
Ship	The date on which the goods or services were shipped to the customer.
Via	The name of the courier or delivery service.
F.O.B.	Free On Board; the point to which the cost of delivery (and loading onto a ship if necessary) is included as part of the cost of goods. It is also the point at which ownership of the goods transfers from the vendor to the customer.

10 Click **Save & Close**.

Viewing, Adjusting and Deleting Sales Invoices

Like payables transactions, you can make changes to a sales invoice, sales order, or sales receipt at any time. To change it, you redisplay it, make the necessary changes, and save the sales transaction again. If you wish to cancel the entire sales invoice, you can delete it.

Learn the Skill

In this exercise, you will learn how to modify a sales invoice processed earlier.

1   Click **Customers**, **Create Invoices** from the menu bar. In the Create Invoices window, click **Find** in the Main ribbon.

2   In the Find Invoices dialog box, click the **Customer:Job** drop-down button, select **District #56 School Board** and click **Find**.

As there is only one invoice outstanding for this customer, it will automatically be displayed. If there were more than one, a Find window would open allowing you to select the one required by double-clicking on the invoice.

3   In the Create Invoices window, add the following item:

    Quantity   5
    Item   Metronome
    Price   44.955

(Since the customer's rate is now educational, the program will calculate the adjusted price to three decimal places. Change this to two decimal places).

If a Price Levels window is displayed regarding flexible pricing, select the **Do not display** checkbox, and then **OK**.

Your screen should resemble the following;

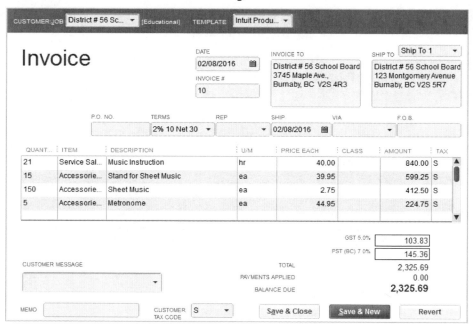

4   Click **Save & Close**.

5   Click **Yes** when the Recording Transaction message displays.

Payments and Credits on Receivables

Receiving Payments

In the Receive Payments window, QuickBooks assumes that all cash receipts come from your customers for payment of unpaid sales invoices. Therefore, the Receive Payments window expects you to select a customer from the customer list, then it will look up the outstanding invoices for that customer (this is called the Open Invoice system). You can also enter discounts (such as early payment discount), and select any credit notes that have been issued to that customer. The process is very streamlined and easy to use. If you wish to cancel the entire payment, you can delete it.

A current receivables report may be needed to ascertain how much a customer owes.

Learn the Skill

In this exercise you will learn how to create a report, and receive payments from customers.

1   Click the **Reports** icon in the Navigation bar. In the Report Centre select **Customers & Receivables**, click **A/R Aging Summary** and then click **Run**.

> You can also display this report by selecting **Reports**, **Customers & Receivables**, **A/R Aging Summary** from the menu bar.

2   Select **Custom** from the Dates field, then click the ▦ **(Calendar)** button, select **March 31, 2016** and click **Refresh**.

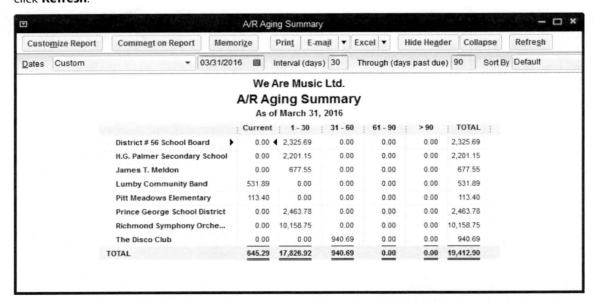

3   Review the clients, and the outstanding amounts. Close the A/R Aging Summary window. Do **not** memorize this report. Close the Report Centre.

Now receive a payment from a customer.

4 In the **Customers** section of the Home Page tab, click **Receive Payments**.

You can also display this screen by selecting **Customers**, **Receive Payments** from the menu bar.

You have received a cheque from a customer, Pitt Meadows Elementary, for the amount of $113.40.

5 Click **Received From** and select **Pitt Meadows Elementary**.

6 Click the 📅 (Calendar) button for the Date field, and select **March 21, 2016**.

7 If necessary click **Pmt. Method** and select **Cheque**.

8 Enter the following data:

Amount   113.40

Cheque #   54321

Notice that QuickBooks has automatically advised that this customer has discounts available. Make sure your highlighter stays on invoice 15. Different discounts may apply to individual invoices if more than one is outstanding.

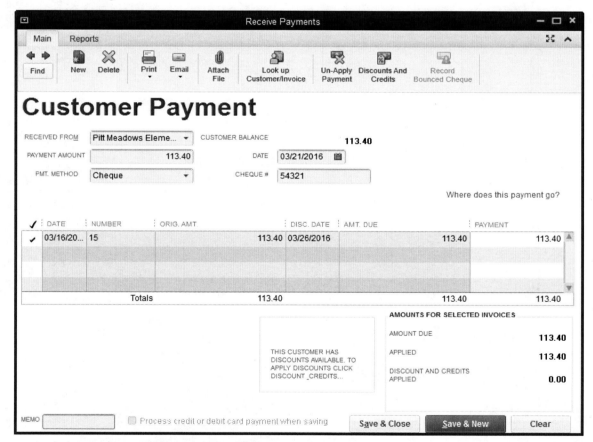

9 Click **Discounts & Credits** in the Main ribbon.

10 In the Amount of Discount field, accept the 2.16 figure QuickBooks assigned.

11 If necessary click **Discount Account** and select **Sales Discounts**.

The Discounts and Credits window should appear as follows:

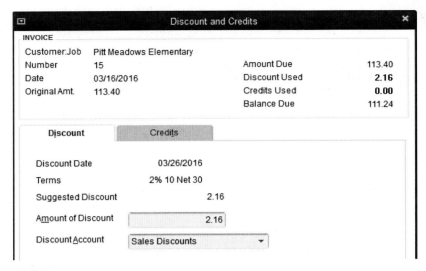

12 Click **Done**.

The completed screen should now appear as follows:

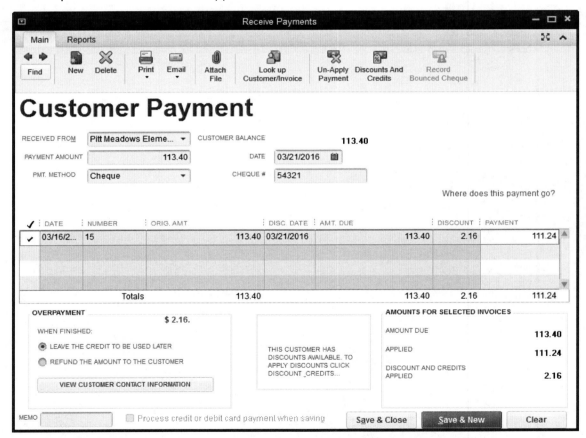

13 If necessary, select **Leave The Credit to be Used Later** then click **Save & New**.

14 Click **OK** in the Payment Credit window.

Learn the Skill

In this exercise, you will enter additional receipts.

1   If necessary, open the **Receive Payments** window.

2   Click **Received From** and select **District #56 School Board**.

3   Click the ▦ **(Calendar)** button for the Date field, and select **March 25, 2016**.

4   If necessary, click **Pmt. Method** and select **Cheque**.

5   Enter the following data:
    Amount   2,325.69
    Cheque #   367

6   Click **Save & New**.

7   Click **Received From** and select **James T. Meldon**.

8   Click the ▦ **(Calendar)** button for the Date field, and select **March 25, 2016**.

9   Click **Pmt. Method** and select **Cheque**.

10 Enter the following data:
    Amount   677.55
    Cheque #   497

11 Click **Save & Close**.

Refunds and Credits

There will be situations where customers will return goods. When you accept the returns, you will either provide an exchange or a refund for that return. If it is an exchange transaction, then two possible situations could occur:

•   If the replacement item is identical, then you do not need to do any accounting for the exchange.

•   If the replacement item is different and the value is different (higher or lower), then you can use the procedure for modifying the sales invoice.

If it is a refund transaction, then you will need to return the value of the item(s) sold, and the following three situations could occur:

•   If the customer has already paid for the item(s), you can refund the purchase price less any applicable return fee.

•   If the customer had purchased on account and had not yet paid, you can cancel the sale of the item(s) and the amount owing on the receivable less any applicable return fee.

•   You can issue a credit note that can be applied on future purchases.

In any of the previous situations, the item may no longer be saleable. If that is the case, then you may be able to return it to the manufacturer or distributor and you will process a purchase return transaction for that.

Notice that a sales return transaction is the reverse of a sales transaction.

If the items returned are unsaleable, then you will have to enter an inventory adjustment transaction to remove them from the inventory (covered in the Level 2 courseware).

Learn the Skill

In this exercise, you will learn how to process a sales return.

1   In the Customers section of the Home Page tab, click **Refunds & Credits**.

2   Click **Customer:Job** and select **Maple Ridge Marching Band**.

3   Ensure the date is **March 16, 2016**.

4   Enter the following item data:

Item	Description	Qty
C-111	Trumpet Case	1

5   Select the **Memo** text box, and enter: Refund on returned item.

The completed screen should appear similar to the following:

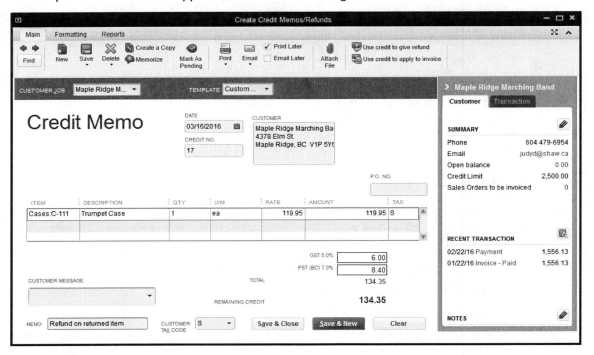

6   Click **Save & Close**.

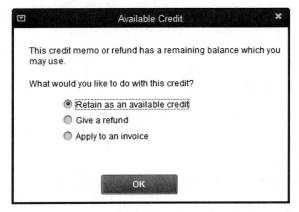

7   In the Available Credit dialog box, select **Retain as an available credit**, then **OK**.

Applying a Credit

When a customer has a credit or refund these funds may be applied to past or future invoices. This can often be determined by communication with the customer as to how the credit funds are to be applied.

 ## Learn the Skill

In this exercise, you will learn how to apply a credit to an invoice.

Maple Ridge Marching Band has recently returned an item and now wants to purchase a different item. The customer has a $134.35 refund credit that can be applied to an invoice. Create the following invoice.

1 In the Customers section of the Home Page tab, open the **Invoices** icon and select **Create Invoices**. Fill in as per the following, and note the Credit Memo listed in the history section under Recent Transactions.

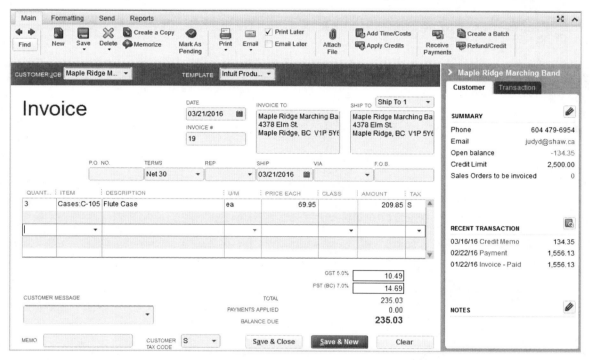

2 Click the **Apply Credits** icon in the main ribbon.

3 In the Recording Transaction window, click **Yes**.

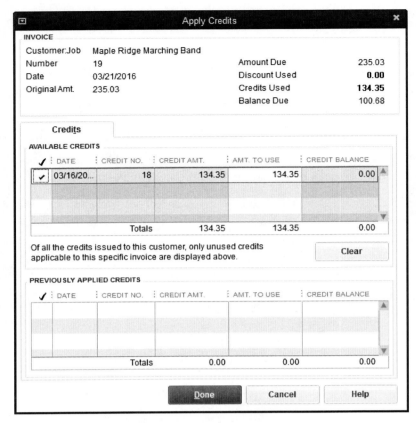

4   Review the information in this window, and note the Balance Due amount of $100.68 after applying the credit to this new invoice. Click **Done**.

5   Your screen should resemble the following:

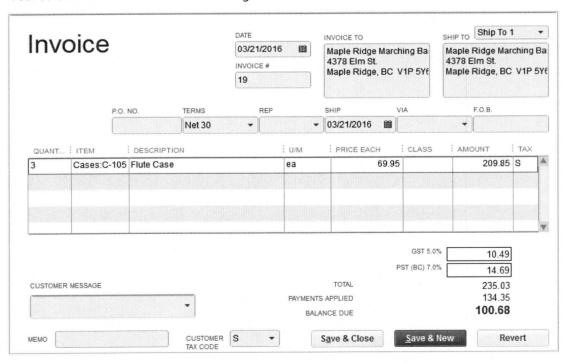

6   Click **Save & Close**.

Adjusting Payments

There may be a time when a payment has been recorded incorrectly. When this happens, the payment amount can be easily adjusted if it has not been recorded as deposited. If it has been deposited, there is a process to adjust the payment, which will be discussed in the Level 2 courseware. At this time we will adjust a payment that has not yet been deposited.

 ## Learn the Skill

In this exercise, you will learn how to adjust a payment that has been received, but recorded incorrectly.

The payment received from District #56 School Board on March 16, 2016 for $2,325.69 should have been recorded as $2,000.00. We now have to adjust the payment to record the correct amount.

1   In the Customers section of the Home Page tab, click **Receive Payments**, and then click ◄ **(Previous)** twice to display the payment from District #56 School Board.

2   Click the **Un-Apply Payment** button (located on the Main ribbon).

3   In the Payment Amount field, enter: **2,000.00** and press ⌨Tab.

4   Click in the ✓ column to select the invoice.

5   If necessary, in the Underpayment notice area, select **Leave this as an underpayment**.

Your screen should resemble the following:

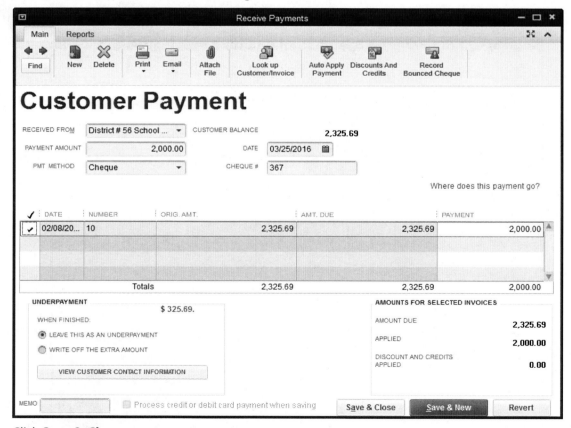

6   Click **Save & Close**.

7   If necessary, click **Yes** in the Recording Transaction window.

Recording Deposits of Payments

In QuickBooks, there are two options regarding methods of depositing payments. You may either record a deposit at the time of accepting the payment, or choose to record all payments in the Undeposited Funds account. This second option more closely resembles the normal banking procedures in business. That is, recording the deposit when a receipt or selection of receipts are taken to the bank. One total will be recorded on the bank statement, which will match the deposit total recorded in QuickBooks. These options are chosen in Preferences.

This data base has been set up for the Undeposited Funds option.

To make a deposit, select Record Deposits in the Banking section. Select all the payment(s) to be deposited in this window. The screen will show all the receipts received and not deposited. You are provided with the Date, Transaction Type, Cheque No., or Reference No., Payment Method, Customer, and the Amount of receipt(s).

 ## Learn the Skill

In this exercise you will deposit the funds now recorded in the Undeposited Funds account.

1   In the Banking section of the Home Page tab, click **Record Deposits**.

> You can also display this window by selecting **Banking**, **Make Deposits** from the menu bar.

2   In the Payments to Deposit window, click **Select All**.

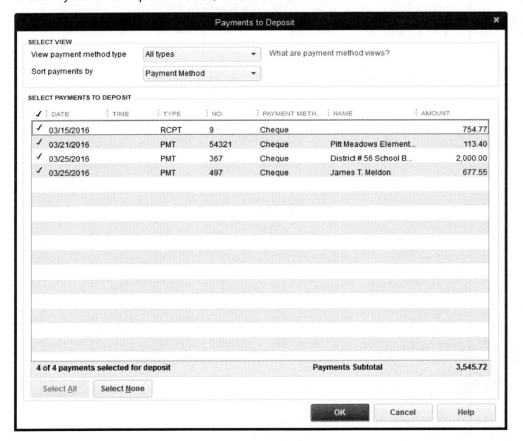

3 Click **OK**.

In the Make Deposits window one of the entries was for a one time customer, and therefore, no name is displayed.

4 Click **Deposit To** and if necessary, select **Royal Bank Chequing Account**.

5 Select **March 28, 2016** as the date.

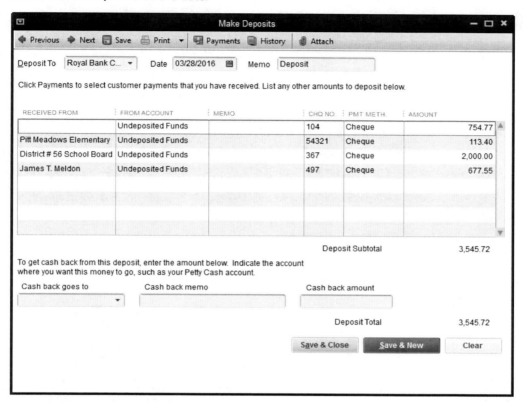

This window provides the option to receive cash back from the deposit, and to have it applied to another bank account or to Petty Cash. A memo regarding the cash back transaction and the amount provide further information for the program.

Use the Print option to print a deposit slip.

6 Click the drop-down list button for **Print**, and select **Deposit Slip** from the submenu.

7 In the Print Deposit Slips window click **Print** if conditions in the lab allow, otherwise, click **Cancel**.

8 In the Make Deposits window click **Save & Close**.

Customer Reports

Like vendors and purchases, QuickBooks has several built-in reports for customers and sales that are easy to run and read.

Learn the Skill

In this exercise, you will learn how to run various customer, sales, and payments reports.

First, print the list of all customers entered in your system.

1   Select **Reports, Customers & Receivables, Customer Contact List** from the menu bar.

The Customer Contact List report is now displayed, showing the customers and selected data. As usual the list will display the current computer date at the top of the report. If it is necessary to change this date, select **Customize Report**, and in the Modify Report: Customer Contact List dialog box, click the **Header/Footer** tab and in the **Subtitle** field change the date to the desired date, for example **March 31, 2016**. If preferred, you can also deselect the Date Prepared and Time Prepared options.

2   Close the report. If necessary, click **No** to the request to memorize the report.

3   Select **Reports, Customers & Receivables, A/R Aging Detail** from the menu bar.

4   Select **Custom** in the Dates field, then click the 📅 **(Calendar)** button, change the date to **March 31, 2016** and click **Refresh**.

The Customer Aged Detail report shows the unpaid amount for every invoice for each customer. The information is also broken up in 30-day increments to help you recognize which invoices are overdue and by how much. Like the customer list report, this should be printed on a regular basis to help you manage your receivables and your cash balance. You should follow up on any invoices that have been outstanding for more than 45 to 60 days and determine whether they are collectible.

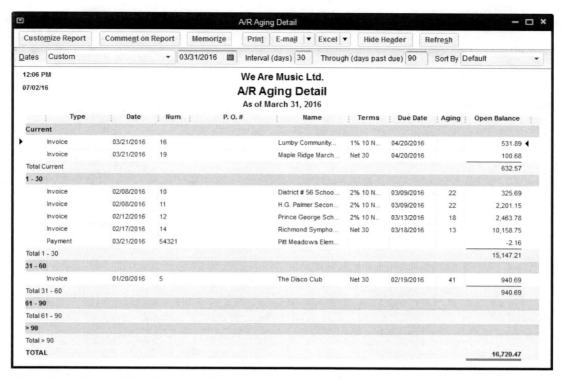

5   Close the A/R Aging Detail report. Click **No** to the request to memorize the report.

6   Select **Reports**, **Customers & Receivables**, **Customer Balance Detail** from the menu bar.

7   Accept the default date of **All.**

The Customer Balance Detail report shows all transactions for each customer that contributed to the current outstanding balance.

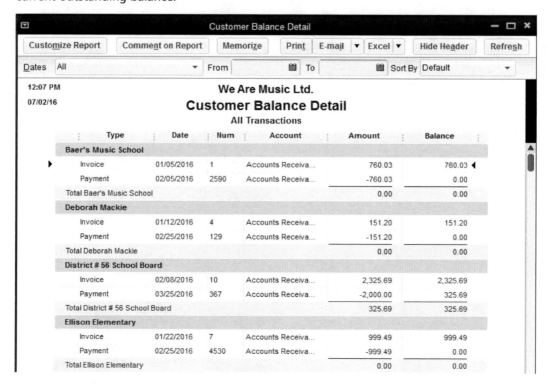

8   Use the scroll bar on the right to view the entire report.

You can adjust this report to show a data range of various dates, such as March 1/16 to March 31/16.

9   Close the report, and do not memorize the report.

10   Select **Reports**, **Customers & Receivables**, **Accounts Receivable Graph** from the menu bar.

11   Click **Dates**.

12   In the Change Graph Dates window, change the date to **March 31, 2016**, and click **OK**.

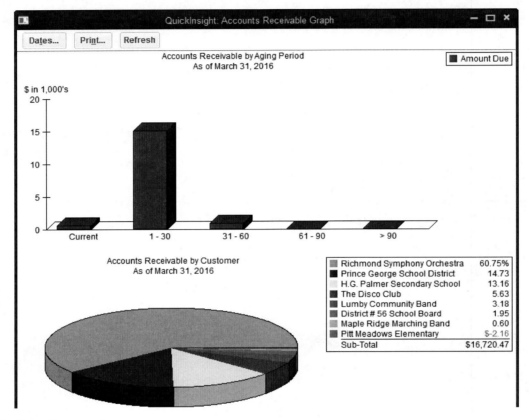

13   Close the report.

14   Select **Reports**, **Sales**, **Sales by Customer Detail** from the menu bar.

15   Change the Dates field to **Custom**. Change the dates to From **March 1, 2016** and To **March 31, 2016**, and click **Refresh**.

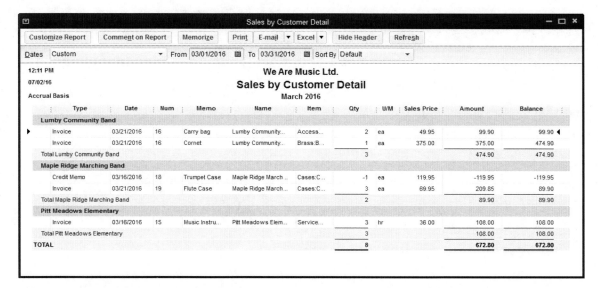

16 Close and do not memorize the report.

You can also select a similar sales report sorted by item number.

17 Select **Reports**, **Sales**, **Sales by Item Summary** from the menu bar.

18 Change the Dates field to **Custom**. Change the dates to From **March 1, 2016** and To **March 31, 2016**, and click **Refresh**.

The Sales by Item Summary report shows all sales made in the time period specified including the gross profit and the gross margin earned on each item. This report is very useful to help you monitor the sales volume and profitability of each item.

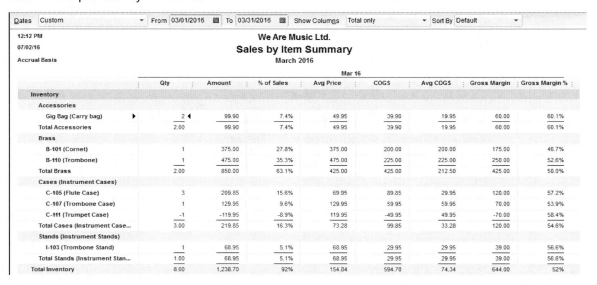

19 Use the scroll bars to view the entire report.

20 Close and do not memorize the report.

21 Backup the file as: `We Are Music Ltd. - Your Name Lesson 4` following the same steps learned in Lesson 1.

Lesson Summary

In this lesson, you learned how to move around in the Customer Section of the Home Page tab, and how to use the components of the Customer Centre. In particular, you learned how to:

☑ work with the Customer Centre

☑ add and modify customer records

☑ understand the workflow

☑ issue sales receipts

☑ record sales orders

☑ create, adjust and delete sales invoices

☑ work with price levels

☑ receive, adjust and delete payments

☑ process refunds and credits

☑ work with undeposited funds

☑ record deposits

☑ run customer reports

 ## Practice the Skill

The following additional exercise covers many of the items discussed in this Lesson. The Practice the Skill exercises are included as extra practice and may be completed by the students in class or on their own. Your instructor has access to the Answer Key for these exercises.

1. Add a new customer.

    Enter the following data at the top of the New Customer window:

Opening Balance	0.00
As of	March 09, 2016

    Enter the following data in the **Address Info** tab:

Mr./Ms./...	Mrs.
First Name	Geraldine
Last Name	Porter

    Click (Tab) to record the Customer Name in the field at the top of the window.

Phone	604 856-6521
Address	8765 Clearview Drive
	Port Moody, BC V1B 4L9

    Click **Copy** to copy the Invoice/Bill To address to the Ship To address field. Click **OK**.

    Click the **Payment Settings** tab and enter the following:

Account No.	5987
Credit Limit	3,000
Payment Method	Cheque

2. Modify the following customers:

Name	Lumby Community Band
Terms	2% 10 Net 30
Credit Limit	3,000

Name	Pitt Meadows Elementary
Account No	56981
Credit Limit	5,000

3. Record a sales receipt:

Customer		Geraldine Porter		
Date		March 15, 2016		
Cheque #		637		
Payment Method		Cheque		
Item	W-105 (1)	Flute	Tax Code	S
Item	C-105 (1)	Flute Case	Tax Code	S
Item	Lessons (3)	Music Instruction	Tax Code	G
Total Sales Receipt		$478.75		

4. Enter an Invoice:

Customer	School District # 93
Date	March 22, 2016
Quantity	2
Item	Music Stand (Educational Rate)
Quantity	1
Item	Metronome (Educational Rate)
Quantity	1
Item	P-103 Drum Set (Educational Rate)
Total Invoice	$529.05 (Note: some rounding may occur with the adjusted rate)

5. Record a Payment:

Customer	Maple Ridge Marching Band
Amount	$100.68
Date	March 31, 2016
Pmt. Method	Cheque
Cheque #	395

6. Make a Deposit:

    Select the following for deposit:

Chq No 637	Geraldine Porter 478.75
Chq No 395	Maple Ridge Marching Band 100.68
Account	Royal Bank Chequing Account
Date	March 31, 2016
Total Deposit	579.43

7. Process a Credit / Refund:

Customer	School District # 93
Date	March 31, 2016
Item	Music Stand
Quantity	1
Rate	35.955 (Educational)
Amount	35.95
Total Credit	40.27 (watch for rounding – taxes are based on the rate, not the amount)
Memo	Refund for returned item

    Retain as an available credit

8. Record a Sales Order:

    Customer   Richmond Symphony Orchestra
    Date   March 31, 2016
    Item S-100   Cello   1
    Total Order $1,596.00

9. Run a report:

    Name   Sales by Customer Detail
    Date Range   March 1, 2016 to March 31, 2016

10. Backup the data file as: The Music Barn - Your Name Lesson 4 Practice.

Review Questions

1. What two guidelines apply when you must decide whether or not to set up a customer in your customer list?

2. What are the steps to retrieve a previously posted invoice?

3. Which of the following accounts is debited when a sales invoice is created?

   a. Chequing

   b. Sales Income Account

   c. Accounts Receivable

4. If a customer is exempt from paying a particular sales tax, this should be recorded in the customer record.

   a. True   b. False

5. What is the purpose of creating and applying Price Levels?

6. What are the two options to record a customer payment in the bank account?

7. In the Receive Payments window, discounts available will be automatically calculated by the system according to the date of the payment transaction.

   a. True   b. False

8. List three methods to memorize a sales invoice.

9. What report will display the individual invoices issued and payments received for each customer?

10. Where would you find the Quick Report button?

   a. Reports, Customers & Receivables on the menu bar

   b. Reports, Report Centre, Customers & Receivables

   c. Customers on the menu bar

   d. Customer Centre

QuickBooks

Premier 2016
Level 1

Lesson 5: Employees and Payroll

Lesson Objectives

In this lesson, you will learn how QuickBooks deals with payroll, and how to manage the Employees List so you can create paycheques and track payroll liabilities. Upon the successful completion of this lesson, you should know how to:

- [ ] set up payroll
- [ ] create a payroll item
- [ ] work with the Employee Centre
- [ ] create employee record defaults
- [ ] add new employees
- [ ] edit employee data
- [ ] maintain current tax tables

- [ ] create payroll schedules
- [ ] produce and print payroll cheques
- [ ] print pay stubs
- [ ] produce and print cheque for payroll liabilities
- [ ] prepare PD7A summary report
- [ ] create payroll reports

To Start This Lesson

Restoring the Exercise File

1. From the **File** menu in QuickBooks, choose **Open or Restore Company**.

    QuickBooks displays the Open or Restore Company window.

2. Select **Restore a backup copy** and click **Next**.

3. Select **Local backup** and click **Next**.

4. In the Open Backup Copy window navigate to your *1761 Student Files* folder.

5. Select the *We Are Music Ltd - 2016 - Student.QBB* file and then click **Open**.

6. In the Open or Restore Company window, click **Next**.

7. Navigate to your *1761 Student Files* folder.

8. In the File name field of the Save Company File as window, type: We Are Music Ltd - Your Name Lesson 5 and then click **Save**.

9. In the QuickBooks Login window enter the password: **Sys2016**.

10. Click **OK** when you see the message that the file has been successfully restored.

11. If necessary, close the QuickBooks Learning Centre and Have a Question windows.

Payroll Overview and Set Up

Payroll processing is a complex topic because of the number of options and calculations involved. For example, income can consist of salaries (a fixed amount), wages (a variable amount that depends on the number of hours worked), commissions (a variable amount that depends on the volume of sales made), bonuses (a variable amount based on a predefined formula), and vacation pay. Deductions will consist of government imposed taxes, government imposed premiums, such as Canada Pension Plan (CPP) and Employment Insurance (EI), and voluntary deductions such as pension plan, insurance, medical and parking. Some of these deductions are based on gross income (before taxes are deducted), or net income (after taxes are deducted). The net pay cheque amount is also affected by taxable benefits in which the employee's income is not affected, but income tax is assessed on the benefit amount.

Because of these variable factors, processing payroll manually can be a complex and time-consuming task, particularly when multiple employees are involved. In addition, manual calculation involves looking up government tax and premiums on either printed tax tables or using either the T4001 Employers' Guide - Payroll Deduction, or T4032 Payroll Deductions tables provided online by the Canada Revenue Agency.

QuickBooks comes with these tables built into the software, and the appropriate deductions will be taken automatically from each pay cheque issued. Deduction rates change, sometimes as many as two or three times in a year. QuickBooks offers a tax table update program to update the government tax and deduction rate tables, whenever they change, and provides software updates as these occur.

At all times, ensure everything you do that is related to payroll in QuickBooks conforms to the provisions of the *Employment Standards Act*. Check and re-check all employee information, set up and input to eliminate errors, which may be very difficult to resolve later. You may have to set up the necessary general ledger accounts that are required for payroll processing. In this courseware, these have already been created for you.

When full payroll features are selected, QuickBooks creates a Payroll Item List for wages and payroll taxes. QuickBooks also adds two accounts to the Chart of Accounts, Payroll Expenses and Payroll Liabilities. In addition, QuickBooks automatically sets up the Receiver General as a vendor to remit payroll liabilities.

> IMPORTANT! You cannot delete default payroll items set up by QuickBooks. These include **Salary**, **Vacation Pay**, **CPP**, **EI**, and **Income Tax**.

Payroll Options

QuickBooks payroll offers five options: Manual, Basic, Enhanced, Enhanced for Accountants, and Assisted Payroll. All but the Manual option have an associated fee for the service. The Manual option requires that you stay on top of all tax law changes, and there is a higher potential for errors and possible penalties. If the Assisted Payroll option is chosen, QuickBooks has a *No Penalties* Guarantee in which Intuit will pay any penalties you incur if you provide proper information in a timely manner and have sufficient funds in your bank account.

You can make the following choices regarding how your payroll options are set up:

- Use Full payroll features (this will include payroll items on your Lists menu, the Employees menu and Employees & Payroll Reports on your Reports menu); Payroll reports only features (Payroll is added to the Other Reports submenu of the Reports menu), or No payroll features.

- Choose the detail displayed on cheques, such as: the employee's address, the company address, sick and vacation information.

- Choose to have the pay period printed in the cheque memo location.

- Create items for salary and hourly rates for completion of the Select Employees to Pay window.

- Input salary amounts that will default to each pay period.

Learn the Skill

In this exercise you will learn how to turn on the payroll feature.

1   Select **Edit**, **Preferences** from the menu bar.

2   Scroll down the list of icons on the left, and select **Payroll & Employees**.

3   Select the **Company Preferences** tab.

4   If necessary, select the **Full payroll** features option button to turn it on.

5   For this exercise click to set the **Last Name** default in the Display Employee List by section.

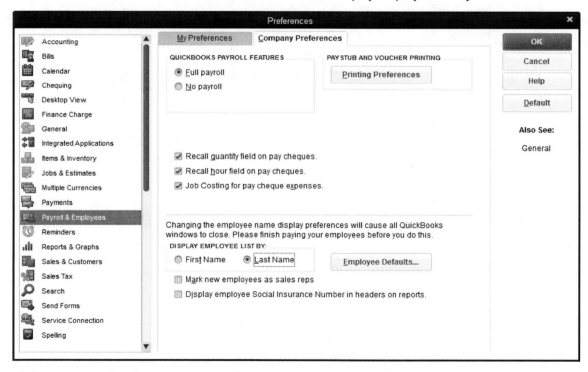

6   Click **OK** to save the changes to the **Preferences**.

QuickBooks will display the warning message "QuickBooks must close all windows to change this preference" to let you know that it is going to close any open windows in QuickBooks.

7   Click **OK** to close the warning message, and then, click **Home** on the Icon bar to display the Home Page.

Payroll Item List

The Payroll Item List is a key lookup list that QuickBooks uses to calculate the taxes and deductions on every employee's pay cheque. Many of these items will be set up when you are creating the company data file.

When you want to make changes to a payroll item or to set up a new one, QuickBooks will run a mini-Interview set of screens to display the settings and choices. You must be careful to select the correct options, as they will affect the amounts calculated on pay cheques.

 Learn the Skill

In this exercise you will review the items in the Payroll Item List and create a new one.

1   Click **Lists**, **Payroll Item List** from the menu bar. Use the scroll bar to review the items in the list.

2   Click the **Payroll Item** button, and select **New**. Read the QuickBooks information and then select **Wage**, click **Next**. In the Wages screen, select **Commission**.

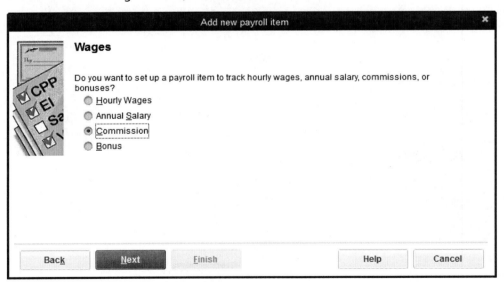

3   Click **Next**. Type: Sales Commission as the name of the payroll item.

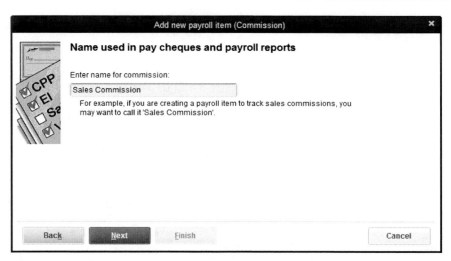

4   Click **Next**. Ensure the Expense account window shows **Payroll Expenses**.

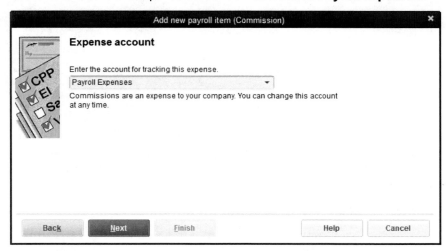

5   Click **Next**. Leave the Record of Employment (ROE) Tracking window unchanged.

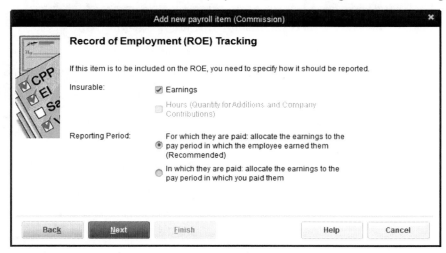

6   Click **Next**. Leave the Default rate window unchanged.

7   Click **Finish**.

8   Review the Payroll Item List, to see the new item in the list and then close the Payroll Item List.

Employee Centre

The Employee Centre displays information about all employees, and their transactions. It can be accessed by clicking the **Employees** icon in the Icon bar, **Employees** in the menu bar, or by clicking on the **Employees** button on the Home page.

The Employee Centre is set up similar to the Inventory, Vendor and Customer Centres.

The tool bar buttons provide access to a variety of tasks, such as creating new employees, manage employee information, and so on.

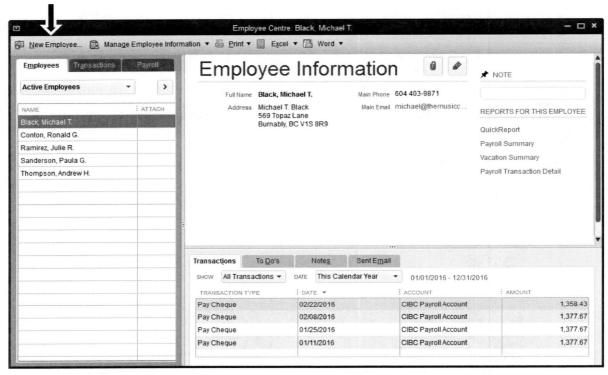

New Employee	Opens the window for New Employee records.
Manage Employee Information	Add/Edit Sales Rep, Change New Employee Default Settings, Set Up YTD Amounts.
Print	Print Pay Cheques, Print/Send Pay Stubs, Employee List, Employee Information, Employee Transaction List.
Excel	Export Employee List, Export Transactions.
Word	Prepare letter to selected employee, prepare employee letters, customize letter templates.

The Employee Centre is divided into three panes.

- The left pane contains three tabs:

    Employees
    - Employee List

    Transactions
    - Pay Cheques
    - Liability Cheques
    - Liability Adjustments
    - Year-To-Date Adjustments
    - Non-Payroll Transactions

    Payroll – Clicking this tab displays three new tabs:
    - **Pay Employees**
        o Create Pay Cheques, Payroll Schedules,
        o Recent Payrolls
    - **Pay Liabilities**
        o Pay Liabilities, Pay Annual Payroll Liabilities, Adjust Liabilities
        o Payment History
    - **File Forms**
        o T4, Relevé (RL-1), Record of Employment (ROE)
        o Filing History
    - All three tabs have links to: Quick Guides, Other Activities, and Reports. (Pay Employees also has a link to Supplies).

- The top-right pane shows the details for the selected Employee, and provides quick access to several reports.

- The bottom-right pane has tabs that show Transactions, To Do's and Notes related to the selected employee.

Employee Records

Creating Employee Defaults

When employee defaults are set up, the information can be selected or overridden when a new employee record is created. If standard information changes for most of your employees, you can edit the default employee information easily in Employee Defaults.

> IMPORTANT! Changing the **Employee Defaults** affects information for new employees only. It does not retroactively change any payroll information for existing employees.

Employee defaults are used to expedite the process of setting up employee records and are used to set up Standard Earnings and Deductions to be used for most employees.

Learn the Skill

In this exercise, you will learn how to set up the default values for all new employee records.

1   If necessary, click **Employees** on the Icon bar to open the Employee Centre. Ensure the Employees tab is selected.

2   Click the **Manage Employee Information** button, and select **Change New Employee Default Settings**.

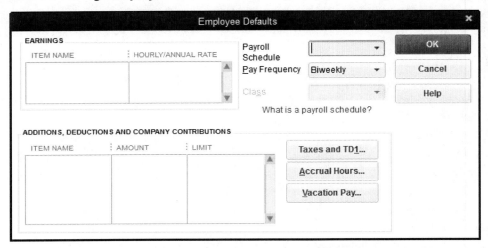

3   In the Employee Defaults window, click the **Pay Frequency** drop-down menu button and select **Weekly**.

4   Click in the **Item Name** field under Earnings and click the drop-down menu button.

The following earnings are already set by the system: **Salary**, **Sick Salary**, **Vacation Salary**, **Hourly Wage**, **Sick Hourly Rate**, **Vacation Hourly Rate**, **VacPay-Accrual Paid Out** and **Advance**. In addition the data file has **Hourly Overtime** and **Time & A Half** set up.

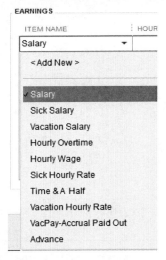

5   Review the list, and then click away from the list to close it.

6   In the Employee Defaults window, click **Taxes and TD1**.

The TD1 and other payroll-related numbers on your computer may be different because of ongoing changes to tax tables.

7   Ensure the Tax Table shows **British Columbia**, and review the Federal and Provincial TD1 amounts.

8   Click **OK**.

9   Click **Accrual Hours**.

This template is used to set up Sick and Vacation Accrual or expense. If your company allows X days of sick leave for every month of service, you would use this template.

10 Click **OK** to close this screen and then click **Vacation Pay**.

11 In the Vacation section, choose **Pay every period**.

12 Accept the 4.0% default as the Vacation pay **Percentage**.

13 In the Earnings section, scroll through the list and select the following Earnings Accounts: **Hourly Overtime**, **Hourly Wage**, and **Time & A Half**.

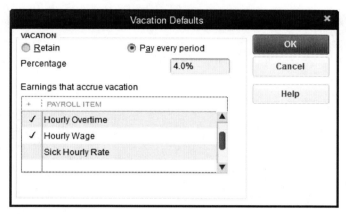

14 Click **OK**.

15 Click **OK** to close the Employee Defaults window. Leave the Employee Centre open for the next exercise.

Adding a New Employee

Learn the Skill

In this exercise, you will learn how to add a new employee record.

1   If necessary, open the Employee Centre and ensure the Employees tab is selected.

2   Click the **New Employee** button at the top left of the Employee Centre window to open the New Employee window.

> You can also press Ctrl + N to activate this feature.

3   In the **Personal** tab, type the following in the respective fields:

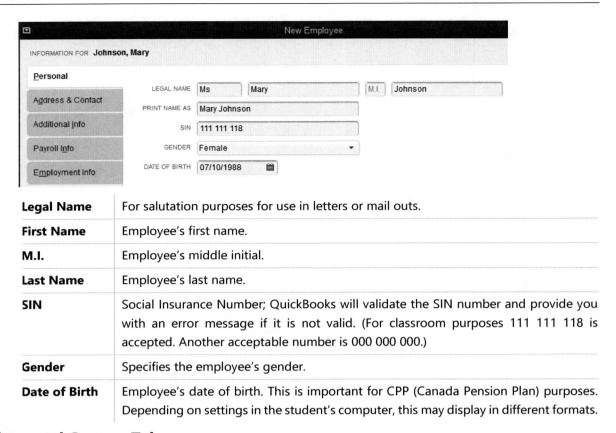

Legal Name	For salutation purposes for use in letters or mail outs.
First Name	Employee's first name.
M.I.	Employee's middle initial.
Last Name	Employee's last name.
SIN	Social Insurance Number; QuickBooks will validate the SIN number and provide you with an error message if it is not valid. (For classroom purposes 111 111 118 is accepted. Another acceptable number is 000 000 000.)
Gender	Specifies the employee's gender.
Date of Birth	Employee's date of birth. This is important for CPP (Canada Pension Plan) purposes. Depending on settings in the student's computer, this may display in different formats.

Address and Contact Tab

4   In the **Address and Contact** tab, type the following in the respective fields.

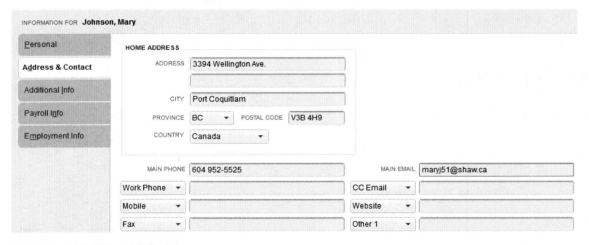

5   Select the **Additional Info** tab.

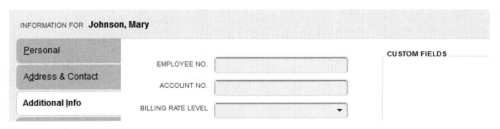

Employee No.	This field is optional, but if the company assigns employee numbers this is where you would input the number.
Account No.	For the employee account number, if applicable.
Billing Rate Level	This field will allow you to input a special rate at which you bill out employees to customers.
Custom Fields	For any custom defined fields you may be using.

6   Click the **Payroll Info** tab and enter the following data in the Earnings section:

Pay Frequency   Weekly

Item Name	Hourly/Annual Rate	
Hourly Wage	18.50	
Hourly Overtime	($18.50 X 2)	37.00
Time & A Half	($18.50 X 1.5)	27.75

> QuickBooks automatically calculates the figures based on defaults and the hourly rate.

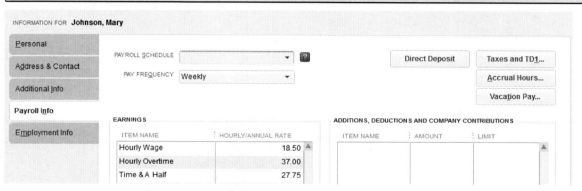

Earnings	Set up all the various earnings for each individual. QuickBooks will default with some of the information from the Employee Defaults.
Payroll Schedule	Select the relative schedule on which the employee is paid.
Pay Frequency	The frequency with which the employee is to be paid.
Additions, Deductions and Company Contributions	Set up deductions for RRSP, medical, etc.
Taxes and TD1	Where you identify the province for tax deductions, TD1 exemption amount, company EI rate.
Accrual Hours	Number of hours the employee has worked which have not yet been paid.
Vacation Pay	The amount of vacation pay owed to the employee.
Direct Deposit	To set up deposit of pay cheques directly into the employee's bank account.

7   Select the **Employment Info** tab, and enter: 03/01/2016 (Mar 1, 2016) as the Hire Date. Enter: Music Instructor in the Occupation field.

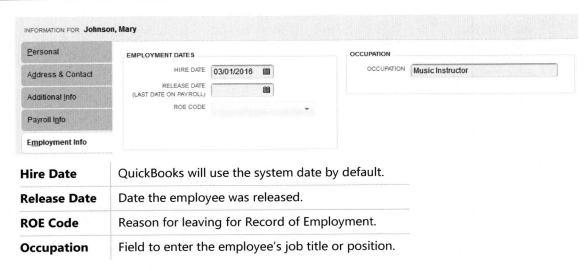

Hire Date	QuickBooks will use the system date by default.
Release Date	Date the employee was released.
ROE Code	Reason for leaving for Record of Employment.
Occupation	Field to enter the employee's job title or position.

8   Click **OK**.

9   In the New Employee: Payroll Info window, click **Leave As Is**.

You will now set up another employee.

10   Click the **New Employee** button, ensure the **Personal Info** tab is selected and enter the following:

Personal tab

Legal Name	Mr.
First Name	Jack
M.I.	S.
Last Name	Lewis
SIN	000 000 000
Gender	Male
Date of Birth	10/21/1995 (October 21)

Address and Contact tab

Address	3355 East 27th Avenue
City	Vancouver
Province	BC
Postal Code	V6R 3L7
Main Phone	604 858-6537
Main E-mail	jslewis@shaw.ca

Payroll Info tab

Pay Frequency	Weekly
Hourly Wage	16.50
Hourly Overtime	33.00
Time & A Half	24.75

Employment Info tab

Hire Date	03/01/2016 (March 1, 2016)
Occupation	Stock Clerk

11 Click **OK**.

12 Click **Leave As Is**.

13 Leave the Employee Centre open for the next exercise.

Editing Individual Employee Data

If you want to make a change to the information of an individual employee, but do not wish to alter the employee template, you can do this easily in QuickBooks through the Employee Centre.

 Learn the Skill

In this exercise you will modify existing employee records.

1 If necessary, select **Employee Centre** to display the Employee Centre window. Ensure the Employees tab is selected.

2 Select **Ronald Conton** from the list of employees.

3 Click the [✐] **(Edit)** button in the Employee Information section to display the Edit Employee screen.

> You could also double-click the employee, or press Ctrl + E to edit it.

4 Change the following for Mr. Conton:

Occupation	Senior Technician
Hourly Wage	22.50
Hourly Overtime	45.00
Time & A Half	33.75

5 Click **OK** to save the changes.

6 Edit the following employees: **Julie Ramirez**, and **Paula Sanderson**. Change the Hourly Wages for each to **18.50**.

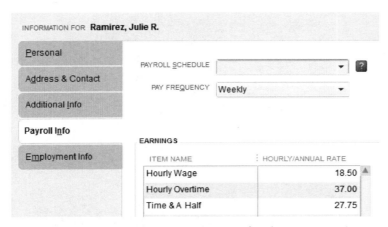

7   Leave the Employee Centre window open for the next exercise.

Maintaining Current Tax Tables

Although QuickBooks has built-in tax tables that are current at the time of production, these tables become outdated as federal and provincial tax laws change. It is important that you ensure your payroll deductions are accurate by having up-to-date tax tables at all times. This is easily done if you subscribe to the QuickBooks Payroll Service. You can then download current tax tables via the Internet. This can be accessed from the **Help** menu by selecting **Update QuickBooks**, then **Update Now**. It should take you less than a minute to install the update and your current data will not be affected.

In order to check for new updates to either the tax tables or the QuickBooks program, select **Help**, **Update QuickBooks**. When the Update QuickBooks window appears, it will indicate whether there are any updates and/or which ones you have already installed. If none of the items in the list are checked, you can click **Get Updates** to update QuickBooks.

> **IMPORTANT!** Some of the tax and payroll calculation results in this courseware may vary from your results if you are using a different tax table.

 Learn the Skill

In this exercise you will check the version of the tax tables currently being used.

1   In the Employee Centre window, select the **Payroll** tab, click the **My Payroll Service** button at the top left of the window, and select **Tax Table Information**.

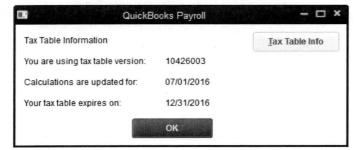

This dialog box provides information on the version currently in use. If you click on the **Tax Table Info** button, it provides more detailed information about the tax tables. Your information may be different, depending on the date and current tax tables in use at the time of taking this course.

2   Click **OK** to close the window.

3   Close the Employee Centre window.

Payroll Cheques and Paystubs

Producing Payroll Cheques

QuickBooks creates accurate pay cheques, ready for printing, once you have entered accurate payroll information for your employees.

Pay cheques for salaried employees are very straightforward to create. Hourly employees have information that must be entered each pay period. Also, employees who have commissions, who have used some sick or vacation time, or who otherwise have unique variations, will require pay cheque data to be manually entered and reviewed.

Once you enter payroll data, QuickBooks performs the necessary calculations, makes deductions, withholds taxes, and maintains employee records for printing pay cheques and creating payroll reports.

When QuickBooks creates a payroll cheque, it also performs many related tasks. It:

- updates the recorded date of the last cheque written for the employee.
- removes the check mark next to the employee in the Select Employees to Pay window.
- increases or decreases the accrued sick hours by the amount entered on the pay cheque.
- increases or decreases the accrued vacation pay based on the rate entered for the employee during set up.
- records an increase in all affected liability accounts.
- writes a payroll cheque ready for printing, with the correct net amount on the cheque and all deductions in the voucher area.
- updates payroll expenses in expense accounts.

 Learn the Skill

In this exercise you will learn how to use QuickBooks to automatically generate each employee's pay cheque, including calculating the payroll-related deductions and withholding taxes.

1   In the Employees section of the Home page, click **Pay Employees** to open the Employee Centre: Payroll Centre window.

The Calendars displayed will always reflect default months based on the current real time date. The display can be adjusted to reflect the desired months by clicking on the directional arrows beside the Month (e.g. Mar 2016).

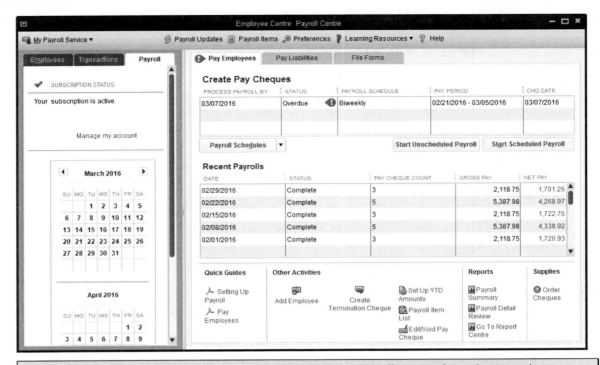

You can also display this window by selecting **Employees**, **Payroll Centre** from the menu bar.

In the Pay Employees section there are several options available:

1. Create Pay Cheques:
   a. Payroll Schedules – New, Edit, or Delete Schedule.
   b. Start Unscheduled Payroll – an unscheduled payroll (this allows you to create a pay cheque when needed, rather than on a regularly scheduled basis).
   c. Start Scheduled Payroll – (this allows you to select and pay specific employees that have a matching pay frequency – such as weekly, biweekly, monthly).

For this particular exercise, we will select the **Biweekly Payroll** as we only have one payroll schedule set up at this time.

2. Click the **Scheduled Payroll** dated 03/07/2016 to select it, and then click **Start Scheduled Payroll** to open the Enter Payroll Information window.

   You may receive a reminder window regarding having current tax tables installed before calculating any payroll deductions. Depending on the current date the figures shown in the following screens may be different, as different tax tables may be in use.

   If the Review Employee TD1 Amounts reminder window displays, click in the **Do not display** box, and then click **OK**. Close the Employee TD1 review list window.

3. In the Salary column, ensure: 80 is entered for both Employees, and then press (Tab).

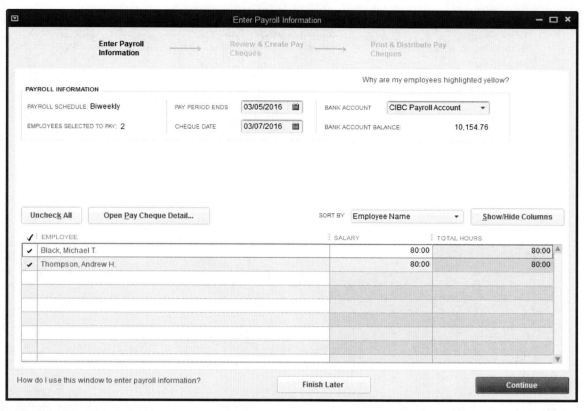

4   Click **Continue**. Click **OK** if a warning message regarding the expiry date of the tax tables is displayed.

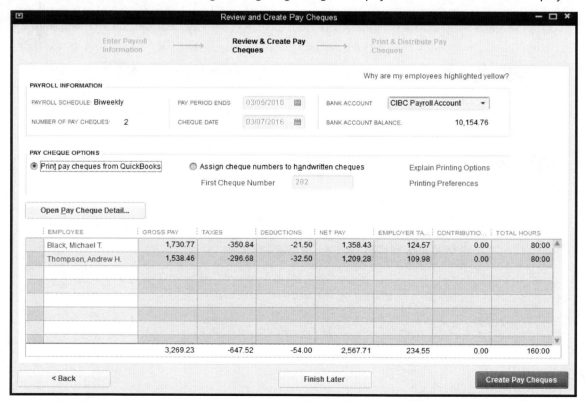

5   If necessary, click to select the **Print pay cheques from QuickBooks** option.

6   Select **Michael Black**, to preview the cheque.

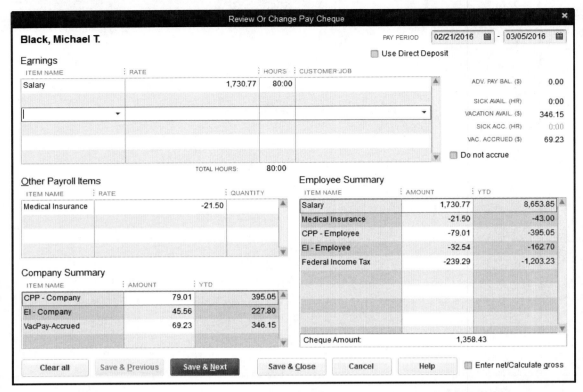

7   Click **Save & Next** to review the pay cheque for Andrew Thompson. Click **Save & Close.**

8   In the Review and Create Pay Cheques window, click **Create Pay Cheques**. Click **OK** if a warning message regarding the expiry date of the tax tables is displayed. Click **Yes** if a date warning is displayed.

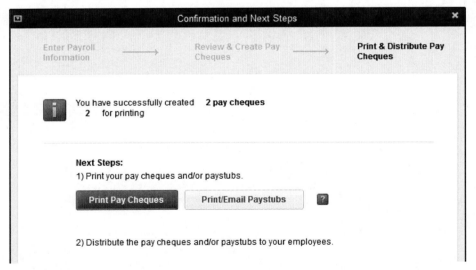

9   In the Confirmation and Next Steps window, review the information and click **Close**.

QuickBooks returns you to the Employee Centre: Payroll Centre window.

10   Close the Employee Centre.

Creating Payroll Schedules

Since we need to pay our weekly employees as well, and in order to do this efficiently, we will create a weekly payroll schedule to include those employees with this pay frequency.

Note that the payroll dates for the weekly employees brought them up to date as of the end of February. We are now into the month of March, and will need to pay both weekly and biweekly employees.

 Learn the Skill

In this exercise you will learn how to create a payroll schedule.

1   From the menu bar, select **Employees**, **Payroll Setup**, **Add or Edit Payroll Schedules** to open the Payroll Schedule List. Note that the Biweekly schedule is shown.

2   Click **Payroll Schedule**, and select **New**.

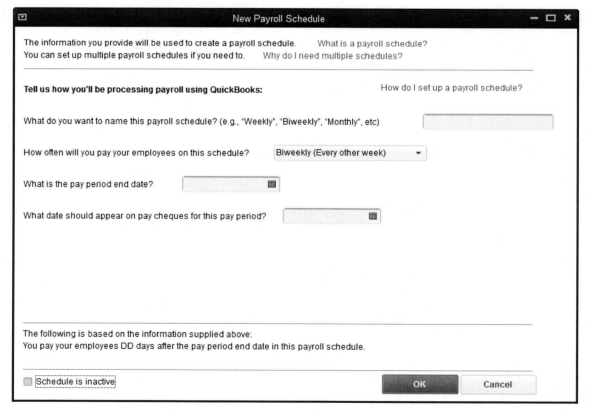

3   In the name the payroll schedule field, type: Weekly.

4   In the next field, click the drop-down menu button and select **Weekly.**

5   In the pay period end date field, type: 03/05/2016 (Mar 5, 2016).

6   In the pay cheques date field, type: 03/07/2016 (Mar 7, 2016).

7   Click **OK**.

8   If a warning about the pay cheque date is displayed, click **Yes**.

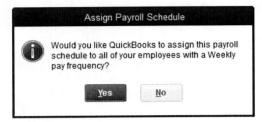

9   In the Assign Payroll Schedule, click **Yes**, and then click **OK** in the next information window.

10 Close the Payroll Schedule List window.

11 Open the Employee Centre, select **Ronald Conton**, and double-click to display the Edit Employee window.

12 Choose the **Payroll Info** tab and view the information displayed.

Note the Payroll Schedule field shows the Weekly schedule.

13 Click **OK** to close the window.

Now that we have a weekly payroll schedule in place, it is time to pay those employees who are due.

14 If necessary, open the Employee Centre; click the **Payroll** tab to open the Payroll Centre.

The weekly payroll schedule is now listed.

15 Click the **Weekly** schedule to select it, and then click **Start Scheduled Payroll**.

16 Enter the following hours:

Ronald Conton	Hourly	37.5
Mary Johnson	Hourly	24
Jack Lewis	Hourly	24
Marie Ramirez	Hourly	37.5
Paula Thompson	Hourly	37.5

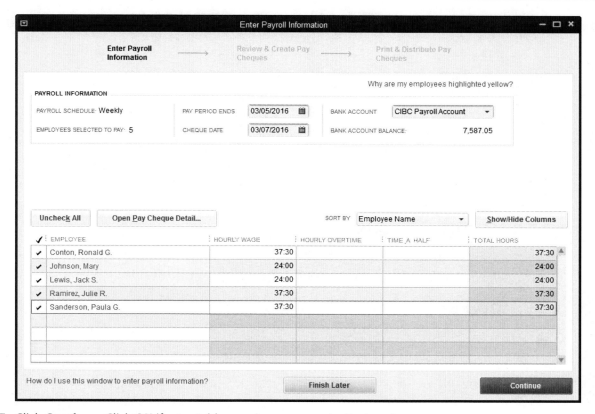

17 Click **Continue**. Click **OK** if a tax table warning message is displayed.

Your screen should resemble the following (a change in tax tables will result in different figures).

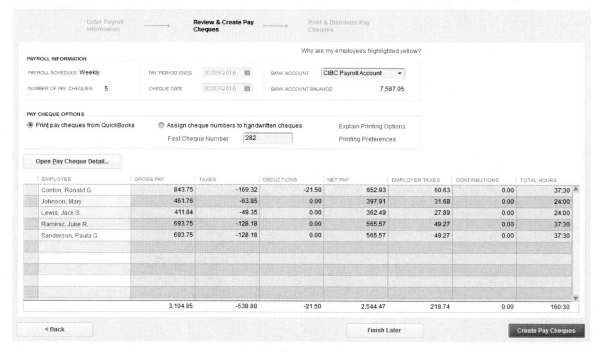

18 Ensure **Print pay cheques from QuickBooks** is selected.

> To view the cheque details for an employee, select the employee, and then click **Open Pay Cheque Detail**.

19   Click **Create Pay Cheques**. Click **OK** in Tax Table warning screen. If necessary, click **Yes** at the Past Transactions message.

20   Click **Close** in the Confirmation and Next Steps window.

21   In the Employee Centre, select the **Employees** tab, click **Ronald Conton**, and view the payroll cheque transaction. Note the change in amount due to the adjusted pay rate and occupation.

22   Close the Employee Centre window.

Printing Payroll Cheques

You can print all your payroll cheques at one time if you selected **To be printed** when you created them. However, you must print payroll cheques separately from other types of cheques in QuickBooks.

 ## Learn the Skill

In this exercise you will print the outstanding payroll cheques from the previous exercises.

1   From the menu bar, select **File**, **Print Forms**, **Pay Cheques**.

The Select Pay Cheques to Print window will display all unprinted pay cheques created from the bank account displayed.

2   Ensure the First Cheque Number is: **282**.

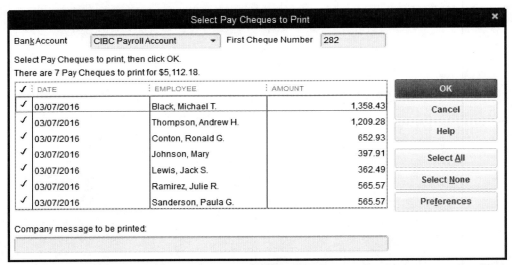

> You can also display this window by clicking the **Print Pay Cheques** button when you are in the Confirmation and Next Steps window.

3   With all employee pay cheques selected, click **OK**.

Review the information and notice the total value of the seven cheques you will print at the top of the Print Cheques window.

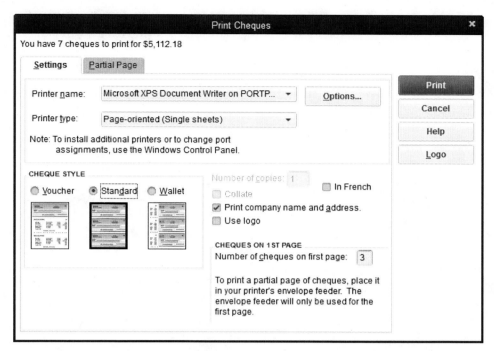

4 In the Cheque Style section, select **Standard** with 3 for the **Number of cheques on first page** and select **Print company name and address**.

Ensure your printer is set up and properly loaded with pay cheque forms to be printed.

5 Click **Print** if lab conditions allow, otherwise, click **Cancel**.

When QuickBooks is finished printing, the following message is displayed:

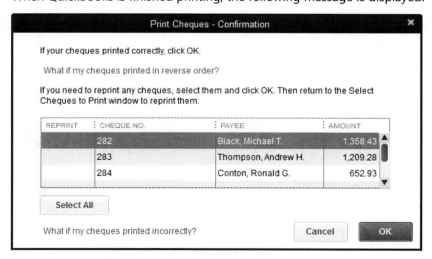

6 Click **OK** to confirm that all pay cheques printed correctly.

Printing Paystubs

If you do not use pay cheques with attached vouchers, you can still print pay stubs to provide your employees with the information that would normally appear on a pay cheque voucher. A pay stub will be printed on a separate blank piece of paper that should be included with the corresponding pay cheque when presented to each employee.

It is a legal requirement to print a pay stub including the following information:

- employee's full name, address, and social insurance number,
- pay period start and end dates,
- salary or hourly rate,
- hours and amount of pay for the pay period,
- deductions from wages,
- additions to wages, and
- gross and net pay.

 ## Learn the Skill

In this exercise you will print the pay stubs for the employees.

1   From the menu bar, click **File**, **Print Forms**, **Paystubs**.

> You can also display this window by clicking the **Print/Email Paystubs** button when you are in the Confirmation and Next Steps window.

2   Change the **Cheques Dated** box to **Mar 1, 2016** thru **Mar 10, 2016**, press ⌨Tab.

The window will display all pay cheques for the selected time period.

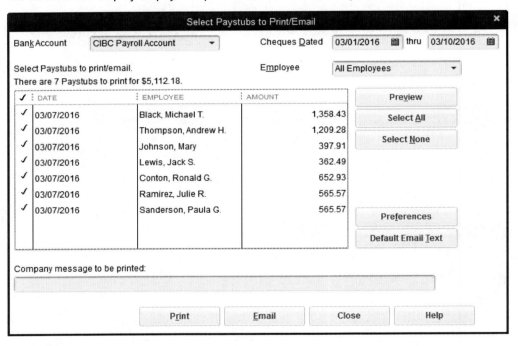

3   Click **Preview**.

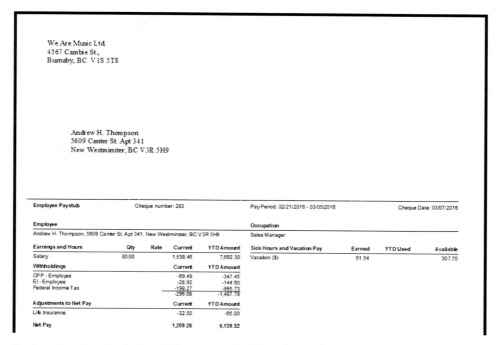

4 Review the Pay Stub Detail Report and click **Print**. After printing, the Select Paystubs to Print/Email window closes automatically.

5 If necessary, close the Employee Centre.

Remitting Payroll Liabilities

An employer is required to remit taxes and other payroll liabilities to Canada Revenue Agency. The exact date that your payments are due will depend on the size of your payroll and what Canada Revenue Agency decides is appropriate. In most instances, you are required to remit by the 15th of the month for the previous month's deductions. You may be required to pay penalties if you do not remit on time.

When it is time to remit payroll liabilities, QuickBooks calculates and displays the amounts for you to preview. You may then choose to pay your liabilities by creating a cheque for them.

After you create a cheque to pay your payroll liabilities, you should also use QuickBooks to create an accompanying PD7A (Statement of Account for Current Source Deductions) form.

 Learn the Skill

In this exercise you will remit the liabilities due.

1 In the Employees section of the Home Page, click **Pay Liabilities**. In the Pay Liabilities tab of the Employee Centre: Payroll Centre window, click **Pay Liabilities**.

> You can also display this window by selecting **Employees**, **Payroll Liabilities**, **Pay Payroll Liabilities** from the menu bar.

2 Change the Dates to read From **February 1, 2016** Through **February 29, 2016**.

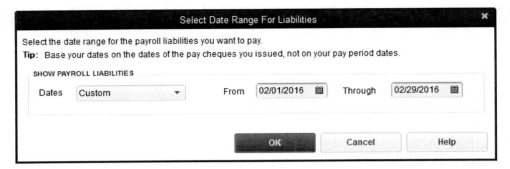

3 Click **OK**.

4 If necessary, select the **To be printed** check box, select the **Review liability cheque to enter expenses/penalties** option.

5 Ensure **Royal Bank Chequing Account** is selected.

6 Change the Payment Date to **Mar 11, 2016**.

QuickBooks will use the Show Payroll Liabilities date information to fill in the PD7A form.

7 Select the **Show all liabilities** check box.

8 Click any of the **Payroll Item** (payable to the **Receiver General**) rows to display the check mark on the left side of each of these items.

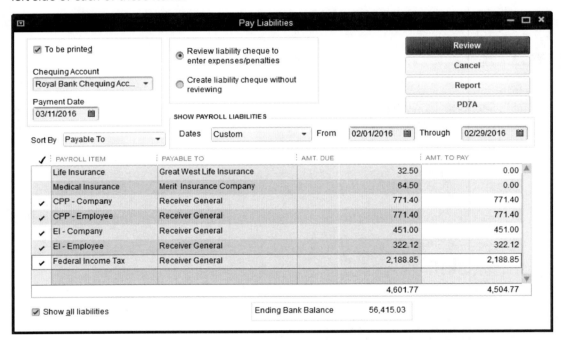

When you click one of the Payroll Item rows, QuickBooks checks off all related payroll liabilities and taxes to be paid to the same vendor – the Receiver General. QuickBooks sets up the Receiver General as a vendor when you indicate in the setup of the data base that you will be using the Payroll feature.

The Workers' Compensation Board is automatically set up by QuickBooks as the vendor to remit Workers' Compensation deductions. However, for private liabilities, such as dental benefits or retirement plans, you will have to set up additional vendors before you can remit payments.

9 Click **Review** to preview the cheque. Ensure **Print Later** is selected.

10 Review the cheque, ($4,504.77) and click **Save & Close** to create the cheque.

11 Repeat steps 1 through 9 to pay the two other liabilities, **Life Insurance**, and **Medical Insurance**. Watch **Chequing Account and the payment dates**. Click **Yes** in the Past Transactions window, if it appears.

12 Close the Employee Centre.

13 Select **File**, **Print Forms**, **Cheques**.

14 In the Bank Account field, verify **Royal Bank Chequing Account**, is selected, and, if necessary, change the cheque number to **119**.

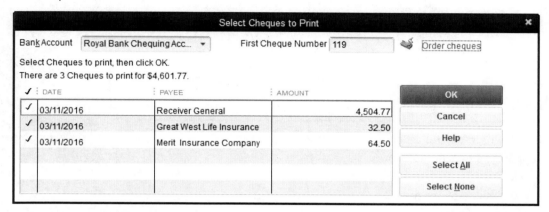

15 Review the three cheques to print and then click the **OK** button.

16 If lab conditions allow, click **Print** in the Print Cheques window, otherwise click **Cancel**.

17 Click **OK** in the confirmation window.

Creating Employee and Payroll Reports

It is necessary to create payroll reports for a variety of reasons, including business management and legal obligations. QuickBooks can help you create payroll reports, pay government liabilities and taxes, fill out your accompanying Statement of Account for Current Source Deductions (PD7A), and fill out your yearly T4 Supplementary forms and T4 Summary report.

 Learn the Skill

In this exercise you will create and print Employee related reports.

1 Select **Reports**, **Employees & Payroll**, **PD7A Summary**.

2 Change the Dates to From **Feb 1, 2016** To **Feb 29, 2016** and click **Refresh**.

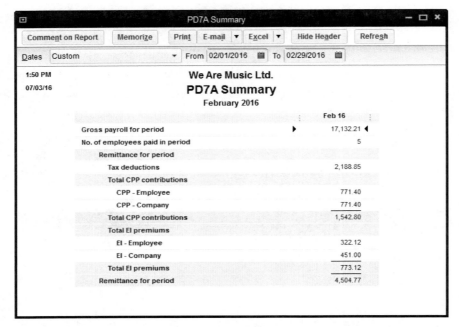

3   Print or note the following information as you will need to enter the amounts on your government-supplied PD7A Summary form.

> Month(s) for which deductions were withheld
>
> Gross payroll for period
>
> No. of employees paid in period
>
> Tax deductions
>
> CPP – Employee
>
> CPP – Company
>
> EI – Employee
>
> EI – Company
>
> Remittance for period

4   If lab conditions allow click **Print**.

5   If the Printing Features information window appears, click **OK**.

6   Review the printer settings and click **Print** for a Summary print out.

7   Close the PD7A Report window.

In order to confirm that YTD information was entered accurately for all employees, you should review the payroll data using QuickBooks payroll reports. There are two reports that are particularly useful for double checking that both employee and liability information is correct. These are: Employee Earnings Summary and Payroll Liabilities reports.

8   Select **Reports**, **Employees & Payroll**, **Payroll Summary**.

9   Change the Dates range to From **Mar 1, 2016** To **Mar 07, 2016**, and click **Refresh**.

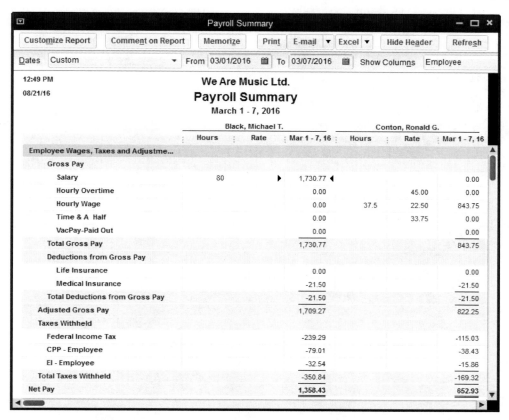

10 Scroll through the report to review the information and close the window. Do not memorize report.

11 Select **Reports**, **Employees & Payroll**, **Payroll Liability Balances**.

12 Change the Dates range to From **Jan 1, 2016** To **Mar 07, 2016**, and click **Refresh**.

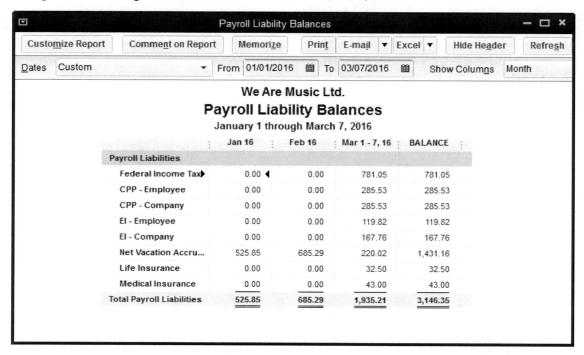

13 Review the information and then close the window. Do not memorize report.

14 Open the Employee Centre window and click the **Employees** tab.

15 Highlight **Ronald Conton**, and click **QuickReport**.

> You can also press Ctrl + Q to access this report.

16 Change the Dates range to From **Jan 1, 2016** To **Mar 7, 2016**, and click **Refresh**.

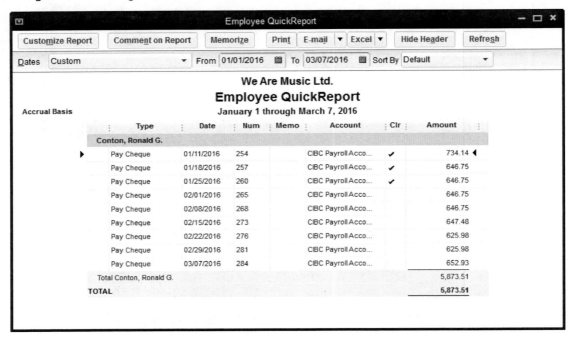

17 Review the information, and then close the Employee QuickReport window.

18 Close the Employee Centre.

19 Backup the file as: We Are Music Ltd - Your Name Lesson 5 following the same steps learned in Lesson 1.

Lesson Summary

In this lesson, you have learned how to set up and work with Canadian payroll. You should now know how to:

☑ set up payroll

☑ create a payroll item

☑ work with the Employee Centre

☑ create employee record defaults

☑ add new employees

☑ edit employee data

☑ maintain current tax tables

☑ create payroll schedules

☑ produce and print payroll cheques

☑ print pay stubs

☑ produce and print cheque for payroll liabilities

☑ prepare PD7A summary report

☑ create payroll reports

Practice the Skill

The following additional exercise covers many of the items discussed in this Lesson. The Practice the Skill exercises are included as extra practice and may be completed by the students in class or on their own. Your instructor has access to the Answer Key for these exercises.

1. Create the following new employee:

Name	Mrs. Helen Blackstone
SIN	111 111 118
Gender	Female
DOB	08/24/1989
Address	5821 Pebble Lane
	Surrey, BC V2R 5Y7
Phone	604 547-3685
E-mail	hblackstone@shaw.ca
Pay Frequency	Biweekly
Payroll Schedule	Biweekly
Hourly Wage	$18.50
Hourly Overtime	$37.00
Time & A Half	$27.75
Hire Date	03/14/2016
Occupation	Bookkeeper
Message	Leave as is

2. Create the following Payroll Item:

Item Type	Wage
Wages	Bonus
Name used	Bonus
Expense account	Payroll Expenses
ROE	Accept defaults

3. Modify the data for the following employees:

Employee	Mary Johnson	Jack S. Lewis
Hourly Wage	$19.00	$17.50
Hourly Overtime	$38.00	$35.00
Time & A Half	$28.50	$26.25

4. Process the weekly payroll schedule as of Mar 12, 2016 with Cheque date of Mar 14, 2016.

Employee	Hourly	Hourly Overtime
Ronald Conton	37.5	3
Mary Johnson	24	
Jack Lewis	30	
Julie Ramirez	37.5	2
Paula Sanderson	37.5	
Total Gross Pay	$3,460.49	

    Create and print the pay cheques (accept first cheque # 289)

5. Prepare the PD7A summary for Mar 1 to Mar 15, 2016.

6. Prepare the Payroll Liability Balances Report for Mar 1 to Mar 15, 2016.

    Total Payroll Liabilities $2,945.17

7. Pay the **Receiver General** for Payroll Liabilities from Mar 1 to Mar 15, as of Mar 31, 2016.

    Total Cheque $2,530.54

8. Backup the data file as: `We Are Music Ltd - Your Name Lesson 5 Practice`.

Review Questions

1. Which of the following payroll items can be deleted?

    a. Salary   c. Income Tax

    b. Hourly Overtime   d. CPP

2. How do you determine if you are working with current tax tables for payroll deductions?

3. Where are the deductions made from employees' pay cheques recorded?

    a. Payroll Expenses   c. Payroll Liabilities

    b. Uncategorized Expenses

4   Why do you set up employee defaults in QuickBooks?

5. Which QuickBooks report will provide you with the total CPP, EI, and Income Tax withheld liability amounts that you must pay to Canada Revenue Agency?

    a. Employee Withholding

    b. Payroll Transactions by Payee

    c. Payroll Liability Balances

6. Why is it so important to ensure that an employee's date of birth in the Employee record is correct?

7. QuickBooks can also be set up to expense WCB premiums on each employee's pay cheque.

    a. True   b. False

8. Which of these reports gives details of total amounts paid to an employee during a specified period?

    a. Payroll Item Detail

    b. Employee Earnings Summary

    c. Payroll Transaction Detail

9. What report gives details of individual pay cheques paid to an employee during a specified period?

QuickBooks

Lesson 6: Reporting, Miscellaneous and Year End Procedures

Lesson Objectives

In this lesson, you will learn how to use the financial reporting functions of QuickBooks, how to report and remit sales taxes, and to carry out year-end procedures. Upon successful completion of this lesson, you should understand how to:

☐ create and print financial reports

☐ use the Company Snapshot report

☐ use the Calendar

☐ use the Reminders List

☐ manage sales tax

☐ verify data integrity

☐ complete year-end procedures

To Start This Lesson

Restoring the Exercise File

1. From the **File** menu in QuickBooks, choose **Open or Restore Company**.

   QuickBooks displays the Open or Restore Company window.

2. Select **Restore a backup copy** and click **Next**.

3. Select **Local backup** and click **Next**.

4. In the Open Backup Copy window navigate to your *1761 Student Files* folder.

5. Select the *We Are Music Ltd - Student.QBB* file and then click **Open**.

6. In the Open or Restore Company window, click **Next**.

7. Navigate to your *1761 Student Files* folder.

8. In the File name field of the Save Company File as window, type: We Are Music Ltd - Your Name Lesson 6 and then click **Save**.

9. In the QuickBooks Login window enter the password: **Sys2016**.

10. Click **OK** when you see the message that the file has been successfully restored.

11. If necessary, close the QuickBooks Learning Centre window.

Creating and Printing Financial Reports

The Reports icon in the Icon bar allows you to display and print a wide range of prebuilt reports. Two categories are used to monitor the financial aspects of your company: Company & Financial, and Accountant & Taxes. There are also reports for specific areas of your business as well as a variety of industry specific prebuilt reports. At this time we will deal only with the financial reports.

1. Click the **Reports** icon on the Icon bar, select ▤ **(List View)**, select the **Company & Financial** category and then use the scroll bar on the right to review the list.

Company & Financial

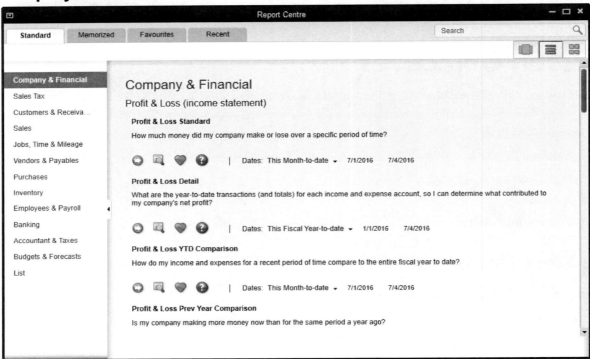

This report category includes the following subcategories:

Profit & Loss	Also known as the Income Statement, these reports show the revenue, expenses and net income of the company for a specified period. There are also comparative reports, relating to a previous month or year, or by job or class, with options for standard or detail, and YTD or Previous Year comparisons.
Income & Expenses	These reports show the gross profit (revenue minus the cost of goods sold) earned for each customer by summary or detail. There are also reports showing the expenses for each vendor by summary or detail. An Income & Expense graph is also available, providing a visual comparison of total revenue to total expenses, and a percentage breakdown of the expenses.

Balance Sheet & Net Worth	This reports the company's assets, liabilities and equity in Balance Sheet format, either summary or detail. You can make this a comparative report—QuickBooks will compare it to a previous month or even a previous year. You can also create a Balance Sheet by Class, and a Net Worth Graph, with option for summary or detail.
Cash Flow	This report shows how your cash position changed over a period of time. It shows the amount of cash earned from profit, where you received additional cash, and where your cash was spent, and with option for previous year comparison and a forecast.

2.   Select the **Accountant & Taxes** category on the left, and review the list.

Accountant & Taxes

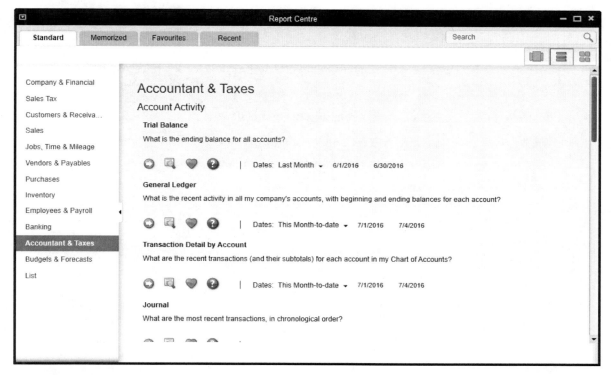

This report category includes the following:

Trial Balance	This is a listing of the general ledger balances in debit and credit columns, with balancing totals at the end of the report.
General Ledger	This lists all General Ledger account details by transaction, showing debit and credit entries and running balance on each account for a specified period.
Transaction Detail by Account	This is a listing of all general ledger transactions grouped together by account.
Journal	This report breaks down each transaction into their component debits and credits. The report is intended to be used by accountants.
Audit Trail	This is a listing of all transactions including any changes.
Closing Date Exception Report	This lists what changes were made, after the last closing date was set, to transactions dated on or before that closing date.

Voided/Deleted Transactions Summary	This report provides summary reports on transactions that have been voided or deleted. This is critical for an audit trail.
Voided/Deleted Transactions Detail	This report provides detail reports on transactions that have been voided or deleted. This is critical for an audit trail.
Transaction List by Date	This provides a list of transactions entered in a specified period of time.
Account Listing	This is a current list of all general ledger accounts including a description and the tax line. The balance sheet accounts balances are displayed.
Fixed Asset Listing	This is a current list of all fixed assets.
Income Tax – Preparation, Summary & Detail	These three reports are used to help you gather the data necessary to fill out your federal tax forms, including the transactions involving tax amounts.

Learn the Skill

In this exercise, you will generate a set of financial reports for February 29, 2016 for We Are Music Ltd.

1   If necessary select **Reports** on the Icon bar.

2   In the Report Centre window, select **Company & Financial.**

3   Select **Profit & Loss Standard** and click on the ⊙ **(Run)** button to open the report.

4   Change the date range to **Jan 1, 2016** to **Jan 31, 2016** and click **Refresh**.

We Are Music Ltd.
Profit & Loss
January 2016

	Jan 16
Ordinary Income/Expense	
Income	
Merchandise Sales	44,482.45
Miscellaneous Income	198.00
Service Sales	
Lessons	2,170.00
Repair Services	2,160.00
Shipping & Handling	375.00
Total Service Sales	4,705.00
Total Income	49,385.45
Cost of Goods Sold	
Cost of Goods Sold	24,024.45
Total COGS	24,024.45
Gross Profit	25,361.00
Expense	
Bank Service Charges	35.00
Computer and Internet Expenses	64.15
Janitorial Expense	374.50
Office Supplies	138.93
Payroll Expenses	14,612.18
Rent Expense	1,550.00
Telephone Expense	134.29
Utilities	240.75
Vehicle Expense	
Fuel	111.87
Total Vehicle Expense	111.87
Total Expense	17,261.67
Net Ordinary Income	8,099.33
Net Income	8,099.33

5   Close the Profit & Loss report. Click **No** to the request to memorize the report.

6 Select the **Balance Sheet Standard** report and click the ⦿ **(Run)** button to open.

7 Change the as of date to **Jan 31, 2016** and click **Refresh**.

We Are Music Ltd.
Balance Sheet
As of January 31, 2016

	Jan 31, 16
ASSETS	
Current Assets	
Chequing/Savings	
CIBC Payroll Account	7,907.60
Royal Bank Chequing Account	63,895.90
Total Chequing/Savings	71,803.50
Accounts Receivable	
Accounts Receivable	19,878.95
Total Accounts Receivable	19,878.95
Other Current Assets	
Inventory Asset	90,131.80
Prepaid Insurance	900.00
Total Other Current Assets	91,031.80
Total Current Assets	182,714.25
Fixed Assets	
Furniture and Equipment	
Accum. Depr.	-2,235.00
Cost	16,350.00
Total Furniture and Equipment	14,115.00
Leasehold Improvements	
Accum. Depr.	-2,500.00
Cost	15,500.00
Total Leasehold Improvements	13,000.00
Vehicles	
Accum. Depr.	-3,425.00
Cost	12,450.00
Total Vehicles	9,025.00
Total Fixed Assets	36,140.00
TOTAL ASSETS	**218,854.25**

8 Use the scroll bars to view the entire report.

9 Close the Balance Sheet report. Do not memorize the report.

10 Open the **Income by Customer Detail** report.

11 Change the date range to **Jan 1, 2016** to **Jan 31, 2016** and click **Refresh**.

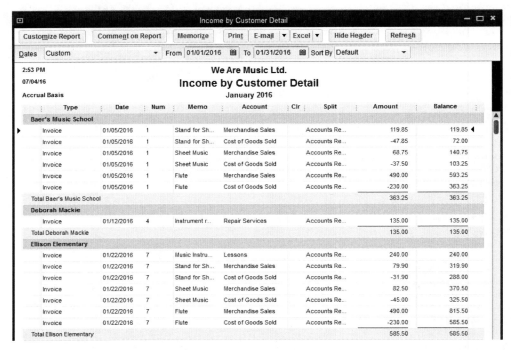

12 Scroll to view the entire report, then close the Income by Customer Detail report without memorizing.

13 Open the **Expenses by Vendor Detail** report. Set the date range as **Jan 1, 2016** to **Jan 31, 2016**.

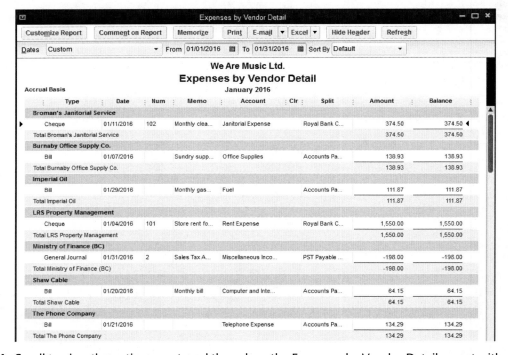

14 Scroll to view the entire report, and then close the Expenses by Vendor Detail report without memorizing.

15 Open the **Income & Expense Graph** report.

16 Click the **Dates** button, select **Custom**, then change the date range to **Jan 1, 2016** to **Jan 31, 2016** and click **OK**. This graph provides several options for display, by Account, by Customer or by Class.

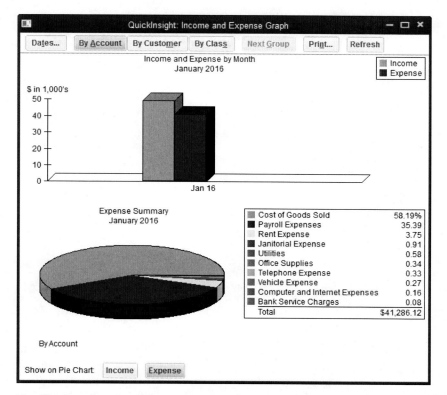

The illustrated report By Account, shows Income and Expenses, and the Expense Summary pie chart.

17 Review, and then click the **Income** button at the bottom of the report to display the Income summary.
Review the new information.

18 Close the Income and Expense Graph.

19 In the Report Centre, select the **Accountant & Taxes** category.

20 In the Account Activity section, locate the **General Ledger** report and click the ⬤ **(Run)** icon.

21 Change the date range to **Jan 1, 2016** to **Jan 31, 2016** and click **Refresh**.

22 Click the **Customize Report** button and in the Columns section select the **Debit** and **Credit** columns
and deselect the **Amount** column. Click **OK** to implement the changes.

We Are Music Ltd.
General Ledger
As of January 31, 2016

Accrual Basis

Type	Date	Num	Name	Memo	Split	Debit	Credit	Balance
CIBC Payroll Account								0.00
Cheque	01/01/2016			Service Cha...	Bank Service...		15.00	-15.00 ◄
Transfer	01/04/2016			Funds Trans...	Royal Bank C...	8,500.00		8,485.00
Pay Cheque	01/11/2016	250	Andrew H. Thomp...		-SPLIT-		1,240.32	7,244.68
Pay Cheque	01/11/2016	251	Julie R. Ramirez		-SPLIT-		589.22	6,655.46
Pay Cheque	01/11/2016	252	Michael T. Black		-SPLIT-		1,377.67	5,277.79
Pay Cheque	01/11/2016	253	Paula G. Sanderson		-SPLIT-		576.20	4,701.59
Pay Cheque	01/11/2016	254	Ronald G. Conton		-SPLIT-		734.14	3,967.45
Pay Cheque	01/18/2016	255	Julie R. Ramirez		-SPLIT-		537.09	3,430.36
Pay Cheque	01/18/2016	256	Paula G. Sanderson		-SPLIT-		537.09	2,893.27
Pay Cheque	01/18/2016	257	Ronald G. Conton		-SPLIT-		646.75	2,246.52
Transfer	01/18/2016			Funds Trans...	Royal Bank C...	5,000.00		7,246.52
Pay Cheque	01/25/2016	258	Julie R. Ramirez		-SPLIT-		537.09	6,709.43
Pay Cheque	01/25/2016	259	Paula G. Sanderson		-SPLIT-		537.09	6,172.34
Pay Cheque	01/25/2016	260	Ronald G. Conton		-SPLIT-		646.75	5,525.59
Pay Cheque	01/25/2016	261	Andrew H. Thomp...		-SPLIT-		1,240.32	4,285.27
Pay Cheque	01/25/2016	262	Michael T. Black		-SPLIT-		1,377.67	2,907.60
Transfer	01/27/2016			Funds Trans...	Royal Bank C...	5,000.00		7,907.60
Total CIBC Payroll Account						18,500.00	10,592.40	7,907.60
Petty Cash								0.00
Total Petty Cash								0.00

23 Scroll to view the entire report, and then close the General Ledger report. Do not memorize.

24 Scroll down to find the **Transaction List by Date** report. Double-click on the area to display the report.

25 Change the date range to **Jan 1, 2016** to **Jan 15, 2016** and click **Refresh**. Click the **Customize Report** button and in the Columns section, deactivate the **Memo** and **Clr** columns. Click **OK**.

The report should resemble the following:

We Are Music Ltd.
Transaction List by Date
January 1 - 15, 2016

Type	Date	Num	Name	Account	Split	Amount
Jan 1 - 15, 16						
Cheque	01/01/2016			CIBC Payroll Acco...	Bank Service...	-15.00 ◄
Cheque	01/01/2016			Royal Bank Chequ...	Bank Service...	-20.00
Transfer	01/04/2016			Royal Bank Chequ...	CIBC Payroll A...	-8,500.00
Cheque	01/04/2016	101	LRS Property Man...	Royal Bank Chequ...	-SPLIT-	-1,627.50
Invoice	01/05/2016	1	Baer's Music School	Accounts Receiva...	-SPLIT-	760.03
Invoice	01/06/2016	2	Kelowna Symphon...	Accounts Receiva...	-SPLIT-	10,080.00
Invoice	01/07/2016	3	Terry Fox Second...	Accounts Receiva...	-SPLIT-	1,275.06
Bill	01/07/2016		Burnaby Office Su...	Accounts Payable	-SPLIT-	-145.42
Sales Receipt	01/09/2016	1	Weekly Cash Sales	Undeposited Funds	-SPLIT-	8,240.76
Pay Cheque	01/11/2016	250	Andrew H. Thomp...	CIBC Payroll Acco...	-SPLIT-	-1,240.32
Pay Cheque	01/11/2016	251	Julie R. Ramirez	CIBC Payroll Acco...	-SPLIT-	-589.22
Pay Cheque	01/11/2016	252	Michael T. Black	CIBC Payroll Acco...	-SPLIT-	-1,377.67
Pay Cheque	01/11/2016	253	Paula G. Sanderson	CIBC Payroll Acco...	-SPLIT-	-576.20
Pay Cheque	01/11/2016	254	Ronald G. Conton	CIBC Payroll Acco...	-SPLIT-	-734.14
Deposit	01/11/2016			Royal Bank Chequ...	Undeposited ...	8,240.76
Cheque	01/11/2016	102	Broman's Janitoria...	Royal Bank Chequ...	-SPLIT-	-392.00
Invoice	01/12/2016	4	Deborah Mackie	Accounts Receiva...	-SPLIT-	151.20
Bill	01/13/2016		Moir Piano	Accounts Payable	-SPLIT-	-18,900.00
Bill	01/14/2016	WOM...	World of Music	Accounts Payable	-SPLIT-	-1,794.71
Jan 1 - 15, 16						

26 Use the scroll bars to review the report. Close the Transaction List by Date report. Do not memorize.

27 Close the Report Centre window.

Company Snapshot

You can use the Company Snapshot to get real-time company information and perform tasks from a single place. To open this report, click **Snapshots** on the Icon bar.

> You can also click **Company, Company Snapshot** on the menu bar.

There are three tabs in the Snapshot window: Company, Payments and Customer; each tab will display a variety of reports specific to each category. In this lesson we will deal only with the Company tab. Payments and Customers will be dealt with in Level 2. *Please note that figures and dates as shown below will be different, based on the actual computer date when this report is created.*

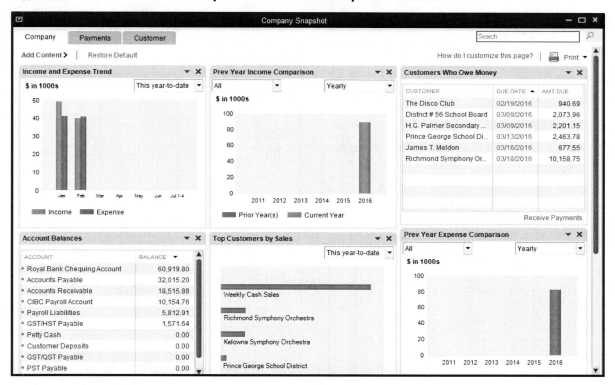

The default settings for the Company display are listed as follows:

Income and Expense Trend	This section shows money going in and out of your business over time. It gives you a quick snapshot of how your business is doing and lets you compare monthly income and expenses.
Previous Year Income Comparison	This section shows how much money you are making this year compared to previous years for any or all accounts. You can view monthly, quarterly, weekly, or yearly comparisons.
Customers Who Owe Money	This section shows balances owed by customers.
Account Balances	This section shows all bank, accounts receivable, accounts payable, credit card, asset, liability, and equity accounts. You can add other accounts by clicking **Select Accounts**.

Top Customers by Sales	This section shows who your top five customers are based on sales for a given period of time.
Prev Year Expense Comparison	This section shows the expenses for the previous and current year and can be set for a variety of fiscal periods.
Expense Breakdown	This section shows your company's biggest expenses. • The default graph view is year-to-date. You can change the date range by clicking the drop-down arrow. • Place your pointer on any wedge in the chart to see the total for that wedge, then right-click to see a breakdown. • Double-click any wedge to view its detail in the Report Centre.

More content is available. To preview additional content, from the Company Snapshot window click **Add Content** to page through the content gallery.

To view the reports available under the Payments, and Customer tabs, select each tab and scroll down to view all reports. Depending on your access permissions, you can add content.

Learn the Skill

In this exercise, you will learn how to add and delete content in the Company category of the Company Snapshot report.

1   If necessary, click **Snapshots** on the Icon bar, ensure the **Company** tab is selected, and review the content by using the scroll bars.

2   In the **Top Customers by Sales** section click on the down arrow beside the date field to review the report options available.

3   Click on the **X** above the date field to close (delete) this section from the company snapshot. Click on **OK** in the Remove Content window that is displayed.

4   In the company snapshot window, scroll to the top of the report, and click **Add Content** to display the content gallery:

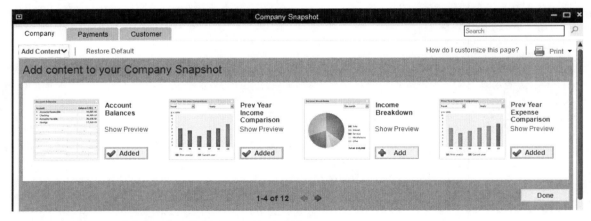

5   Select **Income Breakdown** by clicking on the **Add** button.

The Add button will change to Added to confirm the addition. The program will insert the chosen report at the first position in the Company Snapshot.

6   Click the **Done** button.

To move this report to another position, bring your cursor to the grey area at the top of the Income Breakdown report, and when the four white arrows are showing, hold down the left mouse button, and drag the report to the desired location within the company snapshot window.

7   Drag the Income Breakdown report into the space before the Prev Year Expense Comparison report.

8   Close the Company Snapshot window.

Using the Calendar

The QuickBooks Calendar is a quick way to view transactions and tasks you've entered into QuickBooks. To access the calendar, click the icon in the Company section of the Home Page.

Calendar

> You can also access the calendar by clicking **Company**, **Calendar** from the menu, or by clicking **Calendar** in the Icon bar.

There are three options for viewing the calendar, Daily, Weekly, and Monthly. These can be selected by clicking on the relevant icons shown beside the Date field at the top of the calendar. The illustration above shows the monthly view.

For each day QuickBooks displays a summary of Transactions entered, Transactions that are due, and Tasks you need to complete (to do's).

The transaction detail pane below the calendar displays a list of transactions and to do's for the selected day.

Click the ⋏ icon to hide or show the detail. Double-click a transaction to view or edit it.

On the right side of the window, you see Upcoming: Next 7 Days and Past Due Transactions as of Today.

> QuickBooks uses the current real date as a basis for displaying items in the Upcoming Transactions pane. It also uses the current real date to select the calendar month.

The Add To Do link opens a dialog box where upcoming tasks can be entered.

Type	This field allows a selection of tasks: call, fax, email, meeting, or appointment.
Priority	This can be set to High, Medium, or Low.
With	This field allows the selection of Lead (prospective) Customer, Vendor, or Employee.
Name	This field allows the selection of customer/vendor/employee name.
Due	This field allows the setting of the appropriate date for the task.
Time	Settings for the time of the task.
Details	A field for the details of the task to be undertaken.
Status	The status of the task, active, done, inactive.

Learn the Skill

In this exercise, you will add a phone call to the calendar.

1   If necessary, open the Calendar, and set the Month date to **March 1, 2016** by clicking the **Next** or **Previous** arrows to the left of the month. Click the day **8** to select it. Click the **Add To Do** link to open the dialog box.

2 We are in negotiations with a vendor to adjust the credit terms they offer us. Complete the Add To Do dialog box as follows. Use the arrows beside the fields to select from the drop-down menus, and click the calendar at the right of the Due field to select the date.

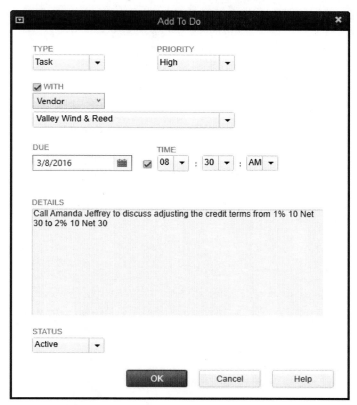

3 Review your screen, and then click **OK**.

4 Click **Mar 8** and note that the item has now been added to the calendar as a To Do (1) as well as into the transaction detail pane below the calendar.

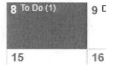

> The calendar reminder section, **Upcoming** or **Past Due** is based on the actual date of the computer, which will control what items are actually shown. Therefore, depending on the actual computer date, this To Do item may not show in the Upcoming or Past Due area of the calendar.

5 Close the Calendar.

Reminders and Alerts

Like the Calendar feature, the Reminders List is a very helpful tool in organizing, by category and date, the many financially related tasks that have to be performed. The most common accounting tasks are organized under various headings, and all pending events are tracked and listed there, saving you the effort of having to run reports to find out what has to be done every day.

To open a transaction or perform the associated task (like paying a bill), double-click the transaction in the list.

The Reminders List can be displayed in its own window, by clicking Company, Reminders, on the menu bar. It consists of several headings that will display reminders such as the following:

> This list can also be displayed by clicking on the reminders icon at the top right of the menu bar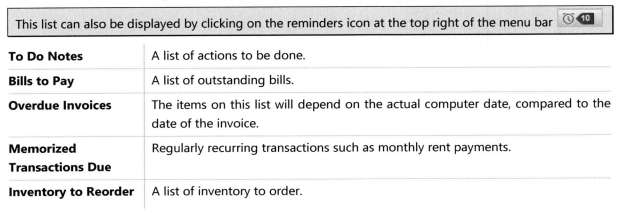

To Do Notes	A list of actions to be done.
Bills to Pay	A list of outstanding bills.
Overdue Invoices	The items on this list will depend on the actual computer date, compared to the date of the invoice.
Memorized Transactions Due	Regularly recurring transactions such as monthly rent payments.
Inventory to Reorder	A list of inventory to order.

Alerts

The Alerts Manager can be displayed by clicking Company, Alerts Manager from the menu bar. Alerts are important messages about QuickBooks or your business. For example, you might receive an alert that there is an update to QuickBooks that you need to download.

 ## Learn the Skill

In this exercise, you will learn how to access and use the Reminders List.

1   Click the **Reminders** icon at the top right of the menu bar.

Since the reminders shown in this window are based on the current date in the computer, your screen may not look exactly like the following. It may show Cheques to Print and To Do Notes among others.

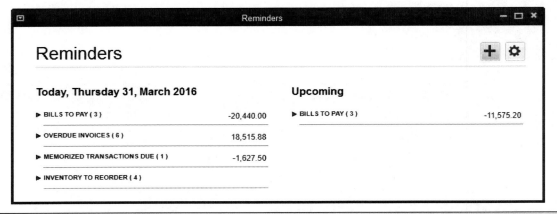

> Clicking the **Open Preferences** ⚙ button will open the Preferences window to allow changes to settings relevant to the Reminders List.

The Reminders window available to the student will show the actual real time date when the exercise is being completed. It may show different items listed.

2 For example the window displayed above, set to March 31, 2016 displays Bills to Pay, Overdue Invoices, Memorized Transactions Due, and Inventory to Reorder. Clicking the chevron to the left of one of the items displayed will activate a listing of the items.

This screen is a reminder only.

3 Close the Reminders window.

Managing Sales Tax

When working with sales tax, there are tasks you perform once (such as setting your company's sales tax preferences), tasks you perform on an ongoing basis (to create and manage your sales tax items and vendors), and tasks you perform occasionally, in preparation to pay sales tax (which can be monthly, quarterly, or at the end of the fiscal year).

The Manage Sales Tax window organizes your sales tax activities in four sections:

- tax accounts and payments,
- tax codes and rates,
- sales tax adjustments,
- sales tax setup.

To view the Manage Sales Tax window:

- Click the **Manage Sales Tax** icon in the Vendors section of the Home page, and if necessary, select **S** in the Sales Tax Codes area; or
- Click **Sales Tax**, **Manage Sales Tax** on the menu bar.

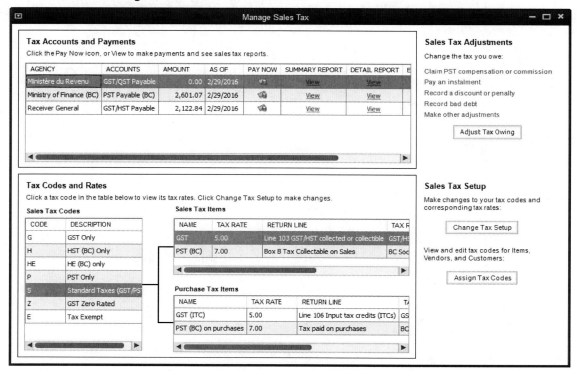

Handling GST/HST Remittances

All GST/HST collected on sales, less the amount of any input tax credits and adjustments must be regularly remitted to Canada Revenue Agency. The frequency varies from business to business, but is normally monthly, quarterly or annually. Amounts to be remitted are calculated using information from QuickBooks and recorded on CRA Form GST34.

- All GST/HST amounts charged on sales are credited to the GST/HST liability account (GST/HST Charged on Sales, or similar) by QuickBooks at the time the sale is posted.

- All GST/HST amounts paid on purchases are debited to the GST/HST liability (contra) (GST/HST Paid on Purchases, or similar) account by QuickBooks at the time the purchase is posted.

- Any GST/HST Adjustments are posted to the GST/HST liability (GST/HST Adjustments, ITC Adjustments or similar) account as necessary.

- Any GST/HST liability account carrying a credit balance represents money owing to CRA.

- Any GST/HST liability account carrying a debit balance represents a refund owing from CRA.

- For each reporting period, the amount of money owing is offset against any refunds to calculate the amount payable to CRA.

To ensure that the GST/HST and PST options are set up:

1. Open the Vendor Centre, right-click **Receiver General**, click **Edit Vendor** and select the **Sales Tax Settings** tab.

2. This company has elected to send remittances quarterly. Ensure the **Reporting Period** of **Quarterly** is selected as illustrated below.

3. Click **OK** to close this window

4. Right-click **Ministry of Finance (BC)**, select **Edit Vendor** and click on the **Sales Tax Settings** tab.

5. Review the information provided, and verify that the Reporting Frequency is **Monthly.**

6. Click **OK** to close this window

7. Close the Vendor Centre.

To view a report of current tax liabilities:

1. Click **Sales Tax**, **Tax Agency Report** on the menu bar.

2. In the Tax Agency field, select **Receiver General**.

3. Set the Dates to: From **Jan 1, 2016** to **Mar 31, 2016** and click **Refresh.**

We Are Music Ltd.
GST/HST Return Report
January through March 2016

	Jan - Mar 16
Line 101 Sales and other revenue	89,438.40
Line 103 GST/HST collected or collectible	4,462.03
Line 104 Adjustments	0.00
Line 105 Total GST/HST and adjustments for period	4,462.03
Line 106 Input tax credits (ITCs)	2,890.39
Line 107 Adjustments	0.00
Line 108 Total ITCs and adjustments	2,890.39
Line 109 Net Tax	1,571.64
Line 110 Instalment and other annual filer payments	0.00
Line 111 Rebates	0.00
Line 112 Total other credits	0.00
Line 113A Balance	1,571.64
Line 205 GST/HST due on acquisition of taxable real prope...	0.00
Line 405 Other GST/HST to be self-assessed	0.00
Line 113B Total other debits	0.00
Line 113C Balance	1,571.64

4. Close the report. Do not memorize.

Learn the Skill

In this exercise, you will learn how to generate a cheque to remit the GST/HST owing to Canada Revenue Agency for the quarter of Jan1, 2016 to Mar 31, 2016.

1 Click **Sales Tax**, **File Sales Tax** on the menu bar.

2 In the Tax Agency field, select **Receiver General**. Set **Custom** dates from **01/01/2016** to **03/31/2016** and press Tab. (We Are Music Ltd. remits the GST/HST every quarter.)

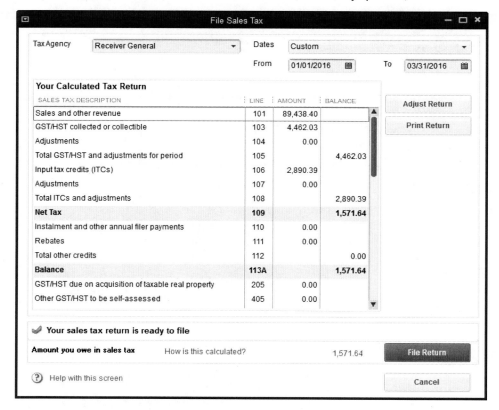

> You can also access this window by clicking the **Pay Now** icon in the Manage Sales Tax window.

Note the **Adjust Return** button. Clicking the button displays the Sales Tax Adjustment window, which allows adjustments to the return. For this exercise, we will not be adjusting the return.

3   In the File Sales Tax window, review the figures, and then click **File Return**.

4   Select **Paper or other filing method** and click **Continue**.

5   Click **No** when asked if you would like to print your return.

6   In the Payment window, select **Pay Now**.

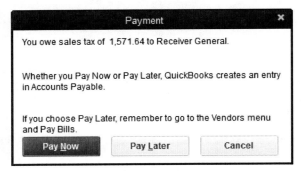

7   Click **OK** in the Filing Process Complete window

8   In the Pay Bills window, select **Receiver General** and enter the following:

Date	March 31, 2016
Cheque	To be printed
Account	Royal Bank Chequing Account

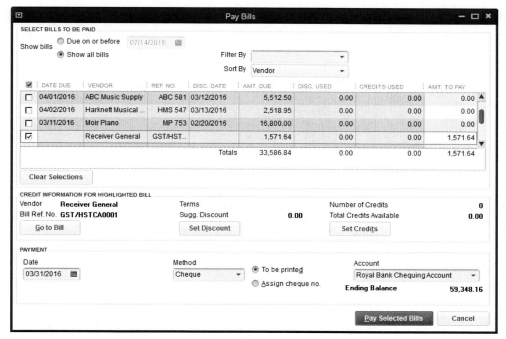

9   Click **Pay Selected Bills**.

10 Click **Done** in the Payment Summary window.

Now verify that the cheque has been entered into QuickBooks.

11 Click **Banking**, **Use Register** on the menu bar, select **Royal Bank Chequing Account**, then **OK** to display the Register.

12 Close the Register window.

Handling and Remitting Provincial Sales Tax

Provincial sales tax that has been charged on sales to customers must be regularly remitted to the appropriate authorities. The provinces in Canada that still charge PST are:

Province	Tax	Rate
British Columbia	PST	7%
Quebec	QST	9.975%
Manitoba	RST	8%
Saskatchewan	PST	5%

> Two provinces have specific names for their Sales Tax, Quebec Sales Tax (QST) in Quebec, and Retail Sales Tax (RST) in Manitoba.

For most businesses, the sales tax charged for the previous month, must be remitted to the Ministry of Finance by the 15th of every month. The Provincial tax agency in the relevant province will advise vendors of the timing and process of submitting the collected taxes. In Manitoba, for example the frequency of filing is determined by the amount of RST collected from your customers. This is determined at the time of registering as a vendor.

As sales transactions are processed by QuickBooks, the amount of PST collected is credited to a liability account called PST Payable or similar, where it is held until it is paid to the authorities. There are no input tax credits permitted on PST remittances, but rather, in some provinces a commission is paid to vendors. When goods are purchased for resale, PST is not charged by the supplier, as this is an exempt transaction (provided the purchaser's PST Number is supplied). All items purchased for use within a business, such as office supplies, are subject to payment of PST, and also some services, telephone and hydro bills for example. Each province has specific rules about what is subject to PST. When PST forms part of the cost of a purchase transaction, the amount of the PST is added to the debit in the general ledger expense account.

Always make sure PST remittances are paid by the required due date. Failure to do so can result in penalty and interest charges, and revocation of the privilege of keeping commission. Although payment may be made by mail, most financial institutions will accept PST payments from their clients.

However, the process of submitting PST to a Provincial agency is identical to that of submitting GST/HST, using **Sales Tax**, **File Sales Tax** from the menu bar. In the File Sales Tax window, select the relevant Tax Agency, **Provincial Ministry**, and proceed as outlined in the GST/HST process.

At the time this manual was created the commission paid to vendors by the Province of BC was as follows:

If Sales Tax Collectable is:	Commission is:
$22.00 or less	Amount of tax collectable
$22.01 - $333.33	$22.00
More than $333.33	6.6% of tax collectable. Maximum amount is $198.00

Learn the Skill

In this exercise, you will learn how to calculate the commission due to the company.

1   Click **Sales Tax**, **Tax Agency Report** on the menu bar.

2   Select **Ministry of Finance (BC)** for the Tax Agency.

3   Set the Dates to **Custom**, from **Feb 1, 2016** to **Feb 29, 2016**, and click **Refresh**.

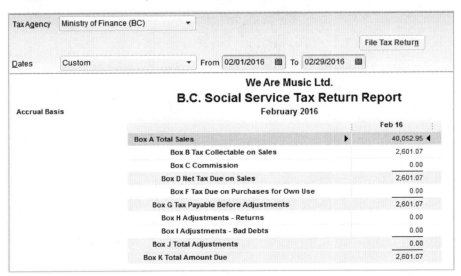

4   Review the Total Amount Due: $2,601.07.

5   Calculate the 6.6% commission on this figure: 2,601.07 * 6.6% = $171.67 which is the commission due to the company.

6   Close the Tax Agency Report window.

 # Learn the Skill

In this exercise, you will learn how to generate a cheque to remit the PST owing to the Ministry of Finance (BC) for the month of February, 2016.

1   Click **Sales Tax**, **File Sales Tax** on the menu bar.

2   Select **Ministry of Finance (BC)** in the Tax Agency field.

3   In the Dates field, select **Custom**, and set the date range from **Feb 1, 2016** to **Feb 29, 2016.** Press (Tab)

4   Click the **Adjust Return** button.

5   Ensure the Adjustment Date is 02/29/2016.

6   Click the arrow on the right of the Sales Tax Item field, and select **PST (BC) Commission** from the drop-down list.

7   Select **Miscellaneous Income** for the Adjustment Account.

8   Type 171.67 in the Amount field, and ensure "Increase Sales Tax line" is selected.

Your window should resemble the following:

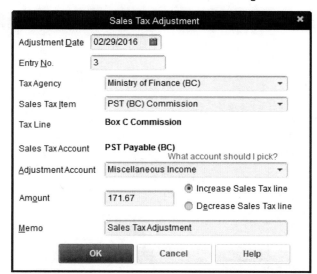

9   Click **OK** to return to the Files Sales Tax window.

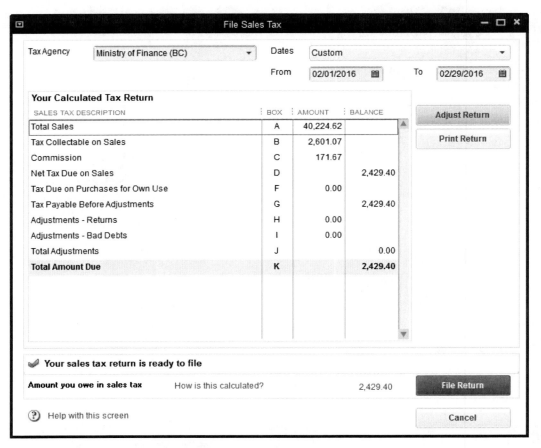

The Total Amount Due of $2,429.40, has been reduced by the Commission amount of $171.67.

10   Click **File Return**.

11   Click **No** when asked if you want to print the return.

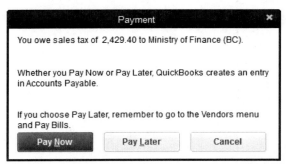

12   Click **Pay Now** in the Payment window.

13   Click **OK** in the Filing Process Complete window.

14   In the Pay Bills window, select the **Ministry of Finance (BC)** bill, and change the Payment Date to **March 14, 2016.**

Your window should resemble the following:

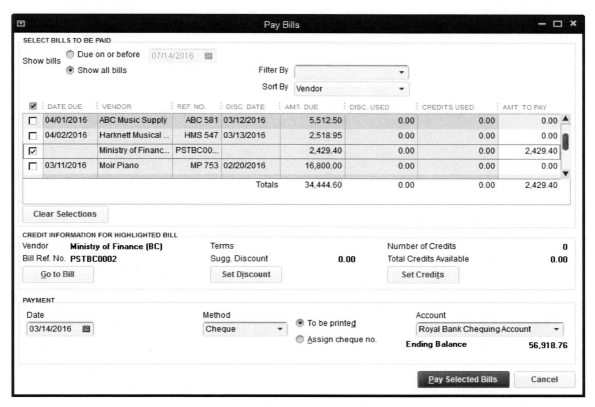

15 Click **Pay Selected Bills**.

16 Click **Done** in the Payment Summary window.

Verifying Data Integrity

At times, the company data file may become damaged. You may suspect that this has occurred if you see cases such as the following:

- Transactions have disappeared for no apparent reason, and they were not deleted as a result of a human error.

- Customer or vendor names are missing from their respective list.

- Transactions are showing very unusual data, such as negative values.

- You receive errors such as Invalid Protection Faults or Fatal Errors when running QuickBooks.

To minimize these problems, you should run the Verify Data function on a regular basis, such as weekly. By doing so, you can detect problems quickly. When you run the Verify Data function, any error found will be written to a file named Qbwin.log. Error messages written to this log file are not deleted, and new messages are added at the bottom of the file. It is common for the Qbwin.log to become very large after you have run the Verify Data function many times.

If the Verify Data function finishes with an error message (indicating that the company data file is damaged), QuickBooks will display a message with instructions for running the Rebuild utility to attempt to repair the damage. You will be prompted to back up your company data file (damaged as it is, you can restore this copy if the Rebuild process causes other problems). You should use a new save location for this copy to prevent overwriting any other recent backup of your company data that you may need to restore. The Rebuild utility will run as soon as the backup completes, and it should only be run once. When the Rebuild process has finished, close your company file and then reopen it in order to refresh the lists in your data file.

If, for some reason, the rebuild process is unsuccessful, you may choose to restore your company data file to a good backup copy of the data. By running the Verify Data function frequently and regularly, you should have a recent good copy of the data file to fall back on, with a minimal loss of data; that is, all data entered since that backup copy was made will now have to be re-entered into QuickBooks.

 ## Learn the Skill

In this exercise, you will learn how to check data integrity.

1   Select **File**, **Utilities**, **Verify Data** from the menu bar.

2   Click **OK** to proceed with verifying the data.

3   Click **OK** to close the Information message.

4   Click **Home** in the Icon bar to open the Home Page.

QuickBooks provides an option to verify data during the Backup process, and it is recommended that you do so each time.

Year-End Procedures

At the end of the calendar year, you should follow these procedures:

- Verify data integrity.
- Back up the data file.
- Print the following payroll reports:
    - Payroll Transaction Detail
    - Employee Summary for all employees
    - Employee Detail for all employees
    - T4 Slips and Summary

Closing the Books

At the end of the fiscal year, there are some steps to complete the accounting cycle, in order to close the books, and begin the next fiscal year. QuickBooks automatically generates year end transactions so that the revenue and expense accounts revert back to zero for the New Year. In addition to bringing the net income or loss to the equity account, you also have to bring the account that tracks owner's draw or shareholder distribution to zero. QuickBooks journalizes and posts the required entries automatically at the end of the fiscal year.

At the time of your company's fiscal year end, you should follow these procedures:

- Verify data integrity and back up data files.
- Reconcile all bank and credit card accounts.
- Print full set of financial statements as at the last day of fiscal year.
- If required by your accountant, create a full General Ledger report for the whole fiscal year.
- Print a complete set of budget reports if this feature is used (Level 2).
- Prepare and input budget figures for the New Year if this feature is used (Level 2).
- Make year-end adjustments when received from the accountant (may be up to a few months later).

Unlike some other accounting software packages, QuickBooks does not require you to close your books at the end of the fiscal year. This feature allows you to continue entering transactions that apply to the previous year—even though you are well into the new fiscal year—so that you can attend to other urgent end of year matters and enter any year-end accounting adjustments prepared by your accountant. To prevent this feature from being abused (and therefore distort your financial picture), you or your accountant may insert a password to prevent transactions from being added into the previous year.

Closing Dates in QuickBooks

QuickBooks allows a choice of whether or not to set a closing date. If you close the books by setting a closing date, QuickBooks does the following for you:

- Transfers the net income or loss to Retained Earnings.
- Restricts access to transactions prior to the closing date by requiring a password.
- Allows you to clean up the data.

> The company file administrator is the only one who can set a closing date and allow or restrict access to prior period transactions.

Since QuickBooks automatically performs some tasks at the end of the fiscal period, there are some pros and cons to setting a closing date.

PROS	CONS
Access can be restricted to prior period transactions by requiring a password.	Prior period transactions cannot be easily accessed.
A closing date exception report displaying any modified transactions that are dated on or before the closing date can be created.	Comparison transaction data reports from prior periods cannot be created.

If your computer has limited data storage or processing power, you may want to condense your company data file by archiving previous years' data and deleting them from your current data file. However when you do this, you will no longer be able to generate comparative financial statements using those previous years' data. If you have a fairly new computer, you should have sufficient storage and processing power to hold several years of data without any performance problems.

Learn the Skill

In this exercise, you will practice preparing for the fiscal year-end of December 2016.

Since we have already verified the integrity of your data file we can skip that step at this time.

1   Backup the file as: We Are Music Ltd. - Your Name Lesson 6 following the same steps learned in Lesson 1.

Assume for this exercise that you do not wish to close your books, condense your data file, or start a new company data file. Instead, you want to retain all of the previous year's details for comparison purposes, and apply a password to prevent anyone from entering transactions in the previous year.

2   Select **Edit**, **Preferences** from the menu bar.

3   Select **Accounting** in the left side of the Preferences window, and then select the **Company Preferences** tab.

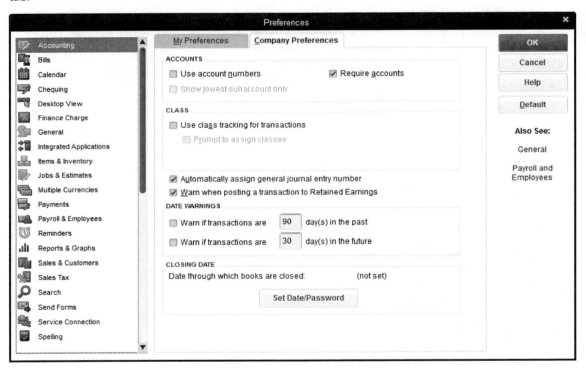

4   In the Closing Date area, click the **Set Date/Password** button.

5   In the next window, click to select the **Exclude estimates...** checkbox.

6   In the Closing Date field enter **December 31, 2016**.

7   In the Closing Date Password field, type: ApR16 (watch the case settings!). Repeat in the **Confirm Password** field.

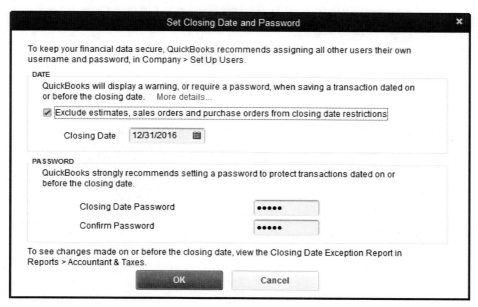

8   As this is a practice session only, click **Cancel** to close the Set Closing Date and Password dialog box.

9   Click **Cancel** to close the Preferences window.

Lesson Summary

In this lesson, you have learned how to use the financial reporting functions of QuickBooks, how to report and remit sales taxes, and to carry out year-end procedures. You should now be able to:

☑   create and print financial reports   ☑   manage sales tax

☑   use the Company Snapshot report   ☑   verify data integrity

☑   use the Calendar   ☑   complete year-end procedures

☑   use the Reminders List

Practice the Skill

The following additional exercise covers many of the items discussed in this Lesson. The Practice the Skill exercises are included as extra practice and may be completed by the students in class or on their own. Your instructor has access to the Answer Key for these exercises.

1.   Create and print the following reports for the month of **Feb 2016**: Do not memorize.
        Expenses by Vendor Summary
        Income by Customer Summary

2.   Find and process the memorized rent transaction due on March 1, 2016. Change the Memo to March rent. Print Later.

3.   In the Reminders List, click **Open Preferences**, and in the Company Preferences tab, change the Remind Me days for Overdue Invoices to: 3, click **OK.** Close the Reminders window, and if necessary, open **My Shortcuts**.

4. Open the Calendar, and set the date to **March 2016**. Add the following **To Do** item:

    Type: Appointment

    Priority: Medium

    With: Customer – Ellison Elementary

    Due: March 22, 2016

    Time: 9:30 AM

    Details: Review details of new contract for music lessons for next semester.

5. Open the Company Snapshot report, and add the following content: **Best-Selling Items**.

6. Backup the file as: `We Are Music Ltd. - Your Name Lesson 6 Practice`.

Review Questions

1. Why is it useful to create regular monthly reports for your company?

2. Which of the following reports is **not** listed in the Company & Financial section of the Report Centre?

    a. Profit & Loss by Job

    b. Expenses by Vendor Summary

    c. Transaction Detail by Account

    d. Net Worth Graph

3. You can print an Income Statement for a specific month, or for the year-to-date.

    a. True   b. False

4. You can process a transaction directly from the Reminders List because it will launch the related function that will display and process it.

    a. True   b. False

5. What are the three view settings available in the Calendar?

6. How do you add a task to the Calendar?

7. What steps do you take to produce a Tax Agency Detail Report?

8. How do you check data integrity?

9. You must close your books at the end of a fiscal year in QuickBooks.

    a. True   b. False

10. Which of the following statements is true?

    a. In a Profit & Loss Report dated January 1, the Revenue and Expense accounts will contain balances.

    b. In a Balance Sheet Report dated January 1, there will be a balance in the Retained Earnings account.

    c. A Profit & Loss Report contains sections for Income, Expenses, and Equity.

11. What safeguard in QuickBooks can ensure that entries will not be posted into the incorrect fiscal year?

QuickBooks

Premier 2016

Level 1

Appendices

Appendix A

Additional Exercises

Appendix B

Glossary of Terms

Appendix C

Index

Appendix A: Additional Exercises

In this appendix, you will practice the skills learned throughout the courseware. You will use a data base for these exercises named *Blue Heron Spa Inc.* These additional exercises are based on the concepts covered in Lessons 1 through 6. Any differences in reports and company balances at the end of these exercises should be the result of having a different set of payroll tax tables. This will be a continuous data file, but it is recommended that you back up the file after each session with the relevant file name for each lesson.

Restoring the Exercise File

1. From the **File** menu in QuickBooks, choose **Open or Restore Company**.

   QuickBooks displays the Open or Restore Company window.

2. Select **Restore a backup copy** and click **Next**.

3. Select **Local backup** and click **Next**.

4. In the Open Backup Copy window navigate to your *1761 Student Files* folder.

5. Select the *Blue Heron Spa Inc - Student.QBB* file and then click **Open**.

6. In the Open or Restore Company window, click **Next**.

7. Navigate to your *1761 Student Files* folder.

8. In the File name field of the Save Company File as window, type: Blue Heron Spa Inc. - Your Name and then click **Save**.

9. In the Enter Password window type: **BlueSpa16** (case sensitive)

10. Click **OK** when you see the message that the file has been successfully restored.

11. Close the QuickBooks Learning Centre window.

Lesson 1

Chart of Accounts

1. Add the following account: Do not set up online services.
   Type: Bank
   Account Name: CIBC Payroll Account

2. Edit the following account:
   Current Name: Esthetics
   New Name: Esthetics Services

3. Make the following accounts subaccounts of Services Income:
   Esthetics Services
   Massage Services

General Journal Entries

The bill from Standard Insurance Inc. dated Dec 31, 2015, was for the annual premium. The monthly portion of the annual premium is due for February; you must now make an entry to record the actual expense.

1. Create the following General Journal Entry as of Feb 29, 2016.

Account	Debit	Credit	Memo
Insurance Expense	125.00		Monthly portion of annual premium
Prepaid Insurance		125.00	Monthly portion of annual premium

Memorize the Entry as follows:

Name	Monthly Insurance
Reminder	Yes
How Often	Monthly
Next Date	Mar 30, 2016

2. Click **OK**, and then **Save & New** in the Make General Journal Entries window.

Now that we have opened a payroll account, it is necessary to transfer funds from the chequing account to the payroll account.

3. In the Make General Journal Entries window record the following entry as of Mar 1, 2016.

Account	Debit	Credit	Memo
CIBC Payroll Account	5,000.00		Funds Transfer
CIBC Chequing Account		5,000.00	Funds Transfer

4. Click **Save & Close**.

Preferences

Set the following Preferences:

1. In **Chequing, My Preferences** set all three default accounts to: CIBC Chequing Account.

2. Select **Company Preferences** and set as follows:

Create Pay Cheques with:	CIBC Payroll Account
Pay Payroll Liabilities with:	CIBC Chequing Account

3. If necessary click **YES** in the Save Changes window.

4. In the **Sales Tax**, **Company Preferences**, make sure the following items have been checked:

Use Customer Tax Codes

Use Vendor Tax Codes

Taxable items: (S)

5. Click **OK**.

Backup Company File

Backup the company file as: Blue Heron Spa Inc. - Your Name - end lesson 1. Continue on with the additional exercises.

Lesson 2

If necessary, open the *Blue Heron Spa Inc.* file, or restore the backup file - *end lesson1*. (Password: BlueSpa16)

Adding Products & Services
Preferences

The company has decided to offer some products as well as services to its clients, so we will need to update some Preferences.

1. Open the Preferences window, and in the **Items & Inventory** category, click **Company Preferences** and click to activate **Inventory and purchase orders are active**.

2. Click **OK** to close the Preferences window.

3. Click **OK** in the warning message, and then click **Home** to open the Home Page.

Item List

1. Open the Item List.

2. Enter the following new items; date Inventory items as of **Mar 1, 2016**.

Type	Inventory Part
Name/Number	Ladies' Robe
Unit of Measure	<Add New>, Count, Each, Box, 10, Purchase: box, Sales: each (Shipping: leave blank, Set Name: Box
Description	Ladies' White Terry Cloth Robe
Cost	9.50
Purch Tax Code	G
COGS Account	Cost of Goods Sold
Sales Price	24.50
Tax Code	S
Income Account	Sales Income <Add New>

Type	Inventory Part
Name/Number	Men's Robe
Unit of Measure	Box:ea
Description	Men's Blue Terry Cloth Robe
Cost	12.50
Purch Tax Code	G
COGS Account	Cost of Goods Sold
Sales Price	29.50
Tax Code	S
Income Account	Sales Income

Type	Non-Inventory Part
Name/Number	Spa slippers (one size)
Unit of Measure	<Add New> Count, Pair, Package: 15 Purchase: package, Sales: pair Set Name: Package
Description	Disposable Terry slippers
Price	1.99 (pr)
Tax Code	S
Account	Linens and Spa Supplies

Type	Non-Inventory Part
Name/Number	Body Wrap Linens
Unit of Measure	Box: ea
Description	Body Wraps
Price	5.95 (ea)
Tax Code	S
Account	Linens and Spa Supplies

Managing Item List Entries

1. Edit the following Items by changing the Account to **Body Treatments**.
   Bikini Wax
   Full leg & Bikini Wax

2. Say **Yes** in the Account Change window for both items. Close the Item List.

Backup Company File

Backup the company file as: `Blue Heron Spa Inc. – Your Name – end lesson 2`.

Lesson 3

If necessary, open the *Blue Heron Spa Inc.* file, or restore the backup file - *end lesson 2*. (Password: BlueSpa16)

Entering Vendors

Enter the following new vendors:

Company Name	Spic & Span Janitorial
Vendor as of date	Mar 1, 2016
Main Phone	250 503-9538
Main Email	btewes@gmail.com
Terms	Net 30
Tax Code	S
Vendor Type	Service Providers
Primary Contact	Bill Tewes
Home Phone	250 503-1685
Email	btewes@shaw.ca

Company Name	Comfort Clothing
Vendor as of date	Mar 1, 2016
Main Phone	250 778-5884
Main Email	info@comfortclothing.ca
Terms	2% 10 Net 30
Tax Code	G
Vendor Type	Suppliers
Primary Contact	June Knox
Mobile	626 828-5734

Modifying Vendor Records

Edit the following Vendor records:

Standard Insurance Inc.

Terms	Net 30
Tax Code	E
Vendor Type	Service Providers

Comox Florists

Account No	52397 Credit Limit 500.00
Terms	Net 30
Account Prefill tab	Miscellaneous Expense
Vendor Type	Suppliers
Primary Contact	Gerry Davison
Mobile	250 778-5694

Adelaide Linen Supplies

Fax	250 534-9660
Terms	2% 10 Net 30
Account Prefill:	Linens and Spa Supplies
Vendor Type	Suppliers
Primary Contact	Janice Bowen
Mobile	250 344-5821

Purchases

We need to purchase both inventory and non-inventory items. Enter the following bills:

Vendor	Comfort Clothing
Date	Mar 4, 2016
Ref. No.	CC 564
Item 1:	Mens' Robe, 1 box, Tax G
Item 2:	Ladies' Robe 1 box Tax G
Total Bill	$231.00

Vendor	North Island Spa Supplies
Date	Mar 7, 2016
Ref. No.	NISS 195
Item	Spa Slippers 2 Pkg Tax S
Total Bill	$66.87

Write Cheques

The monthly rent is due to Island Property Management Ltd. Record the following cheque:

Date	Mar 1, 2016
Order of	Island Property Management Ltd.
Expense	Rent
Tax	G
Amount	1500.00
Memo	March rent
Cheque	247 (assign cheque number)

Pay Bills

There are some outstanding bills which should be paid.

Pay the following bills as of Mar 14, 2016.

North Island Spa Supplies	536.43
Adelaide Linen Supplies	184.80

Print Cheques

Print the above two cheques. Since we wrote out the cheque to Island Property Management Ltd. the first cheque to be printed should be cheque 248.

Purchase Orders

1. We are replacing some of the linens used for the body wrap treatments, and need to place a purchase order for some non-inventory part items as follows:

Vendor	North Island Spa Supplies
Date	Mar 15, 2016
Item 1	Body Wrap Linens 2 Box
Total Order	133.28

We have received the items ordered from North Island Spa Supplies. Record the following Item Receipt:

2. Click the **Receive Inventory** icon, and select **Receive Inventory without Bill**.

Vendor	North Island Spa Supplies - P.O. 1
Date	Mar 18, 2016
Total	$119.00 + tax = 133.28

We have received the invoice from North Island Spa Supplies for the Items Received on Mar 22, 2016.

3. Click **Enter Bills Against Inventory** to record the Bill:

Vendor	North Island Spa Supplies
Date	Mar 22, 2016
Ref.	NISS 592
Expense	Freight Charge <Add New> (Cost of Goods Sold)
Amount	15.00 (Recalculate)
Tax	G
Total Invoice	$149.03

Modifying Bills

Upon opening the item package received from Comfort Clothing we found an extra box of Men's' robes. We need to adjust the bill from this vendor.

1. Click **Enter Bills**, and then click **Previous** three times to open the bill.

2. Change the Men's Robe quantity to 2 bx, and then click **Recalculate**.

3. The new total should be $362.25. Click **Save & Close**. Click **Yes** in the warning screen.

Vendor Reports

If lab conditions allow, print the following reports.

> Create an A/P Aging Summary report as of Mar 31, 2016.
> Create an Accounts Payable Graph as of Mar 31, 2016.

Backup Company File

Backup the company file as: Blue Heron Spa Inc. - Your Name - end lesson 3.

Lesson 4

If necessary, open the *Blue Heron Spa Inc.* file or restore the backup file – *end lesson 3*. (Password BlueSpa16)

Customers

Manage Customer Type

To start, we will modify some customer types.

1. Click **Lists** on the menu bar, select **Customer & Vendor Profile Lists**, **Customer Type List**.

Edit	**Change to**
From advertisement	Advertising

Create New	
Customer Type	**Subtype**
Newspaper	Advertising
Internet	Advertising

Create New Customers

1. Open the Customer Centre, and click **New Customer & Job**, **New Customer**

Customer Name	Wong, Anita C.
Opening Balance	0
As of	Mar 3, 2016
Full Name	Mrs.
First Name	Anita
M.I.	C.
Last Name	Wong
Address	Anita C. Wong
	636 Powell Street
	Duncan, BC V9L 3V7
Main Phone	250 461-4547
Terms	Net 15
Tax Code	S
Customer Type	Advertising: Internet

Customer Name	Donaldson, Samantha E.
Opening Balance	0
As of	Mar 5, 2016
Full Name	Mrs.
First Name	Samantha
M.I.	E.
Last Name	Donaldson
Address Details	Samantha E. Donaldson
	123 Maple Street
	Comox, BC V9M 2L0
Main Phone	250 356 -7712
Credit Limit	500.00
Terms	Net 30
Tax Code	S
Customer Type	Advertising: Newspaper

Credit Sales

Create the following invoices and use the **Intuit Service Invoice** for both sales. Make sure the **Print Later** box is checked for printing later.

Customer:Job	Wong, Anita C.
Date	Mar 07, 2016
Invoice #	3
Invoice To	accept as is
Item	Spa Special
Qty	1
Rate	250.00
Tax	G
Print Later	Yes
Total	262.50

Customer:Job	Donaldson, Samatha E.
Date	Mar 10, 2016
Invoice #	4
Invoice To	accept as is
Item 1	Body Wrap Qty: 1 Rate 120.00
Item 2	Manicure Qty: 1 Rate 50.00
Tax	G
Print Later	Yes
Total	178.50

Print Sales Invoices

Print the two sales invoices just processed.

1. Click **File**, **Print Forms**, **Invoices**.

   Ensure there are two invoices selected for a total of 441.00 to Print.

2. Click **OK** to print if lab conditions allow, otherwise click **Cancel**.

Sales Receipts

Enter the following Sales Receipt:

Customer:Job	Weekly Sales				
Date	Mar 12, 2016				
Sale No.	21				
Item 1	Body Wrap	Qty 5	Rate	120.00	Tax G
Item 2	Manicure	Qty 2	Rate	50.00	Tax G
Item 3	Pedicure	Qty 5	Rate	60.00	Tax G
Item 4	Anti-Aging Facial	Qty 3	Rate	125.00	Tax G
Item 5	Hot Stone Massage	Qty 4	Rate	120.00	Tax G
Item 6	Ladies Robe	Qty 2	Rate	24.50	Tax S
Print Later	Yes				
Total	2,002.63				

Recording Customer Payments

In recording payments, the data file has been set to use Undeposited Funds as a default deposit to account. All payment methods are by cheque.

1. Click **Receive Payments**, and record the following:

Customer:Job	H.K. Lawson & Associates LLP
Date	Mar 15, 2016
Amount	262.50
Cheque No.	450

Customer:Job	Anita C. Wong
Date	Mar 21, 2016
Amount	262.50
Cheque No.	164

Sales Orders

This company uses the Sales Order function to record reservations for group service packages.

1. Issue the following Sale Order:

Customer:Job	Gladys Carmine			
Date	Mar 25, 2016			
S.O. No.	3			
Item 1	Silk Polish	Qty 3	Rate 90.00	Tax G
Item 2	Manicure	Qty 3,	Rate 50.00	Tax G
Item 3	Pedicure	Qty 3,	Rate 60.00	Tax G
Total	$630.00			

Modifying an Invoice

Samantha Donaldson has notified us that the invoice for Mar 16 should also have included a Pedicure.

1. Click **Create Invoices**, and then **Find** from the menu bar.

2. Find and adjust the invoice.

3. The adjusted total should be: 241.50.

Filling a Sales Order

Gladys Carmine and party have received their services. Issue an invoice dated Mar 28, for services received at the spa. While there, they also purchased 2 Ladies Robes. Add these items to the invoice – Total invoice: 684.88. Customer message: Thank you for your business.

Recording Deposits

On March 29, 2016 deposit all funds from the Undeposited Funds account to the CIBC Chequing Account. Deposit total: $2,527.63.

Customer Reports

Create and Print the following reports: Do not memorize.

> Customer Balance Detail Report
>
> A/R Aging Summary Report as of Mar 31, 2016
>
> Accounts Receivable Graph as of Mar 31, 2016

Backup Company File

Backup the company file as: `Blue Heron Spa Inc. - Your Name - end lesson 4.`

Lesson 5

If necessary, open the *Blue Heron Spa Inc.* file or restore the backup file – *end lesson 4.* (Password BlueSpa16)

Edit Payroll Features

1. Select **Edit**, **Preferences** from the menu bar.

2. Select the **Payroll & Employees** category.

3. Click **Company Preferences**.

4. Select **Display Employee List By**: **Last Name**.

5. Click **OK** twice, and then open the Home Page.

Add a Payroll Item

1. Click **Lists**, **Payroll Item List**.

2. Create a new payroll item as follows:

Type	Wage, Bonus
Name	Bonus
Expense Account	Payroll Expenses
ROE	Earnings
Finish	

Add the following Employee

You have decided to hire staff to assist with the day-to-day work.

Legal Name	Mrs. Marie G. Klassen
Print as	Marie G. Klassen,
SIN	123 456 782
Gender	Female
Date of Birth	July 5, 1995

Address and Contact tab

Address	174 Gull Ave
City	Comox
Province	BC
Postal Code	V9M 1L5
Phone	250 356-1234

Payroll Info tab

Hourly	16.50
Double Time	33.00
Time & a Half	24.75
Pay Frequency	Weekly

Employment Info tab

Hire Date	Mar 1, 2016
New Employee info	Leave As Is

Modify Employee Record

Sally Browne's employee record needs to be adjusted to record her Medical Insurance deduction.

1. On the Payroll Info tab, in the Additions, Deductions and Company Contributions area, click in the first line under Item Name, and click **<Add New>**. Add the following new Payroll Item:

Type	Deduction
Name	Medical Insurance
Agency	Standard Insurance Inc.
Number	986257
Liability Account	Accept Default
Tax Tracking	None
Taxes	Click Next
Calculate	Neither
Gross vs. net	Click Next
Default Rate	15.50
Finish	

    Change her pay frequency to Biweekly.

2. Click **OK** in the Edit Employee window to save the changes.

Payroll Schedule

We now have three employees that are paid weekly; we will create a payroll schedule for these employees.

1. Click the **Payroll** tab in the Employee Centre.

2. Click **Payroll Schedules**, **New**.

3. Type: Weekly in the Name field, and select **Weekly** in the next field.

4. Set the Pay Period end Date to: **Mar 5, 2016** and the Cheque date to **Mar 7, 2016**.

5. Click **OK**, and if a warning about the pay cheque date is displayed, click **Yes**.

6. Click **Yes** in the Assign Payroll Schedule window, and **OK** in the QuickBooks Information window.

Pay Employees

1. Click the **Weekly** payroll schedule to select it, and then click **Start Scheduled Payroll**.

2. Click **OK** in the Review Employee TD1 Amounts window. Close the review window.

3. Ensure all 3 employees are selected, and enter 37.5 hours for Kathleen Carson, 24 hours for Marie Klassen, and 37 hours for Sandra Romansky.

4. Ensure **CIBC Payroll Account** is selected, and the pay period end (03/05/2016) and cheque (03/07/2016) dates are correct. Click **Continue**.

    Net Pay should be: Carson 537.13; Klassen 350.73; and Romansky 476.71.

5. Click **Create Pay Cheques**.

6. Click **Close** in the Confirmation and Next Steps window.

7. Close the Employee Centre.

Print Payroll Cheques

To print the Payroll cheques:

1. Click **File**, **Print Forms**, **Pay Cheques** from the menu bar.

    Ensure all cheques are selected for a total of 1,364.57

2. The first cheque number is 1, if lab conditions allow click **OK**. If not, click **Cancel**.

3. If necessary, click "No, and turn off pop-up messages for products and services", then **OK**.

Print Paystubs

As part of payroll requirements, you are required to provide the employee with a detail of what was included on each pay cheque. If lab conditions allow, follow through with the instructions below. If not, click **Close**, to not print.

1. Click **File**, **Print Forms**, **Paystubs** from the menu bar.

2. Print the paystubs for all three employees, ensuring the dates in the Select Paystubs to Print/Email area for Cheques are **Mar 1, 2016** thru **Mar 7, 2016**.

Payroll Liabilities

It is time to remit the Payroll Liabilities for the month of February.

1. Click **Pay Liabilities** in the Employees section of the Home page.

2. In the Pay Liabilities tab of the Payroll Centre, click **Pay Liabilities**.

3. Set the dates From: **Feb 1, 2016** Through **Feb 29, 2016** and click **OK**.

4. Set the bank to **CIBC Chequing Account**, and the Payment Date to **Mar 14, 2016**.

5. Select the **Receiver General** payables, and ensure Review liability cheque... is selected.

6. Click **Review**.

7. Review the cheque – total should be: $974.99 and **Print Later** should be selected.

8. Click **Save & Close**.

9. Close the Employee Centre.

Employee Reports

Create and print the following reports. Do not memorize.
- Payroll Summary from Mar 1, 2016 to Mar 7, 2016
- PD7A Report for the month of Mar, 2016
- Payroll Liability Balances from January 1, 2016 to Mar 7, 2016

Backup Company File

Backup the company file as: Blue Heron Spa Inc. – Your Name – end lesson 5.

Lesson 6

If necessary, open the *Blue Heron Spa Inc.* file or restore the backup file – *end lesson 5*. (Password BlueSpa16)

Printing Reports

Create a **Profit & Loss Standard** for the period of **January 1, 2016** to **Mar 31, 2016**. Compare with the following:

Blue Heron Spa Inc.
Profit & Loss
January through March 2016

	Jan - Mar 16
Ordinary Income/Expense	
Income	
Sales Income	98.00
Services Income	
Body Treatments	13,030.00
Esthetics Services	15,345.00
Facial Treatments	8,400.00
Massage Services	18,300.00
Total Services Income	55,075.00
Total Income	55,173.00
Cost of Goods Sold	
Cost of Goods Sold	38.00
Freight Charge	15.00
Total COGS	53.00
Gross Profit	55,120.00
Expense	
Bank Service Charges	15.00
Insurance Expense	250.00
Linens and Spa Supplies	1,501.92
Miscellaneous Expense	58.85
Office Supplies	149.32
Payroll Expenses	20,593.13
Rent Expense	4,500.00
Telephone Expense	161.58
Uniforms	321.00
Utilities	302.18
Total Expense	27,852.98
Net Ordinary Income	27,267.02
Net Income	**27,267.02**

Create a **Balance Sheet Standard** as at **Mar 31, 2016**. Compare with the following:

Blue Heron Spa Inc.
Balance Sheet
As of March 31, 2016

	Mar 31, 16
ASSETS	
Current Assets	
Chequing/Savings	
CIBC Chequing Account	35,581.38
CIBC Payroll Account	3,635.43
Total Chequing/Savings	39,216.81
Accounts Receivable	
Accounts Receivable	926.38
Total Accounts Receivable	926.38
Other Current Assets	
Inventory Asset	307.00
Prepaid Insurance	1,250.00
Total Other Current Assets	1,557.00
Total Current Assets	41,700.19
Fixed Assets	
Furniture and Equipment	
Accum. Depreciation	-5,743.25
Cost	15,985.00
Total Furniture and Equipment	10,241.75
Leasehold Improvements	
Accum. Depreciation	-5,796.45
Cost	18,950.00
Total Leasehold Improvements	13,153.55
Vehicles	
Cost	18,955.95
Total Vehicles	18,955.95
Total Fixed Assets	42,351.25
TOTAL ASSETS	**84,051.44**
LIABILITIES & EQUITY	
Liabilities	
Current Liabilities	
Accounts Payable	
Accounts Payable	578.15
Total Accounts Payable	578.15
Other Current Liabilities	
GST/HST Payable	2,399.03
Payroll Liabilities	1,130.87
PST Payable (BC)	6.86
Total Other Current Liabilities	3,536.76
Total Current Liabilities	4,114.91
Total Liabilities	4,114.91
Equity	
Opening Balance Equity	53,608.23
Owners Equity	-938.72
Net Income	27,267.02
Total Equity	79,936.53
TOTAL LIABILITIES & EQUITY	**84,051.44**

Create a **Trial Balance** as of **Mar 31, 2016**. Compare with the following:

Blue Heron Spa Inc.
Trial Balance
As of March 31, 2016

	Mar 31, 16 Debit	Credit
CIBC Chequing Account	35,581.38	
CIBC Payroll Account	3,635.43	
Accounts Receivable	926.38	
Inventory Asset	307.00	
Prepaid Insurance	1,250.00	
Undeposited Funds	0.00	
Furniture and Equipment:Accum. Depreciation		5,743.25
Furniture and Equipment:Cost	15,985.00	
Leasehold Improvements:Accum. Depreciation		5,796.45
Leasehold Improvements:Cost	18,950.00	
Vehicles:Cost	18,955.95	
Accounts Payable		578.15
GST/HST Payable		2,399.03
Payroll Liabilities		1,130.87
PST Payable (BC)		6.86
Opening Balance Equity		53,608.23
Owners Equity	938.72	
Sales Income		98.00
Services Income:Body Treatments		13,030.00
Services Income:Esthetics Services		15,345.00
Services Income:Facial Treatments		8,400.00
Services Income:Massage Services		18,300.00
Cost of Goods Sold	38.00	
Freight Charge	15.00	
Bank Service Charges	15.00	
Insurance Expense	250.00	
Linens and Spa Supplies	1,501.92	
Miscellaneous Expense	58.85	
Office Supplies	149.32	
Payroll Expenses	20,593.13	
Rent Expense	4,500.00	
Telephone Expense	161.58	
Uniforms	321.00	
Utilities	302.18	
TOTAL	**124,435.84**	**124,435.84**

Create a **Company Snapshot** report. Set the date for the **Income and Expense Trend** report to **This Year**, and compare with the following:

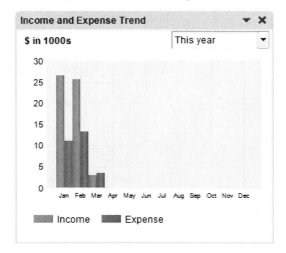

Remove the **Prev Year Expense Comparison** report, and **Add** the **Income Breakdown** report. Move this report after **Top Customers by Sales** report. Compare with the following:

Reminders

1. Click the **Reminders** icon at the top right of the menu bar.

2. Click the chevron beside the Bills to Pay heading.

3. Double click the **Comfort Clothing** bill to open the Enter Bills window and click the **Pay Bill** icon.

4. In the Pay Bills window, set the date to **Mar 22, 2016** and ensure **To be printed** is selected.

5. Click **Pay Selected Bills**.

6. Click **Done** in the Payment Summary window.

7. Close the Enter Bills window.

8. Close the Reminders window.

Sales Tax

We are now going to file the GST return for the Quarter Jan – Mar, and PST for March, and pay the bills to the respective agencies.

1. Click **Sales Tax**, **File Sales Tax** from the menu bar.

2. Select **Receiver General**, set the dates for **01/01/2016** to **03/31/2016**, and then press (Tab).

3. The amount due is $2,399.03. Click **File Return**.

4. Select **Paper or other filing method** and complete the procedure. Do not print the return.

5. Ensure the cheque is dated as of **Apr 15, 2016,** do not print the cheque.

6. Follow steps 1 to 4 to file and remit the PST – **Ministry of Finance (BC)** for the month of Mar, 2016.

7. Since the tax collected is less than the minimum of $11.00, the commission will be the amount collected of $6.86

8. Enter the commission due in the **Adjust Return** screen, using **Uncategorized Income** for the Adjustment Account.

9. Select **PST (BC) Commission** for the Sales Tax Item.

10. Net due after commission should be: 0.00

11. Click **File Return**, click **No** when asked if you would like to print your return, and then click **OK** in the Filing Process Complete window.

Verifying Data

1. Click **File**, **Utilities**, and **Verify Data** from the menu bar.

2. Click **OK** in the Verify Data window.

3. Click **OK** in the QuickBooks Information window, and then open the Home Page.

Closing Date Password

1. Open Preferences, and select **Accounting**, **Company Preferences**.

2. Click the **Set Date/Password** button.

3. Select **Exclude estimates, sales orders and purchase orders from closing date restrictions**.

4. Set **Dec 31, 2016** as the closing date.

5. Set the Closing Date Password as: Dec2016.

6. Confirm the password.

7. Click **Cancel**.

8. Click **OK** to close the Preferences window.

Backup Company File

Backup the company file as: Blue Heron Spa Inc. – Your Name – end lesson 6.

Appendix B: Glossary of Terms

Accounts Payable Account – An account that tracks the amount of money owed by a company to a particular vendor due to outstanding bills (called A/P for short).

Accounts Receivable Account – An account that tracks the amount of money a customer owes to the company due to outstanding invoices (called A/R for short).

Accrual basis accounting – A method of accounting in which expenses or income are recorded at the time a service or an item is purchased or sold, rather than at the time bills are paid or cash is received. Using accrual basis accounting, the time when the original transaction is entered into QuickBooks and the time when cash is paid or received may be two separate events.

Back Order – An additional quantity of goods that a company must manufacture or acquire from its vendors due to an excess of orders over the quantity available for sale. See Short Shipment.

Backup – The process of duplicating data for safety measures, allowing the restoring of the accounting information in the event of destruction, theft, or corruption of the daily working file.

Balance Sheet Account – An account that appears on a Balance Sheet, such as a Bank Account, Accounts Receivable and Payable, or an Equity Account. Reviewing all balance sheet accounts together indicates the financial position of a company.

Canada Revenue Agency – The agency formed by the Canadian government to administer the federal Income Tax Act and collect income taxes (federal & provincial), Employment Insurance, Canada Pension Plan, and other duties and taxes (e.g., GST) levied by the federal government. This agency was formerly called Revenue Canada.

Cash Basis Accounting – A method of accounting in which income or expenses are recorded at the time funds change hands.

Chart of Accounts – A complete list of all accounts of a company.

Classes – A method of categorizing sources of income and expenses. Classes are useful to assign if there is need to classify and track data by department, location, or various business offices or properties.

Credit – A value that is entered on the right side of an account. Also giving a customer the opportunity to pay for goods and services purchased, at a later stage.

Customer Type – A method of categorizing customers in order to classify and track customer types in a way that is meaningful for the business, often for reporting or mailing purposes.

Debit – A value that is entered on the left side of an account.

Default Setting – Suggested information that has been set up or filled in automatically by QuickBooks but can be edited easily by the user.

Depreciation – The amount of the decline in value of a fixed asset over time. Since a fixed asset, such as a large piece of equipment, lasts a long time but also tends to wear out or become obsolete, its financial value is also spread out over the useful life of the asset.

Discount – A reduction in the cost of an item or an entire invoice as an incentive to the customer.

Employee Defaults – Holds data common to most employees with regard to payroll information. Each time a new employee is set up, the information from the employee default is copied into the new employee's record as default suggestions. The user can accept this information or easily edit it. If no employee default is created, there is no prefilled information when a new employee is set up.

Expense – A current cost to the company for the purpose of carrying on business. Unlike inventory, it will always appear on the income statement in the same fiscal period as when it is incurred.

Expense Account – An account that tracks a particular type of expense where a company is spending money.

FIFO (First In First Out) – An inventory valuation method that assumes oldest inventory items are always sold first. Therefore, the cost of inventory is always based on the most recently acquired items.

Filter – A method of selecting particular information (such as specific categories of items or customers from a list) for reporting or mailing purposes.

Fiscal Year – A fixed 12 month period designated by a company as its normal business year for accounting purposes. It may or may not be the same as a calendar year.

FOB – In traditional accounting terms, FOB stands for "Free on Board" and refers to the terms between buyer and seller regarding transportation costs, and the moment at which the buyer assumes ownership of an item. In QuickBooks, this term appears on the Product invoice and is generally used to refer to the site from which a product is shipped or how it will be shipped.

Gross Profit – Calculated as the Sales Revenue earned on the sale of goods and services, less the cost of buying the goods and paying for the labour to deliver the services. The Gross Profit is not the same as the Net Profit.

Gross Margin – Calculated as the Gross Profit divided by the Sales Revenue, and shown as a percentage value.

GST – Goods and Services Tax, levied and administered by the Canadian government (through the Canada Revenue Agency).

HST – Harmonized tax, combining both Provincial Sales Tax and the GST, levied and administered by the Canadian government (through the Canada Revenue Agency).

Historical Data – The data that must be entered into a company's accounts in order to bring the information up to date from the chosen Start Date.

Icon Bar – Appears on the left of the screen and has a range of visual icons which can be clicked to select various forms and activities. It contains four sections: My Shortcuts, Do Today, View Balances and Run Favourite Reports.

Income Account – An account that tracks a particular type of income where a company is earning money.

Inventory Part – An item tracked in QuickBooks purchased for the purpose of resale.

Item – An item is a service or product purchased or sold and entered on a line in a purchase order, invoice or other form. There are eight different types of QuickBooks items, including Services, Inventory Parts, and Other Charges.

Job Type – A method of categorizing a company's jobs in order to classify and track job types in a way that is meaningful for the business, often for reporting or mailing purposes.

Journal – A record "book" that lists details of a certain type of transaction, such as a Sales Journal to record all sales for a given day. In manual accounting systems, journals are used to reduce the number of entries required in the ledger account by entering only the summary total of all of the events.

Ledger – The official record "book" containing the listing of all accounting transactions, grouped into their accounts. In manual accounting systems, each account will typically occupy one or more pages, depending on how active the account is. If an account is very active with many transactions – typically Accounts Receivable and Accounts Payable – a sub-ledger may be used to record the detailed transactions and the summary transaction is recorded in the ledger.

Liabilities – Any money a business owes to someone else, including unpaid bills, loans, or taxes to be remitted to the government.

LIFO (Last In, First Out) – An inventory valuation method that assumes the most recently acquired goods are sold first. Therefore, the cost of the inventory will always be based on the oldest purchased items.

Ministry of Finance – A branch of the provincial government to administer the provincial tax laws and collect sales taxes (PST) on behalf of the provincial government.

Net Income – Calculated as the Gross Profit earned, less all operating expenses for the same time period including various overhead costs such as general wages and salaries, utilities, telephone, vehicle expenses.

Net Worth – Often referred to as Equity, the net worth of a company is equal to the total assets minus the total liabilities.

Non-Inventory Part – Non-inventory parts are items that are purchased (usually on behalf of a specific customer) and then immediately sold or installed, or items that are sold without buying.

Opening Balance – The amount of money in or the value of, an account as of the company's QuickBooks start date.

Owner Password – If set up in Passwords Preferences, allows unlimited access to the company data but must be entered each time the company file is opened.

Payment Terms – The conditions – usually time limits – by which payment must be made, and may include a discount as an incentive for earlier payment.

Payroll Expenses Account – An account set up to track expenses associated with payroll, added automatically by QuickBooks, when the payroll feature is activated.

Payroll Item – Any item associated with payroll that would be a category to appear on a payroll cheque or report. QuickBooks creates several default payroll items, such as CPP, EI, and income tax. The user may add additional items such as union dues, commission, and hourly wages.

Payroll Liabilities Account – An account set up to track liabilities associated with payroll, added automatically by QuickBooks when the payroll feature is activated.

Payroll Password – If full payroll features are selected in Payroll Preferences, a password can be set up allowing only authorized users to enter and edit payroll transactions. An Owner password is also required if a Payroll password is set up.

Paystub – A separate paystub, listing employee data, payroll income and deductions, can be set up and printed on blank 8.5 x 11 paper if voucher cheques are not used for payroll.

PST – Provincial Sales Tax. Levied and administered by the local provincial government. Rates vary from province to province, and some may not have a PST.

Purchase Order – A document sent to a supplier to confirm an order for the purchase of goods or services.

Quick Add – If filling out a QuickBooks form and entering data in a field and the name has not already been added to a QuickBooks list, click the Quick Add button to add the name to the appropriate list at the time of data entry.

QuickFill – By entering the first two letters of any name currently on a QuickBooks list, QuickBooks will fill in the rest of the name automatically.

QuickInsight Graph – From the Graphs menu, a wide range of QuickInsight graphs can be quickly created to convert financial data into a bar or pie chart.

QuickReport – At various locations in QuickBooks, a QuickReport button is available to display a list of transactions for a customer, vendor, or account.

QuickZoom – Allows the display of the original transaction behind a report or graph data. When viewing a QuickBooks report or graph, placing the mouse pointer over a number on a report or a bar or pie slice on a graph and double-clicking when the magnifying glass enclosing Z is displayed.

Reconciliation – The process of comparing two sets of records to verify that they contain the same information. Differences between the two are investigated and corrections or adjustments made. For example, the bank account records kept by the company needs to be reconciled to the statement produced by the bank.

Refundable Tax – A tax item that is paid by the company but is reimbursed by the government body that had levied it; e.g., GST.

Reorder Point – A value that reflects the minimum quantity of a particular inventory item at which point the item should be reordered.

Revenue Canada – See Canada Revenue Agency.

Sales Forms – QuickBooks offers three types of forms for recording sales of services or products — invoices, cash sales, and credit memos. Sales forms formats can be set up to reflect appropriate layouts for Product, Professional, Service or Custom uses and can be modified at any time.

Service Item – Intangible items offered by a company for sale to customers. Because these items usually involve activities that must be performed by an employee, they cannot be verified by physical count. See also Inventory.

Short Shipment – A delivery of goods in which the quantity actually delivered is less than what was originally ordered, due to insufficient stock carried by the vendor. The remainder of the order is placed on "back order".

Shrinkage – Loss of inventory for unknown reasons but often attributed to theft.

Spoilage – Inventory that becomes unsalable before it is sold because of inherent degradation, e.g., fresh produce, goods that are broken on the sales floor.

Start Date – The date that QuickBooks must have a complete list of balance sheet accounts with correct balances entered.

Tax – A cost levied by a level of government in exchange for the privilege of carrying on business in its jurisdiction.

Tax Exempt – An organization or individual that is not required to pay one or more designated taxes, such as GST.

Transaction – A business event that involves an exchange of items of value between two parties. For accounting purposes, that transaction is recorded in monetary terms.

Vendor Type – A method of categorizing the vendors in order to classify and track vendor types in a way that is meaningful for the business, often for reporting or mailing purposes.

Write off – A reduction in the value of an asset – such as an Accounts Receivable amount (bad debt) or a vehicle depreciated to a zero value. The amount of the reduction is transferred to an expense account for the current fiscal period.

Appendix C: Index

S

Sales
    Entering invoices, 116
    Modifying invoices, 119
    Receiving payments, 120
    Refunds and credits, 123
Sales orders, 114

Sales tax
    Remitting GST, 184
    Remitting PST, 187
Service items, 51
Spin button, 7

T

Tax tables, 150

V

Vendor reports, 93
Vendors
    Creating, 62
    Modifying, 67
Verifying data integrity, 191

Y

Year end procedures, 192

*1 7 6 1 - 1 - 0 0 - 0 0 - M A N *